# POPULATION AND CANADIAN SOCIETY

*Johannes Overbeek*

*Butterworths*

Toronto

*CANADA:* BUTTERWORTH & CO. (CANADA) LTD.
TORONTO: 2265 Midland Avenue,
Scarborough, M1P 4S1

*UNITED KINGDOM:* BUTTERWORTH & CO. (Publishers) LTD.
LONDON: 88 KINGSWAY, WC2B 6AB

*AUSTRALIA:* BUTTERWORTH PTY. LTD.
SYDNEY: 586 Pacific Highway,
Chatswood, NSW 2067
MELBOURNE: 343 Little Collins Street, 3000
BRISBANE: 240 Queen Street, 4000

*NEW ZEALAND:* BUTTERWORTHS OF NEW ZEALAND LTD.
WELLINGTON: 77-85 Custom House Quay, 1

*SOUTH AFRICA:* BUTTERWORTH & CO. (SOUTH AFRICA) (PTY.) LTD.
DURBAN: 152/154 Gale Street

**Canadian Cataloguing in Publication Data**

Overbeek, Johannes, 1932-
Population and Canadian society

Includes index.
ISBN 0-409-85740-8

1. Canada - Population. I. Title.

HB3529.083 304.6'0971 C80-094007-5

*To the memory of James Saunders*

# *Preface*

When in 1975 I was invited to teach the "Population and Society" course at the University of Guelph, I realized that no suitable introductory text fitting Canadian needs existed. I decided therefore to give it a try myself.

Throughout the text I will often compare Canadian statistics with those of Canada's mighty neighbour, the United States. I have decided that on occasion comparisons with some European countries and certain developing countries are also in order. I will limit myself mainly (although not exclusively) to Iran as an example of the latter category for the good reason that I lived and taught there for two years.

There is usually something unique about each country and Canada is no exception. Canada, for instance, is the largest nation in the Western hemisphere and the second largest (after the USSR) in the world. Canada is thinly populated by comparison. Her 3,851,809 square miles of territory (more than 40 times the size of Britain) are inhabited by some 23 million people in 1976, which amounts to the very low density of 6 persons per square mile.

If, in approximately 89% of the total land area, there is no permanent settlement, it is because Canada's huge land mass has its limitations. The larger part of Canada is under arctic climate and a great deal of the remainder is rocky or mountainous. Only one seventh of the total land surface is suitable for agriculture. Canada's population is distributed in very much the same way as that of the world as a whole. People obviously cluster in the most favorable and livable areas. Most Canadians live within a strip 200 miles wide along the American border, where the climate is relatively temperate, or on a narrow fringe near the Atlantic or Pacific Ocean.

There is no lack of information about Canada. *Statistics Canada,* established in 1918 as the *Dominion Bureau of Statistics,* is the main collector and publisher of socioeconomic statistical information. This agency also conducts censuses at five- and ten-year intervals. The last five-year census was taken in 1976. Students should learn to use such publications as the *Canada Yearbook* and the census reports which contain a great deal of valuable basic demographic information.

I found the writing of the book an exciting challenge, and I hope that instructors and students at Canadian universities will enjoy it too. Hopefully, my experience in Europe, the United States and Asia has helped to put Canada's demographic issues in proper perspective. Considering the fact that universities in this country turn increasingly to the one-semester system I have tailored the size of the book to fit such needs.

I wish to express my sincerest thanks to Dr. Nesim Tumkaya who was kind enough to read the entire manuscript. He made numerous helpful suggestions and contributed to increasing the quality of the text. I am also indebted to colleagues and students at both the University of Guelph and Pahlavi University for their indirect but helpful input to my thinking. For whatever flaws remain the author accepts sole responsibility.

# Table of Contents

Chapter 1

# *The Nature of Population Study*

A population consists of a number of people inhabiting a geographical area which may be a nation, a province, a city and the like. Populations are obviously the subject of study by population experts. There is an important reciprocal relationship between a population and its social setting. Societies which are predominantly agricultural or industrial do have a number of specific characteristics. When, for instance, a society moves from a predominantly agricultural to a chiefly industrial stage its population characteristics change as well.

It is customary to establish a difference between formal demography and population analysis. Formal demography refers to the statistical description and analysis of human populations. In other words, formal demography aims at statistical measurement of a given population and its evolution.

Population statistics have a logic of their own. If a population grows, it may be because the number of births in a population exceeds the number of deaths or perhaps because the number of immigrants exceeds the number of emigrants. Demographers therefore do not only study the current state of a population but are also interested in its evolution and sometimes predict its future course. We refer here to the difference between a picture and movie. The picture is to be compared to the numerical portrayal of a human population, the movie pertains to the changes taking place over time. The formal demographer studies and analyses both. Formal demography is basically a quantitative discipline. Numbers and measurement are its very basis.

While formal demography limits itself to the study of such subjects as the size, composition and distribution of a population, population analysis or study, leaves the realm of statistical measurement and seeks to explain the determinants and consequences of observed population trends. Population analysis therefore is related to all the social sciences and is by definition interdisciplinary. The population analyst may for example attempt to examine the impact of fast population growth on economic development or investigate the determinants of a decline in fertility which can be social, economic, psychological, etc. Population study uses the data of formal demography and ties them to the concepts of the other social sciences. As Hauser and Duncan state it — demographic analysis is confined to the study and components of population variation and change while population studies transcend this and devote themselves also to the relationships between population changes and social, economic, political, geographical and psychological variables.[1]

## Bibliography

Hauser, P.M., O. D. Duncan, *The Study of Population,* Chicago: University of Chicago Press, 1964.

Henripin, J., *Eléments de Démographie,* Montréal: Librairie De L'Universite De Montreal, 1973.

Thompson, W. S., D. T. Lewis, *Population Problems,* New York: McGraw-Hill, 1965.

---

[1]P. M. Hauser, O. D. Duncan, ''Overview and Conclusions'' in P. M. Hauser, O. D. Duncan, *The Study of Population* (Chicago: The University of Chicago Press, 1964), pp. 2-3.

# Chapter 2

# *The Sources of Information for Demographers*

## A. Population Registers

Demographers need statistical information, and its collection is an essential component of the study of population. Statistical information is gathered in a number of ways. Some countries, for example, maintain continuous population registers which contain full information about the sex, age, marital status, occupation, religion and location of each person in the country.

This system requires local registration offices to maintain a separate card for each individual on which every change in status (e.g. marriage, migration, etc.) is recorded. The system has the advantage of furnishing complete information about the population but it is onerous and time-consuming. Only certain small developed countries such as Switzerland, the Netherlands and the Scandinavian countries maintain such a system. It is nonexistent in Canada and the United States.

## B. Census

The census is an extremely important piece of information for the student of population. Censuses are basically inventories of the entire population at a given time. One could define the census as the entire process of collecting, compiling and publishing demographic and socio-economic data of a defined population living in a specific area at a specific time.

Censuses have been carried out from the earliest civilized times. They were usually implemented for such limited objectives as military conscription and tax purposes. A typical feature of the modern census is its regularity. In many developed and developing countries the inhabitants are enumerated every 10 years. The first modern census system began in Sweden in 1749. This country now has the best historical statistics in the world.

In Canada censuses are taken at five- and ten-year intervals. Statistics Canada is in charge of conducting them. The decennial census has been taken every ten years since 1851 and quinquennial censuses since 1956.[1] The quinquennial cen-

---

[1]In 1851 and 1861 separate censuses were taken for the provinces. The first nationwide census dates from 1871.

sus however, is much smaller in scope. The latest ten-year census took place in 1971 and the latest five-year census in 1976. In the United States, where the first census was taken in 1790, the inhabitants are constitutionally required to be enumerated every ten years.

For the 1971 ten-year census of Canada the specific point of time was midnight May 31/June 1. In practice, however, this amounts to June 1. At that moment everybody alive in Canada was to be enumerated while babies and immigrants arriving after that point of time were to be excluded.

As it is in the United States, taking a census every ten years is a constitutional requirement in Canada. Canada has traditionally used the *de jure* system of census enumeration in which persons away from their homes are counted in with the population as if they were at their regular place of residence. The United States has always practiced the alternative system, i.e., the *de facto* approach whereby persons are actually counted at the location where they happen to be situated on the census date.

Large scale enumerations such as censuses inevitably contain certain errors. Some sources of error are inherent in the periodic character of the census, especially in the problems of staffing. The mobilization of a large staff of enumerators for short-term employment results in problems of selection, incentive and field supervision. Mistakes in the collection and analysis of data are inevitable. However, with existing corrective quality control techniques, the results in a country like Canada are nevertheless satisfactory. In the United States and Canada a typical census is estimated to contain a 2.5% error which still means 97.5% completeness. In the censuses taken in the third world nations, errors are of course far greater.

## C. Sample Surveys

Sample surveys can be thought of as partial censuses. The kind of information which is collected is the same. A small and skilled staff can obtain, relatively cheaply and quickly, vital information from a survey population which is only a fraction of the entire population but related to the total population in a known and regular manner. Partial enumerations are increasingly used especially for data needed in intercensal intervals but also as adjuncts to complete census enumerations.

Surveys can be more accurate than a total census in cases where the skills of the enumerators leave something to be desired. Low income countries sometimes cannot as yet afford censuses because of a lack of qualified interviewers. Surveys then provide a solution because only a small staff is needed. Experienced personnel can even be borrowed from other countries.

Following the example of the United States, which started this method in 1970, Canada adopted for the 1971 census the method of self-enumeration combined with large-scale use of sample coverage. Under this system, a relatively small questionnaire was filled out by most Canadians, while a relatively small number completed a more extensive one. For the 1971 census only three percent of the population (mostly living in remote regions) was enumerated by the traditional canvasser method. This new method of census-taking, possible in a highly literate population, has the advantage of speed, accuracy and low cost.

## D. Vital Statistics

Vital statistics record the incidence of events at or near the time of occurrence. They largely pertain to birth, marriage, divorce and death. The origins of civil registration are ecclesiastical. In some parts of Western Europe the Church authorities have kept lists of baptisms, weddings and burials since the eleventh century. In Quebec the Catholic Church has kept records since 1628.

In Western Europe vital registration occurs on a national scale. In Canada civil registration has traditionally been the responsibility of the provinces and territories. The federal government compiles and publishes the data. Vital registration has been collected and published for all provinces since 1926 and for all territories since 1950.

In the United States vital registration is equally a regional responsibility. The states collect this kind of information on a separate basis, while a Federal Agency, which is part of the Department of Health, Education and Welfare, organizes and publishes the information on a country-wide basis.

## E. International Migration Statistics

A migrant is a person who moves from one political or administrative area to another. A migrant may move within the nation, say from Quebec to Ontario, or he (or she) may actually cross the national boundary and move, for example, to the United States. Countries such as Canada which do not keep continuous population registers usually do not keep a precise record of internal migration either. However, Canadian censuses now collect information about the place of birth and current residence of Canadians. This procedure provides some information about interprovincial migrations. The 1961 and 1971 censuses also included questions seeking to determine the exact locality of habitation of each individual at the date of the previous census five years before. A comparison with the present residence of the same people allows some conclusions regarding the magnitude and direction of internal migration over the period.

With regard to international migration, many countries, including Canada, actually collect and publish information only on immigrants not emigrants. The statistical documentation of immigration is the responsibility of the Department of Employment and Immigration. When immigrants arrive they fill in cards which seek information about sex, age, marital status, profession and the like. Migration statistics are somewhat imprecise. One of the many reasons for this lack of accuracy is that no information is supplied about return migrants, that is, persons who move back to their area of origin.

## Bibliography

Kammeyer, K. C. W., *An Introduction to Population,* San Francisco: Chandler, 1971.

Sauvy, A., *La Population,* Paris: P.U.F., 1970.

Spiegelman, M., *Introduction to Demography,* Rev. Ed., Cambridge: Harvard Univ. Press, 1968.

Thompson, W. S., D. T. Lewis, *Population Problems,* 5th ed., New York: McGraw-Hill, 1965.

# Chapter 3

# *The Growth of Population*

## A. A Sketch of World Population History

We have only vague ideas about the world population in the distant past when people lived in small nomadic groups devoting themselves to basic subsistence activities such as hunting, fishing and food gathering. Numbers were certainly very small as the primitive hunting and food gathering technology could sustain only very few people.

It has been estimated that a million years ago the world community counted some one hundred and twenty-five thousand inhabitants. The population grew to about five or ten million people at the beginning of the agricultural revolution nearly ten thousand years ago. The latter, it will be remembered, involved the cultivation of plants and the domestication of animals.

The radical change in agriculture which occured between the Bronze Age and Iron Age greatly improved the food supplies while making them at the same time more reliable. As a result the population ceiling was moved upwards and population increase was enhanced. In 3500 B.C., the population of the globe had increased to about thirty million.

At the time of the birth of Christ total numbers had multiplied by eight. Toward the death of Emperor Augustus the population of the Roman Empire alone counted between forty-five and eighty million. By 1800 the world community had reached the figure of one billion. Around the sixteenth century the rate of increase rose to one percent per annum and remained at that level until the beginning of the twentieth century.

When the food-gatherers and hunters became plowmen and herdsmen, the first acceleration of population growth occurred. The scientific-industrial revolution which began in the sixteenth and seventeenth century raised the population ceiling again by increasing the food supplies even more and thus sparked another increase in the rate of population growth. The scientific revolution also resulted in improvements in scientific medicine and public health practices. It now became possible to postpone death, and children, who in earlier times might have died before reaching the age of procreation, now survived to become parents themselves and contribute to further population expansion.

While the first billion mark was reached in 1800 it took only 130 years (in 1930) to reach the second billion figure. In 1960 the world population comprised three billion and in the early part of 1976 the four billion mark was attained. Current estimations tell us that in 1985 or 1986 the five billion figure will be reached. The following tables summarize world population growth and the relevant rates of increase.

TABLE 1. Estimated World Population (in millions)*

| Years Ago | Population (in millions) | Cultural Stage |
|---|---|---|
| 1,000,000 | .125 | Lower Paleolithic |
| 300,000 | 1. | Middle Paleolithic |
| 25,000 | 3.34 | Upper Paleolithic |
| 10,000 | 5.32 | Mesolithic (Bronze Age) |
| 6,000 | 86.5 | Neolithic (Iron Age) |
| A.D. 1 | 250. | Early Farming and Handicraft |
| 1650 | 545. | Early Industrial & Scientific Revolution |
| 1750 | 728. | Industrial & Commercial Stage |
| 1800 | 906. | Second Industrial Revolution |
| 1850 | 1,171. | Contemporary Period |
| 1900 | 1,608. | Idem |

***Source:** E. S. Deevey, "The Human Population", *Scientific American,* Vol. CC III (September, 1960), p. 196.

TABLE 2. Estimates of World Population by Regions, 1900-2000 (in millions)*

| Area | 1900 | 1950 | 1970 | 2000 |
|---|---|---|---|---|
| World Total | 1608 | 2400 | 3621. | 6,406 |
| Europe | 401 | 541** | 459. | 540 |
| North America | 81 | 166 | 226.4 | 296 |
| Latin America | 63 | 162 | 284.2 | 625 |
| Russia-USSR | n.f. | 195 | 242.8 | 321 |
| Asia | 937 | 1320 | 2,037.5 | 3,757 |
| Africa | 120 | 198 | 351.7 | 834 |
| Oceania | 6 | 13 | 19.4 | 33 |

***Sources:** A. M. Carr-Saunders, *World Population, Past Growth and Present Trends* (Oxford: Clarendon Press, 1936), p. 42.

United Nations, Department of Economic and Social Affairs, *Concise Report on the World Population Situation in 1970-1975 and Its Long-Range Implications* (ST/ESA/Series A/56) (New York, 1974), p. 5.

**Until 1950 the figures for Europe include the population of the European part of Soviet Russia. Thereafter European figures exclude the USSR population.

TABLE 3. Annual Population Increase in the World (%)*

| Year | Average Rate of Increase |
|---|---|
| 0-1499 | 0.02-0.04 |
| 1500-1779 | 0.2 |
| 1800-1849 | 0.5 |
| 1850-1899 | 0.5 |
| 1900-1949 | 0.8 |
| 1950-1964 | 1.8 |
| 1965-1970 | 1.9 |
| 1970-1975 | 1.93 |

***Sources:** K. Davis, "The World Demographic Transition," *Annals of Political and Social Science,* Vol. CC LXXIII (January, 1945), p. 3.
H. Gerard, G. Wunsch, *Comprendre La Démographie* (Verviers: Marabout Université, 1973), p. 116.
United Nations, *ibid.,* p. 5.

As the table above shows the present rate of increase for the world as a whole is very close to two percent, which implies a doubling time of about 35 years.[1] The demographic rate of growth for the more developed regions taken together is 0.88% for the 1970-1975 period. For the less developed nations this rate attains the 2.36% figure. As we shall see later in this text the relationship between the level of socio-economic development and fertility is usually inverse.

## B. The Present and the Future

The figures shown above demonstrate that the growth rate has increased while being applied to an ever-expanding base. As a result the annual increment in the world population constantly rises. In the early 1970s about 124 million births were recorded each year while the number of deaths stood at some 51 million. The resulting net increment of approximately 73 million people is more than three times the entire Canadian population of the same period.

Long-term projections of population trends are difficult to make and likely to be subject to error. We can be certain, however, that the world population will continue to grow for a long time to come. Fertility, however measured, is high in most Asian, Latin American and African countries. A decline in the number of births per family would imply the deliberate regulation of marital fertility, a custom presently not prevailing in most developing nations. A quick change in the age-old high fertility custom is not to be expected.

Another reason why large increments in the world population are in the offing

---

[1]The formula for finding the doubling time is: $n = \frac{70}{r\%}$ where n = doubling time and r% = the rate of increase.

is that in many populations the younger members outnumber their parents by a large margin. The current generation of parents therefore will be replaced by a larger crop of parents in the near future. This means that even if the fertility of the next generation of parents were to be below present levels, the actual number of children born could still be greater.

One of the reasons for the sharp upturn in world population has been mentioned, i.e., the elevation of the population ceiling resulting from increased and improved food supplies. From the early days of pastoral activity and crude agriculture a constant flow of inventions, such as the plow and the horse-collar, has permitted a more intensive use of the land which could then sustain larger numbers. Under primitive conditions both fertility and mortality are high. When a major check on population growth, in this case inadequate subsistence, is gradually removed, death rates could fall, at least temporarily, and numbers expand.

Another major check on population expansion consisted of the whole spectrum of diseases which destroyed life as carelessly as it was created. With catastrophic onslaughts of killing diseases being the rule, life expectancy at birth was short, usually between twenty-five and thirty years. After the Renaissance knowledge and experience began to accumulate relatively rapidly, and from the 18th century onwards the benefits of improved medicine and sanitation became increasingly available. The drop in mortality — a result of improved sanitary and medical knowledge — encouraged population to grow further and when such achievements as the battle against disease-carrying insects, mass vaccinations, new drugs, sanitary protection of water, and safe garbage collection and disposal were transplanted from the Western countries to the developing African, Asian and Latin American nations, their populations literally exploded. Hopefully, birth rates will follow the decline in the death rates in those areas before catastrophic population densities are attained. For the moment, however, "artificial" and low death rates continue to coexist with high "natural" birth rates.

## C. Population Growth in Canada and the United States

The first 150 years of Canada's demographic chronicle, starting in 1600, consisted almost entirely of French-Canadian history. In 1610 Canada's population counted about 10 Europeans and an unknown number of native Indians. The latter probably did not exceed the 200,000 figure. About 10,000 Frenchmen migrated to Canada between 1600 and 1750, a figure which has grown to over six million in the 1970s, a beautiful example of exponential growth. When in 1763 the Treaty of Paris was concluded between France and England, the French Canadians counted 65,000. Cut off from intercourse with France, they received no further demographic reinforcements. At that time the English-speaking population totalled 20,000.

After the peace treaty which gave the United States its independence (1783), some 30,000 loyalists (loyal to Britain) emigrated from America to Canada.

However, it was especially after 1815 that the British began to enter in large numbers. Between 1815 and 1840 some 500,000 British subjects migrated to Canada. Between 1830 and 1870 about one million British citizens entered Canada, many of whom moved to the United States later in their life.

At the first Dominion Census in 1871 the Canadian population had reached the figure of 3.7 million. Between 1681 and 1851 the average annual growth of the European settlers in Canada has been estimated at 3.2%. The decade 1851-61 was one of rapid expansion with an average annual growth rate of 2.9% for the entire decade. Some 23% of this increment was due to net immigration (about 350,000 persons). During the remaining decades of the 19th century demographic expansion was much slower with an average annual growth of 1%. The main cause for this slowdown was the opening up of the American "West" which attracted many Canadian residents. During the last decade of the 19th century, for example, Canada counted 326,000 immigrants while 505,000 Canadian residents left, mainly to the U.S.A. Immigration to Canada picked up during the 1900-14 period which coincided with the opening up of the Canadian "West" and the completion of a railway network linking the various parts of Canada. During the 1901-11 period the growth rate rose to the 3% per annum figure again. Some 1,782,000 immigrants entered the country while 1,067,000 are estimated to have left leaving a net surplus of 715,000. From World War I onwards the annual population growth dropped. Although between 1911 and 1931 Canada was still a heavy receiver of immigrants (2,787,000), the outflow (2,297,000) almost matched it. During the economic depression of the 1930s birth rates in Canada and elsewhere in the Western World fell while the government virtually closed the frontiers. After World War II the population registered accelerated growth again. This phenomenon lasted until about 1961. As in other western nations, the birth rate was on its way up again. This experience was labeled the "postwar baby boom". Canada's prosperity also attracted many foreign immigrants, a number of whom had been repelled by the chaos which the war had left in Europe. In the 1951-61 period alone the population expanded by 28.2% or 2.7% per year. Especially after 1960 the baby boom began to flag and the number of European immigrants lessened as local economic conditions improved. The growth rate for the entire decade declined to 17.5% while between 1966 and 1971 the annual increase in numbers levelled at some 310,000 a year.

Table 4 and Figure 1 illustrate Canada's population growth since 1851. The 1971 population includes 17,550 Eskimos and 295,215 Indians. Present-day Eskimos and Indians now represent less than two percent of Canada's population.

We stressed earlier the two sources of population growth in Canada, i.e., the excess of births over deaths and the surplus of immigrants over emigrants. With regard to internally generated growth, Canada behaved very much like other countries: its birth rate has so far been higher than its death rate. Immigrants to Canada have tended to come in waves. The first major wave came after the American independence when a number of British loyalists decided to settle in Canada. Another wave came in the 1830s and 1840s. The economic difficulties

TABLE 4. Population Growth in Canada, 1851-1971*
*Increase Over Preceding Census*

| Census Year | Population | Number | % Increase | Average Annual (%) |
|---|---|---|---|---|
| 1851 | 2,436,297 | | | |
| 1861 | 3,229,633 | 793,336 | 32.6 | 2.9 |
| 1871 | 3,689,257 | 459,624 | 14.2 | 1.3 |
| 1881 | 4,324,810 | 635,553 | 17.2 | 1.6 |
| 1891 | 4,833,239 | 508,429 | 11.8 | 1.1 |
| 1901 | 5,371,315 | 538,076 | 11.1 | 1.1 |
| 1911 | 7,206,643 | 1,835,328 | 34.2 | 3.0 |
| 1921 | 8,787,949 | 1,581,306 | 21.9 | 2.0 |
| 1931 | 10,376,786 | 1,588,837 | 18.1 | 1.7 |
| 1941 | 11,506,655 | 1,129,869 | 10.9 | 1.0 |
| 1951** | 14,009,429 | 2,502,774 | 21.8 | 1.7 |
| 1961 | 18,238,247 | 4,228,818 | 28.2 | 2.7 |
| 1971 | 21,568,310 | 3,330,064 | 17.5 | 1.5 |

*__Sources:__ Ministry of Industry, Trade and Commerce, *Canada Yearbook, 1975* (Ottawa: Information Division, Statistics Canada, 1975), p. 162.

L. O. Stone, *et al.*, *The Population of Canada: A Review of the Recent Patterns and Trends* (Paris: C.I.C.R.E.D. Series, 1974), p. 2.

**Census figures include Newfoundland for the first time.

in Britain — the potato famine in Ireland (1846) — induced a large stream of persons to leave the stricken lands. When the Canadian "West" was opened up and millions of fresh acres of land became available, another wave of settlers was pulled in. This occurred between 1900 and the outbreak of the First World War. Finally, during the fifteen years following World War II large numbers of European refugees, war brides and persons who feared that Europe would never rise from her ashes again, established themselves in Canada. The typical situation so far has been that Canada has known short periods of heavy immigration followed by longer periods of gradual losses mainly to the U.S.A. Between 1851 and 1950, for instance, Canada welcomed 7.1 million people and lost 6.6 million. However, about 40% of the emigrants moving out were Canadian-born. Table 5 shows the growth components of the Canadian population between 1851 and 1971.

With regard to the future, it must be admitted that demographic projections are beset with difficulties. Mortality in a country like Canada is low and stable but fertility may change from year to year. The next table and graph summarize the results of three population projections as published in the *Canada Yearbook* of 1974. Projection A assumes a rise in fertility from 2.19 children per woman in 1971 to 2.60 children by 1985. A net annual immigration surplus of 100,000 is

FIGURE 1. Canadian Population from 1851 to 1971*

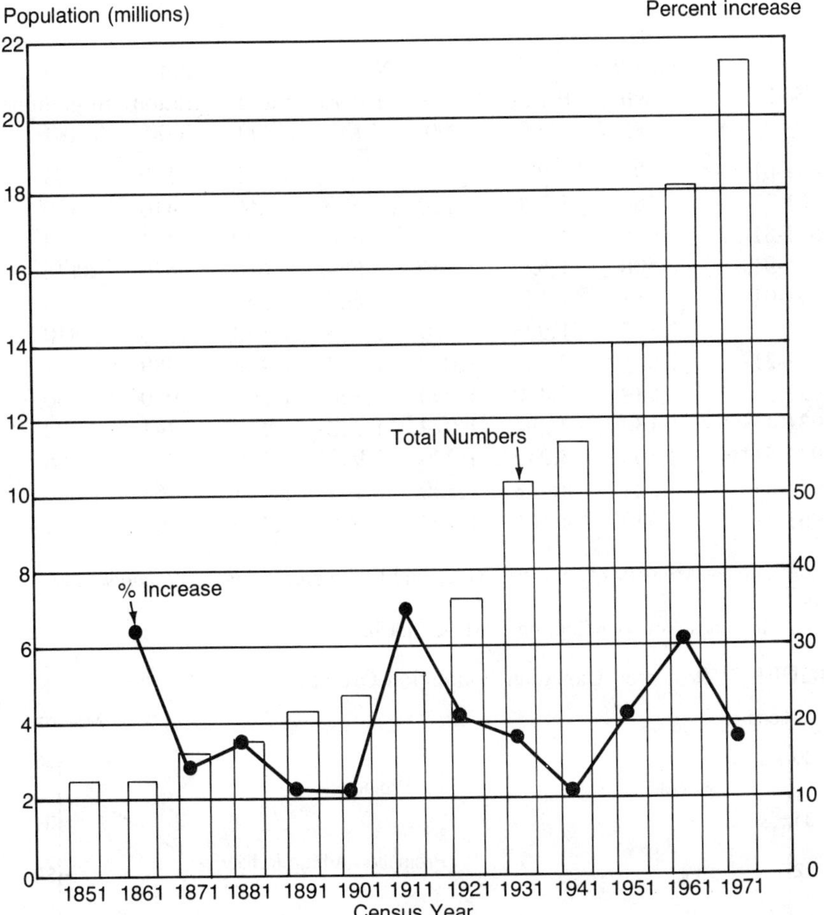


***Source:** Ministry of Industry, Trade and Commerce, *Canada Yearbook, 1973* (Ottawa: Information Division, Statistics Canada, 1973), p. 182.

also expected as well as a slight improvement in mortality conditions. Projection B which is possibly more realistic, conjectures that fertility will remain unchanged at the 2.20 children per woman level with a net annual migration gain of 60,000. Mortality will behave as under assumption A. Projection C hypothesizes that fertility will drop to 1.80 children per woman with migration and mortality behaving as under B. Figure 2 and Table 6 show the three models discussed above.

TABLE 5. Growth Components of the Canadian Population from 1851 to 1971*

| Period | Total Population growth '000 | Births '000 | Deaths '000 | Natural increase '000 | Immi-gration '000 | Emi-gration '000 | Net migration '000 |
|---|---|---|---|---|---|---|---|
| 1851-61 | 793 | 1,281 | 670 | 611 | 352 | 170 | 182 |
| 1861-71 | 460 | 1,370 | 760 | 610 | 260 | 410 | -150 |
| 1871-81 | 636 | 1,480 | 790 | 690 | 350 | 404 | - 54 |
| 1881-91 | 508 | 1,524 | 870 | 654 | 680 | 826 | -146 |
| 1891-01 | 538 | 1,548 | 880 | 668 | 250 | 380 | -130 |
| 1901-11 | 1,835 | 1,925 | 900 | 1,025 | 1,550 | 740 | 810 |
| 1911-21 | 1,581 | 2,340 | 1,070 | 1,270 | 1,400 | 1,089 | 311 |
| 1921-31 | 1,589 | 2,420 | 1,060 | 1,360 | 1,200 | 970 | 230 |
| 1931-41 | 1,130 | 2,294 | 1,072 | 1,222 | 149 | 241 | - 92 |
| 1941-51** | 2,503 | 3,212 | 1,220 | 1,992 | 548 | 382 | 166 |
| 1951-61 | 4,228 | 4,468 | 1,320 | 3,148 | 1,543 | 463 | 1,080 |
| 1961-71 | 3,330 | 4,105 | 1,497 | 2,608 | 1,429 | 707 | 722 |

***Source:** Ministry of Industry, Trade and Commerce, *Canada Yearbook, 1973*, p. 208.

**Includes Newfoundland in 1951 but not in 1941.

FIGURE 2. Projected Canadian Population Growth*

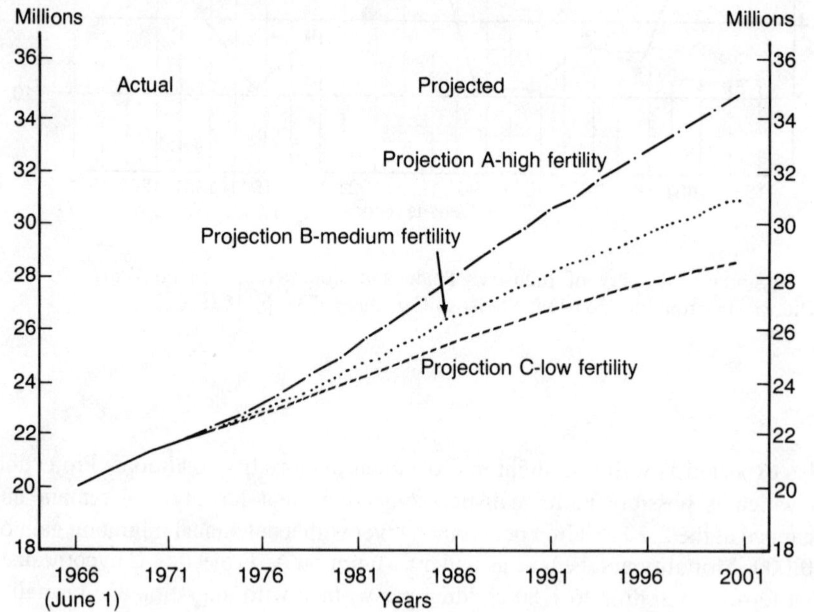


***Source:** Ministry of Industry, Trade and Commerce, *Canada Yearbook, 1974* (Ottawa: Information Division, Statistics Canada, 1974), p. 139.

TABLE 6. Canadian Population Projections to 2001 (in round numbers)*

| Year | Mid-Year Population | | |
|---|---|---|---|
| | Model A | Model B | Model C |
| 1971 | 21,568,300 | 21,568,300 | 21,568,300 |
| 1976 | 23,086,100 | 22,846,300 | 22,772,400 |
| 1981 | 25,311,500 | 24,472,500 | 24,041,400 |
| 1986 | 27,810,900 | 26,258,600 | 25,382,900 |
| 1991 | 30,177,600 | 27,902,100 | 26,591,400 |
| 1996 | 32,347,100 | 29,317,000 | 27,569,700 |
| 2001 | 34,611,400 | 30,655,500 | 28,369,700 |

***Source:** Ministry of Industry, Trade and Commerce, *Canada Yearbook, 1973*, pp. 160-61.

## *Population Growth in the United States*

Starting from a relatively small base, the population of the United States also grew extremely quickly during the 19th century. Fertility dipped in the twentieth century especially during the economic depression of the 1930s. Like Canada, the United States witnessed a baby boom after World War II which lasted until about 1960 after which fertility dropped again. Immigration in the U.S.A. was heavy until the restrictive laws of the 1920s were enacted. The following table illustrates American population expansion from 1790 to present times.

TABLE 7. United States Population, 1790-1975*

| Year | Total Population |
|---|---|
| 1790 | 3,929,214 |
| 1820 | 9,638,453 |
| 1850 | 23,191,876 |
| 1880 | 50,155,783 |
| 1910 | 91,972,266 |
| 1940 | 131,669,275 |
| 1970 | 203,211,926 |
| 1975 | 213,466,000 |

***Sources:** U.S. Bureau of the Census, *Statistical Abstract of the United States, 1975,* 96th edition (Washington, D.C., 1975), p. 5.

## *France, England, Iran*

To conclude this chapter we will picture the growth of Canada's two main "mother" populations, i.e., the French and the English, as well as that of a developing Asian country, Iran. The figures for Iran show clearly that the population explosion occurred after World War II. In 1976 its population was still growing at a rate of 3% per year.

TABLE 8. Population Growth in France, England and Wales and Iran (in millions)*

| Year | France | England & Wales | Year | Iran |
|---|---|---|---|---|
| 1650 | 20 | 5.5 (year 1688) | 1868 | 4.4 |
| 1750 | 21 | 6.5 | 1881 | 7.6 |
| 1800 | 27.5 | 8.9 | 1906 | 9.5 |
| 1850 | 36 | 17.9 | 1926 | 10 |
| 1900 | 39 | 35.5 | 1946 | 15-18 |
| 1950 | 41.7 | 44 | 1956 | 18.9 |
| 1970 | 50.7 | 49 | 1966 | 25.8 |
| 1975 | 52.9 | 49.2 | 1976 | 33.6 |

***Sources:** M. C. Buer, *Health, Wealth and Population in the Early Days of the Industrial Revolution* (London: Routledge, 1926), p. 22.
D. A. Momeni, *The Population of Iran* (1975), p. 29.
A. Sauvy, *La Population* (Paris: P.U.F., 1970), p. 83.
Kayhan Research Associates, *Iran Yearbook* (Tehran, 1977), p. 41.
United Nations, Department of Economic and Social Affairs, Statistical Office of the United Nations, *Demographic Yearbook, 1975* (New York, 1976), p. 146.

## Bibliography

Beaujot, R. P., *Canada's Population: Growth and Dualism,* Population Bulletin Vol. 33, No. 2 (Population Reference Bureau Inc., Washington, D.C., 1978).

Kalbach, W. E., W. V. McVey, *The Demographic Bases of Canadian Society,* Toronto: McGraw-Hill, 1971.

Reinhard, M. R., A. Armengaud, *Histoire Générale de la Population Mondiale,* Paris: Montchrestien, 1961.

Stone, L. O., *et al., The Population of Canada: A Review of the Recent Patterns and Trends,* C.I.C.R.E.D. Monograph, 1974.

Urquhart, M. C., K. A. H. Buckley, *Historical Statistics of Canada,* Toronto: Macmillan, 1965.

Wrigley, E. A., *Population and History,* New York: McGraw-Hill, 1969.

# Chapter 4

## *World Distribution of Population*

### A. The Uneven Distribution of Population in the World

The previous chapter tried to answer the question "how many". The question dealt with in this section is "where do they live".

The total land area on this planet amounts to approximately 516 million square kilometers, while some 374 million square kilometers are covered by oceans. If in 1970 the remaining 142 million square kilometers had been equally divided amongst the inhabitants of the earth each person would have been entitled to 3.76 hectares or some 10 acres. Each doubling of the world population will cut the per capita amount of available land in half.

The quality of the existing land mass, however, varies greatly. About sixty percent is ill-adapted for human settlement and consists of desert regions (17% of world land area), icecaps and tundras (29%), and mountains (12%). The remaining forty percent also differs sharply in quality.

A striking fact is the uneven distribution of mankind over the globe. Some fifty percent of the earth's population lives on five percent of the land area, while two-thirds of all inhabitants live on one-seventh of the existing land mass. The spatial distribution of the world population is highly irregular, as is the regional allocation of people. In the early seventies Canada counted a population of some 22 million people living on a territory of ten million square kilometers which gives us an average density of just over two persons per square kilometer.[1] We are all familiar with the fact, however, that the Canadian population is heavily concentrated in certain areas such as southern Quebec, southern Ontario, southern British Columbia and lives generally close to the American border, leaving the larger spaces of the North nearly uninhabited. The highest population density is found in the Quebec-Windsor axis or the "Grand Trunk Corridor". This region, roughly 700 miles long and between 100 and 150 miles deep, covers only two percent of Canada's total land area but contains 55 percent of the nation's population. This population cluster also includes ten metropolitan areas.

---

[1]The density of a nation or the number of inhabitants per square kilometer (or mile) is found by dividing the population of a country by its total land area. For example, the 1974 Canadian population was estimated at 22,446,000 inhabitants. The total land area amounted to 9,976,139 km$^2$. Thus we obtain a density of $\frac{22,446,000}{9,976,139} = 2.25$ persons per square kilometer or 5.8 persons per square mile.

The same phenomenon can be observed in other countries. If, for example, we take Australia, we note that its population is heavily concentrated in the eastern and western coastal areas leaving the interior virtually empty. The unequal distribution of men over the globe can perhaps best be thought of as a normal adjustment of population to the environment and the earth's resources. Historical and demographic factors also played their role as we shall note later in this chapter.

Among the reasons for the uneven distribution of the world's population, the geographical ones are foremost. Coastal zones, for instance, attract people while high latitudes and continentality repel them. About seventy-five percent of the world's population lives within 1000 kilometers from the sea. Coastal areas and islands enjoy the advantage of easy access to markets and resource areas, while landlocked areas face the problem of high transport costs because of their inaccessibility to and from other regions. High altitudes tend to have low densities which reflect the increased material and psychic costs of living in such areas. Just over 80% of the world's population lives below an altitude of 500 meters (1640 feet).

The relationship between climate and settlement is obvious. The large majority of the earth's empty lands consists of very dry areas (deserts, etc.) and hot-wet lands. The impact of the climate on human settlement is direct and indirect. In spite of technical progress and human ingenuity, excessively high or low temperatures are repellent. Extreme temperatures and the absence of water make agricultural activities and the raising of animals very difficult, which greatly increases the costs of living in those areas. The northern part of Canada is relatively empty. A combination of stony soils and harsh winters discourages permanent settlement. For Canada as a whole there is no permanent settlement in about 89% of the country.

In Iran, for example, the deserts of the east are virtually unoccupied. Densely settled areas are mainly to be found in the north and the north-western part of the country. In the Caspian Sea area of the north humidity is high, whereas the Zagros mountains water the western part of the country. The dryness of the climate is a major factor in Iranian life and people live near the major water supplies. Some regions in the humid tropics, such as Java, are nevertheless densely populated. The combination of humidity and heat makes multiple cropping possible and lessens the need for shelter and clothing. However, the superabundance of heat and precipitation encourages the spread of plant, animal and human diseases.

In certain cases deposits of minerals or fossil fuels may attract population. Those deposits for which there is a strong demand and which are found in relatively few places have the greatest potential to attract people. The rich resources of British Columbia and Alberta have greatly contributed to the bringing of settlers to these provinces.

The influence of the soil, although difficult to dissociate from other factors, is undeniable. The soils, which are the most fertile and therefore most conducive to human colonization are the rich alluvial soils of the deltas (Nile, Mekong, etc.), the volcanic soils, and the black chernozem of certain grasslands. In Canada agricultural operations are conducted on about seven percent of the total land area by a farm population of 1,419,795 persons (1971 figure).

The geographic distribution of mankind has also been determined by demographic and historical factors. The fact that the French colonized Quebec in the 17th century and the fact that the fertility of the French has remained unusually high for a long time are responsible for the six million French-Canadians now living in Quebec. The first settlers in the United States established themselves in the areas closest to Europe, although the bulk of the resources were to be found in the west. As a result the northeastern part of the United States is still the most densely settled part.

Presently some 63% of the world's population lives in four great clusters. Both in North America and in Europe, the heaviest population concentrations are found near the Atlantic Ocean. The populations of these areas are mainly urban, industrialized and enjoy a high standard of living. Asia has two major clusters, one in East Asia (Japan, Taiwan, China and Korea) and another one in tropical South Asia (India, Pakistan, Ceylon). It may be noted that the first Asian cluster borders upon the Pacific Ocean while the second adjoins the Indian Ocean.

## B. Urbanization in the World

The phenomenon of urbanization is closely related to the spatial distribution of people. Urbanization actually implies a redistribution of people resulting in heavy concentrations in certain areas, such as in and around Toronto, Montreal, Edmonton and Vancouver, leaving other regions virtually uninhabited.

Urbanization can be defined as a rise in the proportion of the total population concentrated in urban areas. Urban areas can be characterized as cities of 100,000 or more although each nation seems to use a different yardstick in its definition of urban regions. The latest Canadian (1971) census definition of urban population included all persons living in incorporated cities, towns and villages with a population of 1000 and over, as well as persons living in unincorporated places of 1000 and over, having a population density of at least 1000 per square mile. Equally considered as urban were the built-up fringes of these cities, towns and villages on the condition that they met the criteria of population and density. It would seem rather arbitrary to consider a village of 1000 inhabitants to be urban. In fact, in Europe, where farmers often live together in villages, such a definition would not reflect reality faithfully. In Canada and the United States, however, a village of 700 inhabitants will often be more "urban", economically speaking, than a town of 2000 inhabitants in Europe.

Three conditions seem to determine the existence of towns and cities. First, an agricultural surplus to feed the urban population must be produced by the rural areas. Second, a network of mutually acceptable trade relations must exist between city and countryside. Third, the goods and services produced by the cities must be readily accepted by the rural population willing to trade the agricultural surplus for them.

Urbanization is a recent phenomenon not older than some two hundred years. Cities themselves appeared over 5000 years ago but they were small and encircled by a superabundant rural population. Even the European cities of the Middle Ages and the Renaissance were small, never containing more than a relatively small percentage of the total population. In the fourteenth century, London counted 40,000 inhabitants and an average city would be inhabited by some 10,000 people. The emergence of urbanized societies can be regarded as one of the major events of recent times.

In 1801 England and Wales had less than ten percent of their population in cities of 10,000 or more. A hundred years later in 1901 some 35% of the population lived in such cities. In 1970 the figure had reached 78%. In 1846, some 24.4% of France's population was urban. The figure had risen to 66.2% by 1968.

Urbanization seems to be closely, almost mechanically, related to socio-economic development. Each substantial increase in per capita income seems to result in a migratory stream from rural to urban areas. Basically, one can generalize by stating that in industrialized, advanced societies, the rural population is well below 40%. A transitional nation like Iran, which is already well advanced on the growth-modernization path, has a rural population of 53% while 47% of its population is now classified as urban (1976 figures).

In very low income countries with little industry and infrastructure, the rural population will normally exceed 75%. The two charts below picture the typical evolution of the urbanization process of a nation as it goes through the various stages of development and the percent growth of the American urban population over some 180 years.

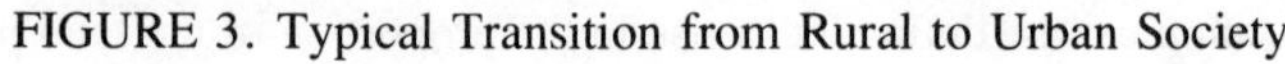

FIGURE 3. Typical Transition from Rural to Urban Society

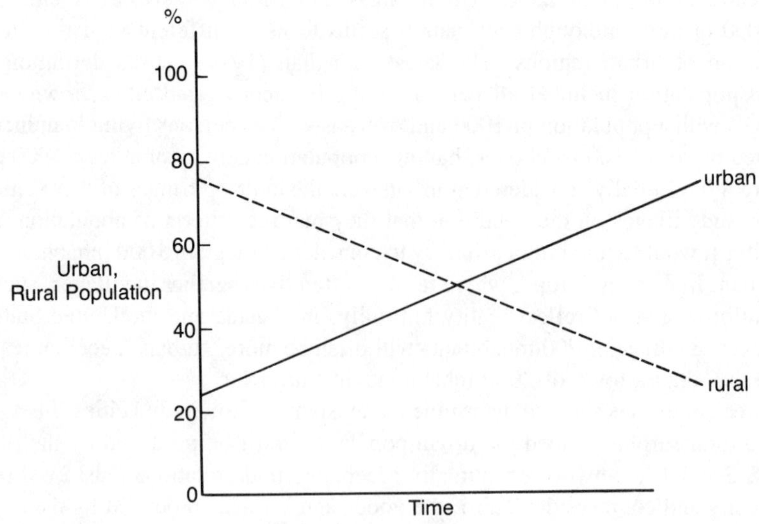

FIGURE 4. Growth of America's Urban Population*

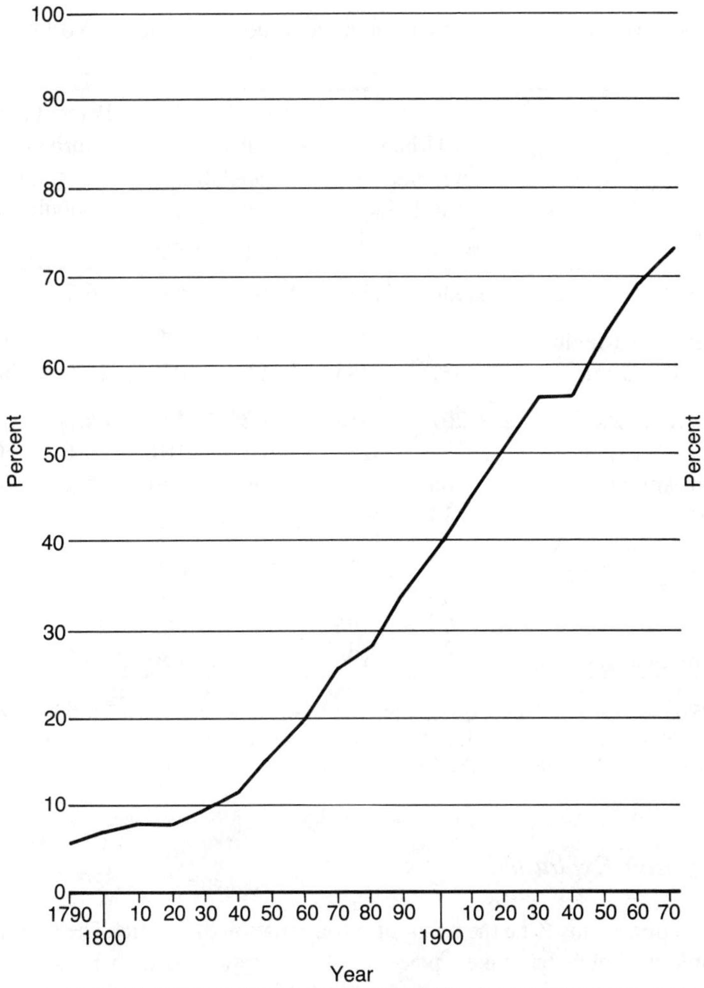


***Source:** U.S. Department of Commerce, Bureau of the Census, *1970 Census of Population,* Vol. I, Characteristics of the Population (Washington, D.C.: Government Printing Office, 1973), p. 32.

43843

The following table pictures the state of affairs with regard to urbanization in the world as a whole.

TABLE 9. Urban and Rural Population in the Major Areas of the World in 1970 and 1975*

| | Urban population (millions) | | Rural population (millions) | | Percentage of urban in total population | |
|---|---|---|---|---|---|---|
| Area | 1970 | 1975 | 1970 | 1975 | 1970 | 1975 |
| World total | 1,330 | 1,548 | 2,291 | 2,439 | 36.7 | 38.8 |
| More developed regions | 699 | 763 | 386 | 370 | 64.4 | 67.4 |
| Less developed regions | 631 | 785 | 1,906 | 2,070 | 24.9 | 27.5 |
| Europe | 297 | 318 | 162 | 156 | 64.6 | 67.1 |
| USSR | 137 | 154 | 105 | 101 | 56.6 | 60.5 |
| Northern America | 168 | 181 | 59 | 56 | 74.2 | 76.5 |
| Oceania | 14 | 15 | 6 | 6 | 69.9 | 71.2 |
| South Asia | 232 | 288 | 879 | 980 | 20.9 | 22.7 |
| East Asia | 245 | 299 | 681 | 706 | 26.5 | 29.8 |
| Africa | 75 | 96 | 276 | 305 | 21.5 | 24.0 |
| Latin America | 161 | 196 | 123 | 130 | 56.7 | 60.1 |

***Source:** United Nations, Department of Economic and Social Affairs, *Concise Report on the World Population Situation in 1970-1975 and Its Long-Range Implications* (ST/ESA series A/56) (New York, 1974), p. 33.

## *Urbanization Explained*

Urbanization seems to be the result of a combination of factors. The revolution in technology which has taken place implied a rationalization of agriculture which greatly increased per capita output and thus the food surpluses needed to sustain the cities. At the same time human energy was increasingly replaced by mechanical energy which resulted in a pressure on the rural population to leave the land. Improvements in transport facilities ended the geographical isolation of the rural areas and facilitated the transfer of labor from rural communities to cities.

As incomes rise and nations become wealthier the demand for city-produced goods and services expands faster than the demand for food items. Beyond a certain threshold, an increased proportion of the rising disposable incomes will be spent on industrial products and urban-type services, which will result in an expansion of those sectors. The latter will then tend to draw labor from the rural areas because of the relatively high wages they can afford to pay.

The clustering of firms in urban areas, moreover, yields important external economies — that is, they result in a number of cost-reducing situations. An industrial environment, in other words, makes it attractive for new firms or companies located elsewhere to establish themselves in such surroundings. Repair and transport services will be more easily available; consultancy, banking and marketing services more accessible; manpower trained by other firms can be hired; the closeness of sources of supply reduces the need for large inventories, etc.

A last economic reason for the increasing concentration of people in the cities has been the revolution in energy and transport. It liberated industries from natural sources of power such as wind or streams. Trains, steamships and trucks could bring the new fuels and raw materials to the cities while formerly distant markets were drawn nearer.

Non-economic factors should not be neglected in this discussion. The level of social and cultural amenities is always higher in cities than in the rural areas and this attracts people to the cities.

After World War II the phenomenon of suburbanization or metropolitan dispersion was superimposed on the urbanization process. This occurred mainly in the developed countries of the Western World. The outward expansion of the cities has been made possible by the same forces which facilitated urbanization: the widespread availability of electrical energy, the improvements in motor transport, the highway systems, better communications, etc. With electricity available and rapid, cheap and efficient transport possible, many commercial and industrial activities become less location-bound. Once the city has reached a certain density, people and industries tend to move to the suburbs where land is cheaper, the taxes lower and life less congested and more convenient. With the growth of the areas surrounding city and town, agglomerations keep growing without the inconveniences of greater density.

Historically the urbanization process has been accompanied by rural out-migration which, first, reduced the growth rate of the rural population and, finally, caused the absolute size of some rural communities to decline. Since 1851 the rural population of England and Wales has declined in absolute numbers. This helped farms to consolidate in larger and more viable units relying on modern implements and mechanical energy. As a result of the modernization of the countryside, ten percent or less of the population produces enough food for the remaining ninety percent and large quantities for export. This, at least, is the situation in Canada and the U.S.A.

In a number of less developed countries, however, the situation is wholly different. In some developing countries, such as Iran, the growth of urban population is accompanied by a corresponding industrialization, and development of transport and communication and the like. This modernization-development process is of course greatly facilitated by the inflow of large amounts of oil earnings. In some other countries, however, people move to the cities while no economic expansion is occurring. If a rural exodus occurs while employment opportunities in the urban areas do not improve, excessive accumulation of labor in marginal service activities and substandard housing are bound to occur. While in the West urban fertility ranks below rural fertility, this is often not the case in low-income areas. In those areas city growth, as a result of the natural increase of the city dwellers, is much faster than it has ever been in the West. Moreover, some low-income countries, such as India and Pakistan, have a densely settled countryside. The question which arises here is "how can the cities in such nations absorb some sixty percent of the rural population once modern technology is introduced on the farm?" If on top of this the cities themselves have very fertile populations the emergence of giant cities containing more than twenty million people becomes inevitable. For the time being, because of overall high fertility in the low-income countries, the rural population of many of these areas will rise steadily until the end of the century in spite of a heavy outflow of country people to cities and towns.

## C. The Regional Distribution of Canada's Population

The unevenness of population settlement in Canada matches that of the world and very much for the same reasons. The subarctic and polar regions of high latitudes are thinly populated. The Rocky Mountains of the Canadian west defer people as other mountainous areas do. The highest population concentrations live in the most hospitable and/or fertile regions and in coastal districts which enjoy the advantages of good location and accessibility. Canada has reliable data from 1851 onwards when for the first time separate censuses for the provinces were taken. The available data show that from then onwards the Canadian population has been continually redistributed.

In 1851 almost all Canadians lived in eastern and central Canada (the Maritime provinces, Quebec and Ontario). Since then the Maritime provinces have experienced a decline relative to Quebec and Ontario. After 1901 the western provinces gained a greater share of Canada's population. The peak was reached in 1931 when 29.5% of the Canadian population lived in the four western provinces. Since then Manitoba and Saskatchewan have been relatively slow growers while Saskatchewan's population marked an absolute decline between 1966 and 1971. British Columbia and, recently, Alberta contain ever growing proportions of Canada's population.

In Canada, as in the U.S.A., the industrialization process as well as the development of the service sector have altered the pattern of population distribution. Nowadays people tend to concentrate in certain metropolitan areas with an especially favorable location for these types of activity. Ontario, Quebec, British Columbia and Alberta contain rapidly growing industrial urban populations which live mainly in and around Toronto, Montreal, Vancouver and Edmonton. The rapid internal migration towards these urban centers coincides with a flow of immigrants from abroad moving in the same direction.

The overall picture as it manifested itself in the early 1970s is as follows: Ontario, British Columbia and Alberta receive the largest share of internal and

TABLE 10. Percentage Distribution of Population, Canada and All Provinces, 1851-1971*

| Province | 1851 | 1861 | 1871 | 1881 | 1891 | 1901 | 1911 | 1921 | 1931 | 1941 | 1951 | 1961 | 1971 |
|---|---|---|---|---|---|---|---|---|---|---|---|---|---|
| Canada | 100.0 | 100.0 | 100.0 | 100.0 | 100.0 | 100.0 | 100.0 | 100.0 | 100.0 | 100.0 | 100.0 | 100.0 | 100.0 |
| Nfld. | ... | ... | ... | ... | ... | ... | ... | ... | ... | ... | 2.6 | 2.5 | 2.4 |
| P.E.I. | 2.6 | 2.5 | 2.6 | 2.5 | 2.3 | 1.9 | 1.3 | 1.0 | 0.8 | 0.8 | 0.7 | 0.6 | 0.5 |
| N.S. | 11.4 | 10.2 | 10.5 | 10.2 | 9.3 | 8.6 | 6.8 | 6.0 | 4.9 | 5.0 | 4.6 | 4.0 | 3.7 |
| N.B. | 8.0 | 7.8 | 7.7 | 7.4 | 6.6 | 6.2 | 4.9 | 4.4 | 3.9 | 4.0 | 3.7 | 3.3 | 2.9 |
| Quebec | 36.5 | 34.4 | 32.3 | 31.4 | 30.8 | 30.7 | 27.8 | 26.9 | 27.7 | 29.0 | 29.0 | 28.8 | 28.0 |
| Ontario | 39.1 | 43.2 | 43.9 | 44.6 | 43.7 | 40.6 | 35.1 | 33.4 | 33.1 | 32.9 | 32.8 | 34.2 | 35.7 |
| Manitoba | ... | ... | 0.7 | 1.4 | 3.1 | 4.7 | 6.4 | 6.9 | 6.8 | 6.3 | 5.5 | 5.1 | 4.6 |
| Sask. | ... | ... | ... | ... | ... | 1.7 | 6.8 | 8.6 | 8.9 | 7.8 | 5.9 | 5.1 | 4.3 |
| Alberta | ... | ... | ... | ... | ... | 1.4 | 5.2 | 6.7 | 7.1 | 6.9 | 6.7 | 7.3 | 7.6 |
| B.C. | 2.2 | 1.6 | 1.0 | 1.1 | 2.1 | 3.3 | 5.5 | 6.0 | 6.7 | 7.1 | 8.3 | 8.9 | 10.1 |
| Yukon & N.W.T. | 0.2 | 0.3 | 1.3 | 1.4 | 2.1 | 0.9 | 0.2 | 0.1 | 0.1 | 0.2 | 0.2 | 0.2 | 0.2 |

***Source:** Stone *et al.*, *The Population of Canada: A Review of the Recent Patterns and Trends, . . .*, p. 72.

foreign migrants. Quebec, Manitoba and Saskatchewan receive a net inflow of foreigners but lose by internal migration. The Atlantic provinces lose both more foreign-born and Canadian-born citizens than they attract. The following table shows the population redistribution pattern from 1851 to 1971.

Presently, most internal migration is no longer rural-urban because urbanization is a finite process. In Canada the rural-urban transition has been completed with 76.1% of the population registered as urban in 1971. The majority of Canadians work in the industrial, trade and service sectors. Hence, most migrants now move from one urban area to another. Some 90% of all foreign immigrants also settle in urban areas.

## D. Urbanization in Canada

We observed the unprecedented magnitude of modern urbanization in the world in a preceding section. This change in settlement pattern was closely connected to the transition from agriculture to other economic pursuits. Canada, as we noted, has not escaped the migration from rural to urban settlements and a general increase in the proportion of people living in cities.

In Canada, as in other countries, different definitions of "urban" localities have been used. In the 1941 census the population of all incorporated cities, towns and villages, irrespective of size was counted as urban, the remainder being rural. The 1951 census, however, stipulated that all places of at least one thousand population, incorporated or not, were considered urban. The population living on the fringe of Canada's largest fourteen cities, now defined as metropolitan areas, was also to be counted as urban. This modification was made in order to account for the suburbanization process.

The change made in the 1956 census raised the total counted as urban even further because now the definition of urban included the population in the unincorporated fringe of "other major areas" which were defined regions in which the largest incorporated unit had a population of more than 25,000. The fringe areas of the metropolitan orbits were also enlarged. The new definition of "urban" in the 1971 census has been discussed previously. If we apply the 1941 definition of urban and rural for all figures up to 1941 and the concurrent definitions for subsequent totals, we get an interesting picture of the continued population gains in urban areas as they occurred at the expense of rural regions. Canada's transition from a predominantly rural society to one which is primarily urban visibly took place in the period under consideration.

Table 12 shows that more than 75% of the Canadian population is living in urban areas. Ontario's population is the most urbanized and that of Prince Edward Island the least. Ontario and Quebec ranked above the national average. A subdivision of the rural population into farm and non-farm population would indicate that between 1961 and 1971 the rural farm population declined from 11.4% to 6.6%.[2]

---

[2]The rural farm population includes people living in dwellings situated on farms in rural areas according to the census definition.

TABLE 11. Distribution of Canada's Urban and Rural Population 1871 - 1971*

| Year | Total Population | Urban | Rural | Urban | Rural |
|---|---|---|---|---|---|
| 1871 | 3,689,257 | 722,343 | 2,966,914 | 19.58 | 80.42 |
| 1881 | 4,324,810 | 1,109,507 | 3,215,303 | 25.65 | 74.35 |
| 1891 | 4,833,239 | 1,537,098 | 3,296,141 | 31.80 | 68.20 |
| 1901 | 5,371,315 | 2,014,222 | 3,357,093 | 37.50 | 62.50 |
| 1911 | 7,260,643 | 3,272,947 | 3,933,696 | 45.42 | 54.58 |
| 1921 | 8,787,949 | 4,352,122 | 4,435,827 | 49.52 | 50.48 |
| 1931 | 10,376,786 | 5,572,058 | 4,804,728 | 53.70 | 46.30 |
| 1941 | 11,506,655 | 6,252,416 | 5,254,239 | 54.34 | 45.66 |
| 1951 | 14,009,429 | 8,628,253 | 5,381,176 | 61.59 | 38.41 |
| 1961 | 18,238,247 | 12,700,390 | 5,537,857 | 69.64 | 30.36 |
| 1971 | 21,568,310 | 16,410,785 | 5,157,525 | 76.10 | 23.90 |

***Sources:** Urquhart, Buckley, *Historical Statistics of Canada* (Toronto: Macmillan, 1965), p. 14.

Department of Trade and Commerce, *The Canada Yearbook, 1952-53* (Ottawa: Cloutier, 1953), p. 144.

Ministry of Industry, Trade and Commerce, *Canada, 1974* (Ottawa: Information Canada, 1974), p. 163.

Stone, *et al., The Population of Canada* . . ., p. 81.

TABLE 12. Number and Percentage of the Population Classified as Urban and Rural by Province, 1971*

| Province or Territory | Total Population | Percentage | Urban | Percentage | Rural | Percentage |
|---|---|---|---|---|---|---|
| Newfoundland | 522,100 | 100.0 | 298,800 | 57.2 | 223,305 | 42.8 |
| Prince Edward Island | 111,640 | 100.0 | 42,780 | 38.3 | 68,860 | 61.7 |
| Nova Scotia | 788,960 | 100.0 | 447,405 | 56.7 | 341,555 | 43.3 |
| New Brunswick | 634,560 | 100.0 | 361,145 | 56.9 | 273,410 | 43.1 |
| Quebec | 6,027,765 | 100.0 | 4,861,245 | 80.6 | 1,166,520 | 19.4 |
| Ontario | 7,703,105 | 100.0 | 6,343,630 | 82.4 | 1,359,475 | 17.6 |
| Manitoba | 988,250 | 100.0 | 686,445 | 69.5 | 301,800 | 30.5 |
| Saskatchewan | 926,240 | 100.0 | 490,630 | 53.0 | 435,610 | 47.0 |
| Alberta | 1,627,875 | 100.0 | 1,196,255 | 73.5 | 431,620 | 26.5 |
| British Columbia | 2,184,620 | 100.0 | 1,654,405 | 75.7 | 530,215 | 24.3 |
| Yukon | 18,390 | 100.0 | 11,220 | 61.0 | 7,170 | 39.0 |
| N.W.T. | 34,810 | 100.0 | 16,830 | 48.3 | 17,980 | 51.7 |
| Total | 21,568,310 | 100.0 | 16,410,785 | 76.1 | 5,157,525 | 23.9 |

***Source:** Ministry of Industry, Trade and Commerce, *Canada, 1974* . . ., p. 108.

## *Urbanization in the U.S.A.*

That in the United States an identical evolution has taken place is demonstrated in the following short table.

TABLE 13. Percentage Distribution of Urban and Rural Population, U.S.A., 1970*

| Year | Urban | Rural | |
|---|---|---|---|
| 1910 | 45.6 | 54.4 | |
| 1920 | 51.2 | 48.8 | Previous Urban Definition |
| 1930 | 56.1 | 43.5 | |
| 1940 | 56.5 | 43.5 | |
| 1950 | 64.0 | 40.4 | |
| 1960 | 69.9 | 30.1 | Current Urban Definition |
| 1970 | 73.5 | 26.5 | |

***Source:** U.S. Bureau of the Census, *Statistical Abstract of the United States: 1975* (Washington, D.C., 1975), p. 19.

As in Canada, the definition of what is an urban population has changed in the U.S. Prior to 1950, urban places chiefly consisted of incorporated locations of 2500 inhabitants or more. In 1950, however, the concept of "urbanized area" was adopted by the Bureau of the Census. The new definition of "urban" now includes both incorporated and unincorporated concentrations of a minimum of 2500 inhabitants and unincorporated territory included in "urbanized areas."

### Bibliography

Clarke, J. I., *Population Geography,* Toronto: Pergamon Press, 1972.

Davis, K., "The Origin and Growth of Urbanization in the World," in *Population and Society,* ed. C. B. Nam, Boston: Houghton Mifflin, 1968.

Firestone, O. J., *Canada's Economic Development,* 1867-1953, London: Bowes & Bowes, 1958.

Hugon, P., *Démographie,* Paris: Dalloz, 1971.

Kalbach, W. E., W. W. McVey, *The Demographic Bases of Canadian Society,* Toronto: McGraw-Hill, 1971.

United Nations, Department of Economic and Social Affairs, *The Determinants and Consequences of Population Trends,* Vol. I (ST/SOA/SER.A/50), New York, 1974.

Zelinsky, W., *A Prologue to Population Geography,* New Jersey: Prentice Hall, 1966.

## Chapter 5

# *The Use of Absolute and Relative Numbers in Demography*

Statements of frequency of a given trait or process in different populations are basic in demographic work. Such accounts facilitate comparisons between populations and subgroups of a given population with respect to the trait or process in question. The simplest form of a frequency statement is in absolute numbers.

Much of the demographic material published in yearbooks, census reports and the like is presented in terms of absolute numbers. We encounter such statements as "this year 150,000 immigrants entered Canada". Such absolute figures are useful. This particular text contains large numbers of them.

## *Relative Numbers*

Relative numbers such as ratios and rates are abundantly utilized in demographic analysis. They usually express a relationship between two or more numbers and/or they summarize data or an aspect of a set of data. The relative numbers are derived from the absolute ones, which remain the most basic raw material. Relative numbers are especially relevant when we attempt to compare the behavior of a population at different points of time or when we make international comparisons. They greatly enhance the readability of numerical findings. If, for instance, we want to bring into analogy mortality in Canada with mortality in the United States (the latter country has a population about ten times greater), we could do so by setting side by side the total number of deaths in each nation. Such a comparison in absolute numbers would not make much sense. If, however for both countries we relate the number of deaths in some way to the population which produces them, a comparison can become more meaningful.

Ratios are a widely used category of relative numbers. A ratio is the relation between two numbers or quantities expressed as a quotient or fraction. It is a way of comparing two numbers by division. If for example we take the ratio of x to y we can write it as $\frac{x}{y}$ which also means: so many x per unit of y. The two quantities making up a ratio are called the terms of the ratio. The first term is the antecedent and the second term the consequent. The antecedent which precedes the word "to" becomes the numerator and the consequent which follows "to" becomes the denominator. The quantities of a ratio must be expressed in terms of the same universe. If the numerator population is restricted to a subgroup (say males) of a given population (for example, that of Canada), the denominator (say females) should be limited to the same population. A well-known example of a demographic ratio is the sex ratio which summarizes the sex composition of a population in the shortest possible way. It is given by the quotient:

$$\frac{\text{No. of males in an area in a given year}}{\text{No. of females in the same area, in the same year}}$$

The calculation for Canada in 1971 is as follows:

$$\text{Sex Ratio (Canada 1971)} \ \frac{10{,}795{,}000 \text{ males}}{10{,}773{,}000 \text{ females}} = 1.00 \text{ males per female}$$

The sex ratio of immigrants in Canada in the year 1973 was:

$$\frac{94{,}768 \text{ males}}{89{,}432 \text{ females}} = 1.06 \text{ males per female}$$

For every female immigrant in 1973 there were 1.06 males. Obviously 1.06 is an awkward number. In order to avoid such figures the quotient of the fraction form of the ratio is multiplied by a convenient number such as 100 or 1,000 which we call a "constant" designated by the small letter "k". Customarily all rates, ratios and proportions are multiplied by an arbitrary number such as 100 or 1,000 in order to express them in a more understandable manner. The above ratio, for example, then takes the form of $\frac{x}{y} \times k$ and expresses the number of x per 100 or 1,000 units of y. This minor change does not modify the significance of the ratio but merely the way it is expressed. If, in the above example, k = 100 we then obtain 106 male immigrants for every 100 female immigrants. The sex ratio in Canada in 1962 stood at 102. The sex ratio at birth in Canada has fluctuated between 105 and 107 since about 1921.

A rate is computed as a ratio. With rates, however, we express a relative incidence of vital events in a given period of time, usually a year. Stated differently, a rate is a measure of the relative frequency of occurrence of an event. Taking births as an example, we can affirm that the birth rate expresses the number of births during a year per 1,000 inhabitants of a given country. Birth rates, like death rates, are usually per 1,000 persons (‰).

$$\text{Crude Birth Rate (1951)} = \frac{381{,}092 \text{ Births}}{14{,}009{,}000 \text{ Population}} \times 1{,}000$$

$$= 27.2 \text{ per } 1{,}000 \text{ persons living} = 27.2‰$$

Per cent is yet another relative number. Per cent means by the hundred. The term is derived from the Latin "per centum". Thus rate per cent can be defined as the ratio of two similar quantities expressed in hundredths. For example, five per cent means 5 hundredths or 5 out of every 100 or $\frac{5}{100}$. The symbol % can be thought of as replacing the denominator 100. Thus, for example, $\frac{5}{100} = 5\%$ and so on. In conclusion, per cents are ratios with 100 as a common denominator while this denominator can be replaced by the symbol "%".

In demography a proportion is a special type of ratio. Its main feature is that the numerator is included in the denominator. A proportion therefore relates a total number to one of its parts. It shows the ratio of one part to the whole or base number. We can think of such examples as the proportion of Indians in the Canadian population. The computation is as follows:

$$\text{Proportion Indian (Canada 1971)} = \frac{295{,}215 \text{ Indians}}{21{,}568{,}310 \text{ Canadian Population}} \times 100$$

$$= 1.36\% \text{ or 136 Indians per 10,000 Canadians}$$

The proportion of blacks in the 1960 American population is calculated as follows:

$$\frac{18{,}860{,}000 \text{ Negroes}}{178{,}464{,}000 \text{ Total Population (Negroes + non-Negroes)}} \times 100$$

$$= 10.57\% \text{ or 1,057 blacks per 10,000 Americans.}$$

## Bibliography

Barcley, G. W., *Techniques of Population Analysis,* New York: Wiley, 1958.

Blalock, H. M., *Social Statistics,* 2nd ed., New York: McGraw-Hill, 1972.

Landes, P. H., P. K. Hatt, *Population Problems,* New York: American Book Company, 1954.

Pressat, R., *Demographic Analysis,* Chicago: Aldine-Atherton, 1972.

# Chapter 6

# *Mortality*

## A. Basic Measures of Mortality

Contemporary demographers have a tendency to discuss mortality before analysing the two other basic demographic processes — fertility and migration. One reason is that mortality itself requires very little explanation. For instance, one may quarrel over definitions of migration or fertility. With mortality, however, there is no problem. It is simply the termination of a condition called life. Questions of motivation also need not be considered. There are many studies and arguments as to why people migrate or have babies. However, with mortality, there is no motivation unless one considers the unusual case of suicide.

A large number of instruments are used to measure and analyse mortality. First, one can measure the *absolute number of deaths* in a country during a given period (usually a year). The total number of deaths in Canada in 1974 amounted to 166,794. Such a figure, as we explained in the previous chapter, has only minimal significance because it does not take the exposed population into account. As a result the use of absolute figures does not permit comparisons between different periods of history or analogies between nations.

### *The Crude Death Rate*

The *crude death rate* (C.D.R.) is the most frequently used measure of mortality. It records the total number of deaths per thousand persons in any given population.
As formula we have:

$$\text{C.D.R.} = \frac{\text{Number of Deaths per Year}}{\text{Population}} \times 1{,}000 = \frac{D}{P} \bullet k$$

where D = Deaths in the Year
P = Midyear Population, and
k = an arbitrary factor of 1,000

The population in the denominator represents the size of the exposed population at midyear (30th of June or 1st of July). In 1974, the C.D.R. in Canada was

7.4‰, while in the U.S.A. the rate stood at 9.2‰. Thus, the Canadian C.D.R. was computed as follows:

$$\frac{166{,}794}{22{,}446{,}000} \times 1{,}000 = 7.4‰$$

The following table shows the historical downward trend of mortality in Canada as measured by the C.D.R.

TABLE 14. Crude Death Rates per 1,000 Population, Canada, 1851-1974*

| Year | | C.D.R. |
|---|---|---|
| (Average) | 1851-1861 | 22 |
| ” | 1861-1871 | 21 |
| ” | 1871-1881 | 19 |
| ” | 1881-1891 | 18 |
| ” | 1891-1901 | 16 |
| ” | 1901-1911 | 13 |
| ” | 1911-1921 | 13 |
| | 1930 | 10.7 |
| | 1940 | 9.8 |
| | 1950 | 8.5 |
| | 1960 | 8.0 |
| | 1970 | 7.3 |
| | 1974 | 7.4 |

***Source:** Ministry of Industry, Trade and Commerce, *Canada Yearbook, 1975 . . .*, p. 174.

The Canadian death rate compares favorably with that of the United States, as the following table demonstrates.

TABLE 15. Crude Death Rates per 1,000 Inhabitants, United States, 1940-1975*

| Year | C.D.R. |
|---|---|
| 1940 | 10.8 |
| 1950 | 9.6 |
| 1960 | 9.5 |
| 1970 | 9.5 |
| 1975 | 8.9 |

***Sources:** U.S. Bureau of the Census, *Statistical Abstract of the United States: 1977* (Washington, D.C., 1977), p. 55.

United Nations, Department of Economic and Social Affairs, Statistical Office of the United Nations, *Demographic Yearbook, 1975* (ST/ESA/STAT/SER.R/4) (New York, 1976), p. 312.

The C.D.R. has the advantage of showing the level of mortality of the entire population. Its calculation is quick and easy and its meaning is rapidly understood. It also has important limitations. The C.D.R. expresses the frequency of death in a given population without regard for such important characteristics as age and sex structure. A population which contains a larger proportion of older people, other things being equal of course, will have a higher death rate than a "younger" population. The C.D.R., in other words, is heavily affected by a population's age composition. The death rate in Canada is still affected by the relative youth of its population. But, because of the lengthening of life and the decline in the birth rate which started in the 1960s, the Canadian population is now ageing, which will eventually cause the number of deaths in the numerator to rise.[1]

## *Age-Specific Death Rate*

Because of the limitations inherent in the C.D.R., demographers have developed category-specific death rates which remove the effect of population composition. The best known rate in this class is the so-called *age-specific death rate* (A.S.D.R.) which expresses the number of deaths at age i or age interval i in a given year to the total population of age i.[2] Hence the A.S.D.R. informs us of death rates computed separately by age group and thus gives us a reliable picture of mortality as dissociated from the age structure of the population. For reasons of precision and comparison the age-specific death rates are often computed separately by sex. The general formula is:

$$\frac{\text{Deaths of Persons of Age i}}{\text{Midyear Population of People aged i}} \times 1{,}000 = \frac{Di}{Pi} \times 1{,}000$$

where Di = number of deaths of age group i
Pi = the mid-year population of that age group
k = 1,000

Clarifying this with a Canadian example we can compute the average age-specific death rate in 1971 for the age group 20-24. Applying our formula we obtain:

$$\frac{2{,}256}{1{,}889{,}400} \times 1{,}000 = 1.2‰$$

For all nations, the death rates roughly conform to a U-shaped distribution. The reason for this synonymity of the curves showing age-specific mortality is the fact that the earliest period in life is one of high susceptibility to lethal diseases while the processes of physical deterioration are an effect of old age.

---

[1]Chapter 11 will explain in detail how populations grow older and younger.

[2]As Barcley explains: "Small letters designate a portion of the total instead of the total and the letter i designates the i th category in the population (that is, any category we may specify)"; see Barcley, *Techniques of . . .*, p. 22.

The curve shown below hits its lowest point between age 10 and 14 after which it begins to rise. Especially after age 50, the upturn becomes very steep.

FIGURE 5. Age-Specific Death Rates, Canada, 1970*

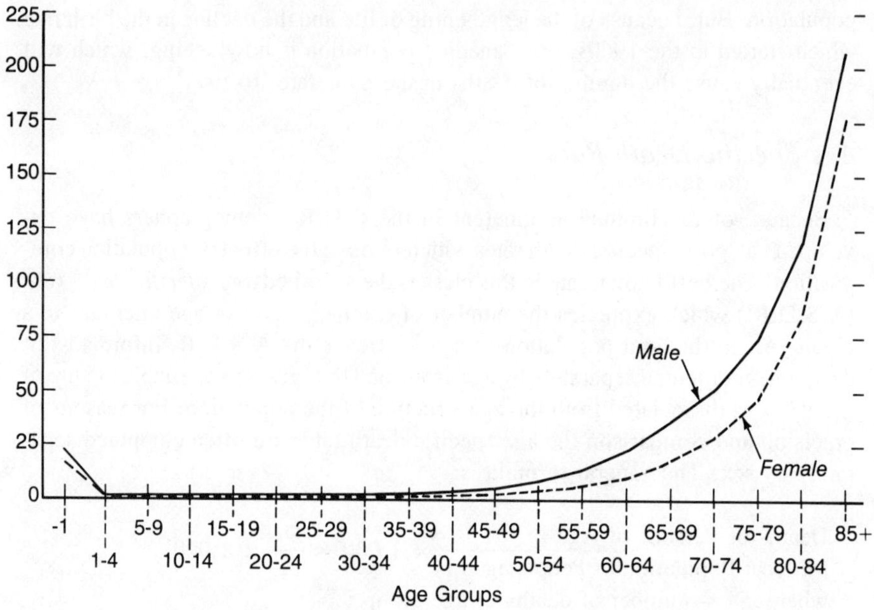

***Source:** Ministry of Industry, Trade and Commerce, *Canada Yearbook, 1972* (Ottawa: Information Division, Statistics Canada, 1972), p. 259.

As can be seen from the curves shown above, the rates are the lowest for Canadian women. In most modernized nations women tend to have lower death rates at all ages than men. This is also true for the earliest period in life. In the United States, moreover, the rates are also lower for whites than for nonwhites except for ages 75 and above. For the less developed countries the curves lie typically above those of the more developed countries, which is due to better health conditions in the high-income modernized nations.

In a country like Canada the curve has continually declined over time, this being due to better health conditions and hygienic improvements.

As noted previously, age-specific death rates can be computed for one-year intervals. In practice, however, five- and even ten-year periods are more commonly used. For most purposes the five-year intervals give sufficient information to get a correct picture of the mortality of the various age-groups.

TABLE: 16 Deaths by Age and Sex, Canada, 1971 (per 1,000; 5 year intervals)*

| Sex/Age Group | Rate | Sex/Age Group | Rate |
|---|---|---|---|
| Male | | Female | |
| Under 1 year | 19.9 | Under 1 year | 15.1 |
| 1- 4 years | 0.9 | 1- 4 years | 0.8 |
| 5- 9 | 0.6 | 5- 9 | 0.4 |
| 10-14 | 0.5 | 10-14 | 0.3 |
| 15-19 | 1.4 | 15-19 | 0.6 |
| 20-24 | 1.8 | 20-24 | 0.6 |
| 25-29 | 1.5 | 25-29 | 0.6 |
| 30-34 | 1.6 | 30-34 | 0.9 |
| 35-39 | 2.2 | 35-39 | 1.3 |
| 40-44 | 3.6 | 40-44 | 2.1 |
| 45-49 | 5.7 | 45-49 | 3.0 |
| 50-54 | 9.3 | 50-54 | 4.6 |
| 55-59 | 14.6 | 55-59 | 7.2 |
| 60-64 | 22.9 | 60-64 | 11.0 |
| 65-69 | 34.7 | 65-69 | 17.3 |
| 70-74 | 51.9 | 70-74 | 28.3 |
| 75-79 | 79.0 | 75-79 | 48.1 |
| 80-84 | 118.8 | 80-84 | 82.4 |
| 85 years and over | 198.5 | 85 years and over | 163.3 |
| Total, all ages | 8.5 | Total, all ages | 6.1 |

***Source:** Ministry of Industry, Trade and Commerce, *Canada Yearbook, 1975 . . .*, p. 178.

Comparisons between crude death rates which show the actual mortality per 1,000 of population are problematic in the sense that C.D.Rs do not always provide a true test of mortality conditions. As we observed earlier, crude death rates are affected by the age constitution of the population in various communities. Obviously, an ''old'' high-mortality-risk population will have a higher death rate than a population containing a high proportion of young people. As stated before, the problem can be solved by comparing the age-specific death rates of two populations or more. This implies, however, that relatively large amounts of figures must be set side by side. Actually, this process necessitates as many separate comparisons as there are age groups.

## *Standardization of Death Rates*

For obvious reasons it has been considered desirable to express genuine mortality differences between communities by one single figure which would imply the elimination of the impact of differences in age constitution. The procedure called *standardization* does precisely this. Standardization or adjustment is a process which allows us to compare the death rates of two or more communities while "holding constant" the effect of age composition. In other words, the method allows us to compare the mortality of several communities each retaining its own set of age-specific death rates while identical age compositions are simulated.

The method works as follows (we shall only discuss the "direct" standardization technique here). First we select a "standard population". For a long time the Canadian Dominion Bureau of Statistics used population of England and Wales in 1901. But the standard population can be any population or even the sum of two populations. Second, we apply to the appropriate age and sex groups in the standard population the age-specific death rates of the actual population under observation. For every age group we thus obtain an "imaginary" number of deaths. These are the deaths which would have occurred if the actual population had the age distribution of the standard population. Third, we sum up the expected or imaginary deaths, divide them by the standard population and multiply the quotient by one thousand. The result is the standardized death rate in per thousand terms for the observed population.[3]

In the 1930s and 1940s the Canadian yearbooks commonly published figures on the standardized death rates by sex and province. The standard population selected was the "standard million" based on the age and sex distribution per million of the population of England and Wales in 1901. This standard million which had the same age distribution as the population of England and Wales of 1901 had been set up for methodological reasons. Other countries such as the United States have used it as well. The structure of that standard million, which comprised a large proportion of young adults, was so different from the age

TABLE 17. Age and Sex Distribution of the "Standard Million"

| Age Group | Both Sexes | Males | Females |
|---|---|---|---|
| All ages | 1,000,000 | 483,543 | 516,457 |
| Under 5 years | 114,262 | 57,039 | 57,223 |
| 5- 9 years | 107,209 | 53,462 | 53,747 |
| 10-14 | 102,735 | 51,370 | 51,365 |
| 15-19 | 99,796 | 49,420 | 50,376 |
| 20-24 | 95,946 | 45,273 | 50,673 |
| 25-34 | 161,579 | 76,425 | 85,154 |
| 35-44 | 122,849 | 59,394 | 63,455 |
| 45-54 | 89,222 | 42,924 | 46,298 |
| 55-64 | 59,741 | 27,913 | 31,828 |
| 65-74 | 33,080 | 14,691 | 18,389 |
| 75 years and over | 13,581 | 5,632 | 7,949 |

[3]Hence: Standardized Death for observed population $= \frac{\text{Sum of Expected Deaths}}{\text{Total Standard Population}} \times 1{,}000$

composition of Asian, African and Latin American populations, which contain a very high proportion of children, that it was abandoned after World War II. The age and sex distribution of the "standard million" mentioned above is shown in Table 17.

As can be seen from the above table, the English 1901 population and the standard population which reflected it comprised relatively few infants and young children and only a relatively small proportion of aged people and formed, therefore, a standard favorable to low mortality. The particular age composition of England and Wales was due to the decline in fertility which had set in after the 1870s. Before that period fertility had been higher but the children born in the high-fertility period had already become adults by 1901.

*The Canada Yearbook* of 1945 shows the following crude and standardized death rates between 1931 and 1943. As can be seen from the table, the standardized death rates ran below the crude death rates during the period.

TABLE 18. Crude and Standardized Death Rates by Sex, Canada, 1931-1943*

| Year | Crude | | | Standardized | | |
|---|---|---|---|---|---|---|
| | Male | Female | Total | Male | Female | Total |
| 1931 | 10.5 | 9.6 | 10.1 | 10.1 | 9.0 | 9.5 |
| 1932 | 10.3 | 9.5 | 9.9 | 9.7 | 8.8 | 9.2 |
| 1933 | 10.0 | 9.2 | 9.6 | 9.3 | 8.4 | 8.8 |
| 1934 | 10.0 | 8.9 | 9.5 | 9.2 | 8.1 | 8.7 |
| 1935 | 10.2 | 9.2 | 9.7 | 9.4 | 8.3 | 8.8 |
| 1936 | 10.2 | 9.3 | 9.8 | 9.3 | 8.2 | 8.7 |
| 1937 | 10.9 | 9.7 | 10.3 | 9.9 | 8.6 | 9.2 |
| 1938 | 10.3 | 8.9 | 9.6 | 9.1 | 7.7 | 8.4 |
| 1939 | 10.4 | 9.0 | 9.7 | 9.0 | 7.6 | 8.3 |
| 1940 | 10.5 | 9.0 | 9.8 | 9.0 | 7.5 | 8.2 |
| 1941 | 10.8 | 9.1 | 10.0 | 9.3 | 7.5 | 8.4 |
| 1942 | 10.6 | 8.8 | 9.7 | 8.9 | 7.2 | 8.0 |
| 1943 | 10.9 | 9.1 | 10.1 | 9.0 | 7.4 | 8.1 |

***Source:** Dominion Bureau of Statistics, Department of Trade and Commerce, *The Canada Yearbook, 1945* (Ottawa: Cloutier, 1945), p. 153.

## *Infant Mortality*

The data shown in Table 16 and Figure 5 show the prevalence of a specific pattern of mortality during the first four years of life. The high mortality of that period becomes more pronounced the younger the child. The first year of age has the highest incidence of mortality. Mortality during this period is particularly interesting to analyse for several reasons. First, mortality under age one has an important impact on other indices of mortality such as the C.D.R. Second, infant mortality is a good indicator of the stage of socio-economic development of a nation, its health conditions, the availability of medical care, its food intake and the like. Thus the *infant mortality rate* denotes the deaths under the first year of age and is written as follows:

$$\text{I.M.R.} = \frac{\text{Number of Deaths Below Age 1 per Year}}{\text{Number of Live Births in the Same Year}} \times 1{,}000 = \frac{\text{Do}}{\text{B}} \bullet \text{k}$$

where Do = number of deaths below age 1 in a given year in a given country
B = number of live births occurring during the same year in the same nation
k = 1,000

In 1972, for example, the number of live births in Canada amounted to 347,319. The number of deaths of children below age one was 5,938. Hence, an infant mortality rate of $\frac{5{,}938}{347{,}319} \times 1{,}000 = 17.1‰$. One can of course compute separate rates for male and female infants.

In order to get the correct view of infant mortality it is necessary to distinguish between exogenous and endogenous causes of infant mortality. Exogenous causes of death could have been prevented by proper medical treatment or public health measures. Endogenous causes are related to congenital malformations, weakness of the fetus, difficult labor and the like. We may note here that, in Canada (1972), of all infants who died during the first year, 61.1% died during the first week and 41.4% on the first day of their life. Most of the death causes were endogenous. Because of their weakness, new-born babies are extremely sensitive to the availability of hygienic conditions, medical care and the like. This explains why, on the average, during the 1965-69 period, infant mortality ranged from 27‰ in the more developed countries to 140‰ in the less developed nations. The infant mortality rate for Iran (1975) is estimated at about 100 per thousand; that of Iraq at 89 per thousand for the same year.

Before the 18th century, infant mortality was high in Western nations and could easily have reached levels of 300-400 per thousand although 200‰ was perhaps a more common rate. For 18th century French Canada, infant mortality has been estimated at 245‰. In the West, the downward trend in infant mortality started after the 1850s. In France, for example, the I.M.R. amounted to around 200/250‰ in 1750. For the year 1850 we find a figure of about 170‰. A hundred years later again (1950), the figure had been reduced to about one third — 53‰. Around 1960 the rate had been cut in half (27.4‰) and by 1973 it had dropped to a low 12.9‰. In Sweden, to take another example, infant mortality stood at 209 per thousand in 1770 declining to 132‰ in 1870. In 1970 it had fallen to a low of 11‰.

Under exceptional circumstances the I.M.R. can rise again as it did in Soviet Russia during World War II. During the siege of Leningrad in 1942, infant mortality rose to 748‰. The following table shows the drastic decline in infant mortality which has taken place in Canada since 1920. The Canadian I.M.R. is compared with that in the Netherlands, whose figures are amongst the lowest in the world. Low as the 1974 Canadian figure is, more progress is still possible as the figures for the Netherlands show.

TABLE 19. Infant Mortality Rates, Canada and the Netherlands, 1920-1973*

| Year | I.M.R. Canada | I.M.R. Netherlands |
|---|---|---|
| 1920-21 | 102 | 82.5 |
| 1930 | 91 | 51.3 |
| 1940 | 58 | 39.4 |
| 1950 | 42 | 26.7 |
| 1960 | 27 | 17.9 |
| 1970 | 18.8 | 12.7 |
| 1971 | 17.5 | 12.1 |
| 1972 | 17.1 | 11.7 |
| 1973 | 15.5 | 11.5 |
| 1974 | 15.0 | 11.3 |

***Sources:** Urquhart, Buckley, *Historical Statistics of Canada* . . ., p. 40.
Ministry of Industry, Trade and Commerce, *Canada Yearbook 1976-77* (Ottawa: Statistics Canada, 1977), p. 206.
Centraal Bureau voor de Statistiek, *75 Jaar Statistiek van Nederland* (S'Gravenhage: Staatsuitgeverij, 1975), p. 30.

## *The Life Table*

Rates and ratios do not answer all questions regarding mortality. A major example is: "What is the average remaining lifetime for persons who have attained a given age?" Another one would be: "How long can a baby born in Canada in 1975 expect to live?" The answers to such questions are given by *life tables* or mortality tables as the French call them.

The life table is not, strictly speaking, a standardization procedure but rather a method of summarizing mortality. Life tables express in compact form the age-sex specific mortality trends of a given period and place. If we were able to observe a cohort (everyone born in the same country during the same year) until all members had died, we could give a detailed mortality account of this group and construct a "longitudinal" or "generation" life table. Since this type of life table can only be constructed after the death of all the members of the cohort, the practical usefulness of such an endeavor is decidedly limited. A second type of life table which *does* have practical significance is called a "cross-sectional", "period," or "time-specific" life table. This is the one which is widely used by demographers and planners as well as insurance companies. Such life tables are produced by starting in a given year with a hypothetical cohort of 100,000 at age zero called the "radix" of the life table. The age-specific death rates prevailing during that calendar year are then applied to the radix. The life table then proceeds to determine how many members of the life table cohort will die in each interval and how many remain at the end of each year. The process continues until all members of the radix have died. In other words, the life table takes a set of age-specific death rates and applies them to the entire lifetime period of a hypothetical cohort. A full life table proceeds by single years while an abridged life table may, for example, use 5-year age classes. For most purposes abridged life tables are adequate.

Life tables are usually constructed separately for males and females because of the difference in the death rates between the two sexes. In the U.S.A. different life tables are also drawn up for whites and blacks for the same reason.

Life tables provide important information, such as the expected number of years to be lived by a newborn child. Life tables also make it possible to calculate each year the total number of person-years to be lived by the entire cohort before the last one dies. Dividing this figure by the number of survivors yields the average number of years to be lived by each after exact age x. The symbol x always refers to birthday age in years. At birth a person has exact age 0 and at exact age 5, a person has lived exactly five years and so on.

Normally abridged life tables comprise 7 columns although the Canadian yearbooks limit themselves to 5. In the seven column system the first column (x to x + n) portrays the interval between two birthdays or the period of life between two exact ages. This section is entitled "age interval". For instance, 1-5 means the five-year interval between the first and the fifth birthdays.

Column 2 (nqx) discloses the probability of dying before reaching the next birthday if the life table proceeds by single years. Stated differently, this column shows the proportion of those people in the cohort who, having reached age x, will fail to survive to age x + n. The Qx values are a set of mortality probabilities for the cohort as it begins a new year of life. They are calculated per 100,000. For example, according to Table 20 the proportion dying between age 10 and age 15 is 0.0020 which means that out of every 100,000 persons living and exactly 10 years old, 20 will die before reaching exact age 15. The Qx values are sometimes computed per 1,000. They are then called life table mortality rates. Returning to our example stated above, 20 per 100,000 will become 0.2 per thousand. The rates showing the probability of dying are derived from and very close to the age-specific death rates. The procedures for computing these probabilities are complicated and of no interest at this point. It is sufficient to remember that they approximate the age-specific death rates but that as a rule they are a little lower.

Column 3 (1x) is the survivor column and shows the number of persons alive at the beginning of each age interval. It starts, for example, with the original cohort of 100,000 from which number the quantity of deaths during the time period under consideration are subtracted. The remainder is placed under the 100,000 figure, etc.

Column 4 (ndx) bearing the title "number dying during age interval" shows the number of deaths which occurs during any given age interval (x to x + n). The column ends when the last person of the life-table cohort dies. The sum total of this column must add up to the original life-table cohort of say 100,000.

Column 5 (nLx) is the years-lived column and discloses the number of person-years lived by the remainder of the cohort between the ages of x and x + n. According to Table 20, the residual of the radix of 100,000 would live 489,077 years between age five and ten. Of the 97,925 persons attaining age five, 97,722 also reach age 10. This category lives five years which makes a total of 488,610. For the sake of simplicity we assume that the 203 persons who die in the interval lived an average of 2.5 years. This gives us 2.5 × 203 = 508. The grand total thus becomes 488,610 + 508 = 489,118. That still makes a difference of 41 with the figure stated in the life table. This situation is due to our simplifying assumption that those who died in the interval all lived 2.5 years. The column is entitled "stationary population in the age interval." Column 5 and 6 refer to what is called a stationary population or life table population. A life table assumes that each year another cohort of 100,000 babies is born and added to the life table population. The same age-specific mortality rates are applied to them as well. When the first cohort has died the population is stationary which means that its age-composition experiences no further change.

Column 6 (Tx) exposes the total number of person-years still to be lived by the surviving cohort when it enters age x. The column is entitled "stationary population in this and all subsequent age intervals."

The last column, number 7 ($\mathring{e}x$) is the expectation of life column. It makes known the average number of remaining years to be lived by a person entering age n. The figure is found by the fraction $\frac{Tx}{lx}$ or column 6 divided by column 3. In our Table 20, limiting ourselves to age interval 1-5 we obtain the following result: $\frac{7,035,631}{98,237} = 71.6$.

*Life expectancy at birth* or the average number of years to be lived at birth is the best recapitulation of mortality conditions in a country. It is used for international comparisons and for contrasting different historical periods and is not affected by that nation's age composition. The higher that life expectancy, the more effectively a given nation grapples with the preservation of life and the combat against death. Persons born in the real-life population to which the life table cohort is compared normally have somewhat higher life expectancies because in reality preventive and curative medical knowledge will continue to advance while public health measures may still improve. Age-specific mortality rates can therefore be expected to decline somewhat over time.

Table 20 is an abridged life table of the United States total population and Table 21 an abridged life table (Canadian) by sex. The latter appeared in the Canadian yearbook of 1974.

In all Western nations life expectancy at birth, both sexes taken together, now surpasses 70 years. For a number of these countries, life expectancy was only around 40 years during the middle of the 19th century. In the United States, the figure stood at 47.3 in 1900. By 1940 it had risen to 68.2, while the 1970 figure shows 70.9. At least since 1900, males live shorter lives than females, while the white population always lives longer than the black.

Table 22 shows the gains made in Canada between 1951 and 1971. A disturbing feature is that the difference between life expectancy at birth for males and females seems to be growing as much in Canada as in other Western countries.

TABLE 20. Abridged Life Table, United States Total Population 1973.*

| Age Interval | Proportion dying | of 100,000 born alive | | Stationary population | | Average remaining lifetime |
|---|---|---|---|---|---|---|
| | Proportion of persons alive at beginning of age interval dying during interval | Number living at beginning of age interval | Number dying during age interval | In the age interval | In this and all subsequent age intervals | Average number of years of life remaining at beginning of age interval |
| (1) | (2) | (3) | (4) | (5) | (6) | (7) |
| x to x + n | $_nq_x$ | $l_x$ | $_nd_x$ | $_nL_x$ | $T_x$ | $\mathring{e}_x$ |
| Total | | | | | | |
| 0 - 1 | 0.0176 | 100,000 | 1,763 | 98,436 | 7,134,067 | 71.3 |
| 1 - 5 | .0032 | 98,237 | 312 | 392,201 | 7,035,631 | 71.6 |
| 5 - 10 | .0021 | 97,925 | 203 | 489,077 | 6,643,430 | 67.8 |
| 10 - 15 | .0020 | 97,722 | 198 | 488,163 | 6,154,353 | 63.0 |
| 15 - 20 | .0056 | 97,524 | 544 | 486,372 | 5,666,190 | 58.1 |
| 20 - 25 | .0073 | 96,980 | 710 | 483,157 | 5,179,818 | 53.4 |
| 25 - 30 | .0072 | 96,270 | 688 | 479,654 | 4,696,661 | 48.8 |
| 30 - 35 | .0083 | 95,582 | 789 | 476,029 | 4,217,007 | 44.1 |
| 35 - 40 | .0117 | 94,793 | 1,109 | 471,376 | 3,740,978 | 39.5 |
| 40 - 45 | .0176 | 93,684 | 1,651 | 464,587 | 3,269,602 | 34.9 |
| 45 - 50 | .0278 | 92,033 | 2,559 | 454,233 | 2,805,015 | 30.5 |
| 50 - 55 | .0408 | 89,474 | 3,655 | 438,772 | 2,350,782 | 26.3 |

| | | | | | | |
|---|---|---|---|---|---|---|
| 55 - 60 | .0638 | 85,819 | 5,472 | 416,170 | 1,912,010 | 22.3 |
| 60 - 65 | .0929 | 80,347 | 7,466 | 383,968 | 1,495,840 | 18.6 |
| 65 - 70 | .1314 | 72,881 | 9,577 | 341,370 | 1,111,872 | 15.3 |
| 70 - 75 | .1948 | 63,304 | 12,334 | 286,576 | 770,502 | 12.2 |
| 75 - 80 | .2885 | 50,970 | 14,707 | 218,708 | 483,926 | 9.5 |
| 80 - 85 | .3914 | 36,263 | 14,192 | 145,115 | 265,218 | 7.3 |
| 85 and over | 1.0000 | 22,071 | 22,071 | 120,103 | 120,103 | 5.4 |

***Source:** U.S. Department of Health, Education and Welfare, *Vital Statistics of the United States 1973,* Vol. II, Section 5, Life Tables.

TABLE 21. Abridged Life Table for Males and Females, Canada, 1971.*

| Age | Male | | | | Female | | | |
|---|---|---|---|---|---|---|---|---|
| | Number living at each age | Number dying between each age and the next | Probability of dying before reaching next birthday | Expectation of life | Number living at each age | Number dying between each age and the next | Probability of dying before reaching next birthday | Expectation of life |
| At birth | 100,000 | 2.002 | .02002 | 69.34 | 100,000 | 1.544 | .01544 | 76.36 |
| 1 year | 97,998 | 126 | .00128 | 69.76 | 98,456 | 113 | .00115 | 76.56 |
| 2 years | 97,872 | 92 | .00094 | 68.85 | 98,343 | 72 | .00073 | 75.64 |
| 3 years | 97,780 | 83 | .00084 | 67.91 | 98,271 | 60 | .00061 | 74.70 |
| 4 years | 97,697 | 69 | .00071 | 66.97 | 98,211 | 56 | .00057 | 73.74 |
| 5 years | 97,628 | 232 | .00061 | 66.02 | 98,155 | 179 | .00050 | 72.79 |
| 10 years | 97,396 | 267 | .00039 | 61.17 | 97,976 | 157 | .00028 | 67.91 |
| 15 years | 97,129 | 682 | .00106 | 56.33 | 97,819 | 262 | .00046 | 63.02 |
| 20 years | 96,449 | 872 | .00178 | 51.71 | 97,557 | 279 | .00057 | 58.18 |
| 25 years | 95,575 | 730 | .00164 | 47.16 | 97,278 | 315 | .00060 | 53.34 |
| 30 years | 94,845 | | .00152 | 42.50 | 96,963 | | .00077 | 48.51 |

| | | | | | | | | |
|---|---|---|---|---|---|---|---|---|
| 35 years | 94,072 | 773 | .00188 | 37.83 | 96,530 | 433 | .00112 | 43.71 |
| 40 years | 93,035 | 1,037 | .00291 | 33.22 | 95,886 | 644 | .00173 | 38.99 |
| 45 years | 91,390 | 1,645 | .00464 | 28.77 | 94,898 | 988 | .00260 | 34.37 |
| 50 years | 88,821 | 2,569 | .00761 | 24.52 | 93,433 | 1,465 | .00403 | 29.86 |
| 55 years | 84,761 | 4,060 | .01213 | 20.57 | 91,197 | 2,236 | .00618 | 25.53 |
| 60 years | 78,719 | 6,042 | .01918 | 16.95 | 87,896 | 3,301 | .00931 | 21.39 |
| 65 years | 70,044 | 8,675 | .02961 | 13.72 | 83,092 | 4,804 | .01449 | 17.47 |
| 70 years | 58,575 | 11,469 | .04436 | 10.90 | 75,995 | 7,097 | .02337 | 13.85 |
| 75 years | 44,788 | 13,787 | .06552 | 8.47 | 65,624 | 10,371 | .03876 | 10.63 |
| 80 years | 29,976 | 14,812 | .09701 | 6.41 | 51,237 | 14,387 | .06514 | 7.88 |
| 85 years | 16,332 | 13,644 | .14355 | 4.74 | 33,628 | 17,609 | .10766 | 5.67 |
| 90 years | 6,491 | 9,841 | .20977 | 3.43 | 16,620 | 17,008 | .17137 | 3.99 |
| 95 years | 1,600 | 4,891 | .30027 | 2.45 | 5,252 | 11,358 | .26132 | 2.76 |
| 100 years | 191 | 1,409 | .41969 | 1.71 | 835 | 4,427 | .38255 | 1.89 |

***Source:** Ministry of Industry, Trade and Commerce, *Canada Yearbook, 1974* . . ., pp. 179-180.

TABLE 22. Expectation of Life (in Years), Canada 1951, 1961, 1966 and 1971.*

| Age | 1951 | | 1961 | | 1966 | | 1971 | |
|---|---|---|---|---|---|---|---|---|
| | Male | Female | Male | Female | Male | Female | Male | Female |
| At birth | 66.33 | 70.83 | 68.35 | 74.17 | 68.75 | 75.18 | 69.34 | 76.36 |
| 1 year | 68.33 | 72.33 | 69.50 | 74.98 | 69.53 | 75.71 | 69.76 | 76.56 |
| 2 years | 67.56 | 71.55 | 68.63 | 74.11 | 68.64 | 74.81 | 68.85 | 75.64 |
| 3 years | 66.68 | 70.66 | 67.71 | 73.18 | 67.71 | 73.88 | 67.91 | 74.70 |
| 4 years | 65.79 | 69.74 | 66.78 | 72.23 | 66.77 | 72.93 | 66.97 | 73.74 |
| 5 years | 64.86 | 68.80 | 65.83 | 71.27 | 65.82 | 71.97 | 66.02 | 72.79 |
| 10 years | 60.15 | 64.02 | 61.02 | 66.41 | 61.00 | 67.12 | 61.17 | 67.91 |
| 15 years | 55.39 | 59.19 | 56.20 | 61.51 | 56.16 | 62.22 | 56.33 | 63.02 |
| 20 years | 50.76 | 54.41 | 51.51 | 56.65 | 51.50 | 57.37 | 51.71 | 58.18 |
| 25 years | 46.20 | 49.67 | 46.91 | 51.80 | 46.94 | 52.52 | 47.16 | 53.34 |
| 30 years | 41.60 | 44.94 | 42.24 | 46.98 | 42.29 | 47.68 | 42.50 | 48.51 |
| 35 years | 37.00 | 40.24 | 37.56 | 42.18 | 37.62 | 42.88 | 37.83 | 43.71 |
| 40 years | 32.45 | 35.63 | 32.96 | 37.45 | 33.01 | 38.15 | 33.22 | 38.99 |
| 45 years | 28.05 | 31.14 | 28.49 | 32.82 | 28.55 | 33.51 | 28.77 | 34.37 |
| 50 years | 23.88 | 26.80 | 24.25 | 28.33 | 24.31 | 29.02 | 24.52 | 29.86 |
| 55 years | 20.02 | 22.61 | 20.30 | 24.01 | 20.38 | 24.70 | 20.57 | 25.53 |
| 60 years | 16.49 | 18.64 | 15.73 | 19.90 | 16.81 | 20.58 | 16.95 | 21.39 |
| 65 years | 13.31 | 14.97 | 13.53 | 16.07 | 13.63 | 16.71 | 13.72 | 17.47 |
| 70 years | 10.41 | 11.62 | 10.67 | 12.58 | 10.83 | 13.14 | 10.90 | 13.85 |
| 75 years | 7.89 | 8.73 | 8.21 | 9.48 | 8.37 | 9.94 | 8.47 | 10.63 |
| 80 years | 5.84 | 6.38 | 6.14 | 6.90 | 6.36 | 7.26 | 6.41 | 7.88 |
| 85 years | 4.27 | 4.57 | 4.46 | 4.89 | 4.79 | 5.16 | 4.74 | 5.67 |
| 90 years | 3.10 | 3.24 | 3.16 | 3.39 | 3.60 | 3.60 | 3.43 | 3.99 |
| 95 years | 2.24 | 2.27 | 2.20 | 2.32 | 2.71 | 2.48 | 2.45 | 2.76 |
| 100 years | 1.60 | 1.59 | 1.49 | 1.56 | 2.04 | 1.69 | 1.71 | 1.89 |

***Source:** Ministry of Industry, Trade and Commerce, *Canada Yearbook, 1974 . . .*, p. 180.

## B. Differential Mortality

Our discussion of the various measures of mortality was limited to overall mortality. The fact is that some fractions of the population have higher mortality rates than others. Such differences in mortality levels between different segments of the population are termed *differential mortality*.

We all know that mortality levels vary widely within the international community. The expectation of life at birth for the more developed regions (1970-1975 period) has been estimated at 71.2 years. The less developed regions taken together scored 53.9 years. The Canadian figure for 1971 was just under 73 for both sexes taken together whereas the Iranian figure for the same period has been estimated at 52-53 years. Within nations, however, mortality levels also differ. Such differences in mortality are often measured with the yardstick of crude death rates although age-specific mortality rates, infant mortality rates and life expectancies at birth are also used.

## *Sex*

We have already mentioned that in countries such as Canada, the United States or the United Kingdom, women have lower age-specific mortality rates than men. Mortality affects both sexes differently. Greater occupational hazards, such as work in mines, and the greater pressures on men to achieve in their work are often given as explanations. Females also seem to be superior in resisting infections while their reduced susceptibility to degenerative disease has also been noted. Women also more frequently admit being ill and seem more prepared than men to seek treatment for minor diseases and disorders. It has also been argued that women more easily release and express their emotions as compared to men. This would contribute to greater mental health. In a number of low-income countries where prenatal care is nonexistent and delivery services poor, female mortality will tend to be greater than male mortality.

## *Place of Residence*

Differences in mortality levels also tend to exist between rural and urban areas. Historically, cities have always been places characterized by high death rates. With people living close to each other and streets being narrow, infectious diseases could spread easily. Besides garbage was often not collected but thrown in the streets while streams and brooks were used for sewage as well as drinking purposes.[4] In the more developed countries the rural-urban mortality differences have narrowed in the twentieth century and are now close to zero. A number of cities are beset with environmental problems, but this is compensated for by the greater availability of proper medical care. In so far as rural mortality remains below urban mortality, the variations must be accounted for by differences in age composition of the two populations or the fact that the higher income groups tend to move out of the cities and into the suburbs while the lower socioeconomic groups tend to move into the larger towns and cities.

In the developing countries, however, urban mortality is usually below rural mortality. One reason is that it is the cities which benefit first from the transplantation of public health discoveries from the more to the less developed countries. The drinking water is first purified in the towns, and only later in the countryside. Other innovations are introduced in the same order. A second reason is the greater concentration of medical facilities and personnel in cities and towns.

---

[4]A sight still common in Shiraz (Iran) consists of people washing their faces and mouths with the dirty water which runs in the open conduits that crisscross the city.

The Central Province in Iran with Teheran as its main city contains about one fifth of the population of Iran. Yet 5,650 out of Iran's 12,000 medical doctors practice in that area. Such at least are the figures for the 1975-76 period.

### *Socioeconomic Rank*

Differences in death rates exist also among people belonging to different social classes. Before the eighteenth century mortality levels were very much the same (and always high) for all socioeconomic groups. Medical care was ineffectual and the inability to consult a physicain did not make much difference. Class specific mortality increased during the industrialization process when certain sections of the population were exposed to long working hours in factories and workshops, low wages and crowding in unwholesome dwellings. The middle and upper classes, however, benefited increasingly from improved medical care and facilities. At present, in most countries those groups which have achieved the highest socioeconomic status as measured by education, occupation and income have the lowest mortality. However, in many developed nations such as Sweden, the Netherlands and Canada, where mortality has reached very low levels, class-specific mortality tends to disappear.

The explanations for class-specific mortality are both biological and social. Through a process of competitive selection the stronger and more able types tend to reach the higher-status occupations leaving the less desirable activities to the others. Once the occupation is entered, there is always the fact that the less desirable employments sometimes involve rather dangerous activities such as climbing, the use of explosives, exposure to high temperatures, or they may imply working in a polluted atmosphere — the breathing-in of chemicals, dust and the like. Since occupation determines to a large extent one's income, the higher income groups can afford good medical care, balanced nutrition, proper clothing and adequate housing. The lower income groups do not have equal access to the advantages mentioned above and have therefore a higher mortality incidence.

### *Educational Achievement*

The educational attainment of the parents, especially of the mother, seems to bear an important relationship to infant mortality. The relationship is clearly inverse. It seems that infant mortality is even more sensitive to the level of instruction of the parents than to their income. Ignorance is apparently more deadly than poverty.

### *Ethnic Differences*

If a nation is inhabited by several ethnic or racial groups, differences in mortality levels may be encountered. A flagrant example of this is the United States. In

1900 the life expectancy at birth for the white population, both sexes taken together, totalled 47.6 years and for the blacks the figure was 33.0 years. The figures for 1970 were respectively 71.7 and 65.3. In other words real progress has been achieved. In those 70 years the gap has narrowed from 14.6 to 6.4 years. In Canada, mortality levels are also likely to be higher for non-whites than for whites but precise figures are not available.

It is unlikely that there is a biological basis for this race-specific mortality. The whites are usually better educated and therefore enjoy higher incomes than the non-whites. The higher incomes imply better medical care, more favorable housing conditions, better nutrition, etc. The higher education levels of the whites entail a greater willingness to use the available medical facilities, better knowledge of what a proper diet consists of and so forth.

### *Marital Status*

Another consistent feature of mortality is that death rates from all major causes of death are significantly higher for widowed, divorced, and single people than for married people. The widowed have higher death rates than the unmarried while the divorced have the highest death rates of all. One major reason for this state of affairs is that mating tends to be selective. Males and females generally tend to prefer the healthiest members of the opposite sex as spouses. Good health therefore increases one's marriageability. Those with health problems will thus tend to remain in the "single" category, contributing to the higher mortality levels in that group. With all the exceptions which confirm the rule, married people, especially men, also tend to lead more orderly and harmonious lives than the non-married. They eat more regularly, their diet tends to be better balanced and they get more sleep. They enjoy regular company, sexual or otherwise, and are better taken care of in case of sickness. Lonelinesss can easily lead to depression, sometimes to excessive drinking, eating poorly, exercising too little and generally neglecting one's body. The widowed suffer the same disadvantages as the single but they also feel the pain of the loss of their loved one. It is the divorced who have the highest mortality rates of all the categories mentioned. In all likelihood there are among them a disproportionate number of persons who have not been able to adapt themselves to a "normal" existence. This may be due to physical and/or psychic inferiority which exposes persons in this class to an above-average casualty rate.

## C. Causes of Death

With regard to the *causes of all deaths,* an interesting evolution has taken place in the more developed countries. It is probable that at least some developing nations will repeat this pattern. Before 1900, infectious and respiratory diseases as well as illnesses of the digestive tract were the main killers in practically all nations. In Great Britain around the 1650s nearly 75% of all deaths were attributable to infectious diseases, malnutrition and maternity complications. Such ailments were typically limited to the younger age groups. Around 1900 when the expectation of life at birth was still only about fifty years in most Western countries, some 30% of all deaths were due to infectious, respiratory and parasitic diseases. The gradual disappearance of the above-mentioned illnesses reflects a better understanding of the nature and transmission of those maladies as well as the development of powerful drugs, vaccines and the like. At the same time the general environment had been improving a great deal since about the 1880s. From almost every point of view the environment in countries like Canada and the U.K. is now safer and cleaner than a hundred years ago. Besides, houses are now built of better materials; the availability of coal first and oil later facilitated their heating; personal and public hygiene made progress; and, the perfected means of transport brought a number of new articles such as citrus fruits to the markets of the industrialized countries. The diet improved in quality and the resistence to infectious diseases grew. After 1950 when in the West life expectancy at birth had come close to the 70 years limit, only 5.7% of all deaths were attributable to infectious, parastitic and respiratory ailments. Now that most of those diseases have either been eradicated or brought under control, most deaths occur on account of non-communicable degenerative diseases such as afflictions of the nervous system (intracranial vascular lesions etc.), disorders of the circulatory system and cancer. Because of an ever increasing private automobile ownership, mortality from motor vehicle accidents has also risen sharply. This shift from the age of infectious diseases to an age of degenerative and man-made sicknesses has been called the ''epidemiologic transition''. In 1973 for instance, in Canada, 49% of all deaths were attributable to cardiovascular diseases, 20.2% were due to cancer while accidents accounted for 8%. Only some 6.6% of all deaths were due to respiratory aliments. The Canadian situation is illustrated in Figure 6.

There is little doubt about the fact that children and young women have been the main beneficiaries of this evolution. The diseases which used to decimate them are now well controlled. Most deaths in the modernized societies occur from degenerative ailments which are in a sense byproducts of the ageing process. As the populations of the developed countries grow older an increased prominence of diseases characteristic of middle and older age is inevitable.[5] However, even if adjustment for changes in age composition is made, the incidence of malignant neoplasms and certain heart and circulatory diseases is on the rise. They seem to increase wherever Western ways of life are being adopted and may be related to certain dietary habits such as an excessive intake of saturated fats, a lack of physical exercise and stressful emotional states.

The pattern of mortality in the underprivileged parts of the world is markedly different. The leading causes of death in the developing countries are now very much the same as they used to be in the technically advanced nations in the last

---

[5]As noted earlier, Chapter 11 will explain how populations can age or rejuvenate themselves.

FIGURE 6. Evolution of Main Causes of Death, Canada, 1931-1970*

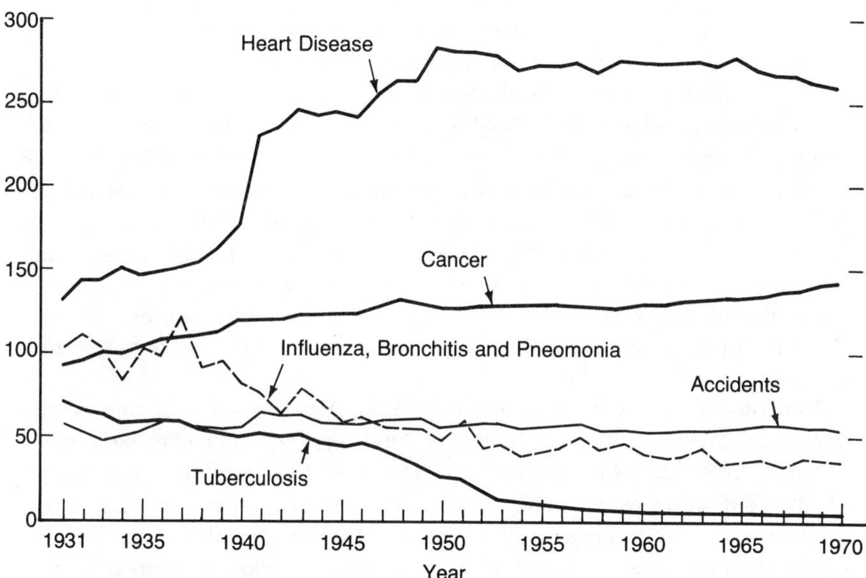


***Source:** Ministry of Industry, Trade and Commerce, *Canada Yearbook, 1972* (Ottawa: Information Division, Statistics Canada, 1972), p. 262.

century. They include gastro-enteritis, diarrheal diseases, pneumonia, tuberculosis, bronchitis, influenza, tetanus, typhoid fever and the like. Momeni reports that in 1967 there were five leading causes of death in Iran, i.e. infective and parasitic diseases (8.6% of all deaths), diseases of the circulatory system (15.4%), diseases of the respiratory system (12.1%), diseases of the digestive system (13.2%) and lastly certain unspecified diseases of early infancy (9.9%). Together they add up to 59.2%.[6] Again, as in the Western countries before World War I, these diseases particularly affect the infants and young adults. As health provisions improve and the general state of resistance against diseases increases, the developing nations are likely to follow the pattern of the Western countries and Japan.

At the risk of being repetitive, we should before ending this chapter briefly survey the evolution of mortality from past to present.

## D. Trends in Mortality

### *Traditional Mortality*

Premodern mortality, that is, mortality before 1750, was high and fluctuating

---

[6]D.A. Momeni, *The Population of Iran* (Shiraz: 1975), p. 169.

in all areas of the world. Life expectancy at birth in Rome some 2000 years ago levelled perhaps at 22 - 25 years. It was little more than 30 in Europe around 1750. Although high, mortality was not uniformly high over this period. Its level was determined by political, economic and environmental conditions and even by the climate. In times of security, order and favorable weather conditions, mortality could drop to relatively low levels, only to rise sharply in times of wars, famines, epidemics or internal political disturbances. In Europe, food shortages and famines were common until the nineteenth century when the well-known Irish famine decimated the Irish population. Famines also devastated Asia at frequent intervals. Malnutrition or deficient diets were less spectacular but perhaps even more deadly than famines. Until the end of the nineteenth century, protein and vitamin deficient diets were exceedingly common in Europe and the remainder of the Western World. They still are in Asia, Africa and Latin America. Inadequate diets lead to weakness and reduced resistence to infectious diseases.

Until about 150 years ago, and even later, there was hardly any defense against the infectious illnesses such as typhus fever, typhoid and malaria, which regularly took their heavy toll of lives. The same held true for such infant and children's diseases as enteritis, measles, whooping cough and the like. Proper sanitation was also lacking. Until the middle of the nineteenth century, garbage, refuse and rubbish were commonly thrown in the streets. Small streams sometimes served simultaneously as sewers and sources of water supply. Public water systems and municipal sewage systems only became available towards the end of the last century. Living and working quarters were often unskilfully built, damp and poorly lighted. Plumbing was absent and the dirt and congestion attracted rodents and lice which are known to spread diseases such as the plague. Personal uncleanliness was fearful by our standards and the regular use of water and soap to wash the human body was practically unheard of until some one hundred years ago. The adding up of all these factors more than explains the low life expectancy at birth until quite recently.

With the advent of the Industrial Revolution all this changed. The secular decline in mortality has manifested itself in the Western World from about 1750 onwards. The fluctuations in mortality tended to become less drastic and have ultimately disappeared. The drop in mortality was slow at first but tended to accelerate towards the end of the nineteenth century. Initially, the fall in mortality was conditioned by economic circumstances rather than by medical and public health discoveries. In England, for instance, the Industrial Revolution was preceded by an Agricultural Revolution which involved emphasis on commercial farming and a change in the land tenure systems. Advances were made in crop rotation systems; irrigation and drainage methods were improved; and, new tools and implements were invented. Storage facilities were also perfected. As a result, the supply of food improved and became more reliable in time. At the same time significant improvements in transport, such as better roads and the digging of canals which connected the rivers, tended to wipe out local food shortages.

The subsequent Industrial Revolution increased the quantity and quality of commodities available per person. Incomes in such countries as England rose, especially after the 1850s, implying that people could afford better and more food, warmer clothes and improved houses.

The second part of the nineteenth century witnessed a medical and public health revolution which ultimately helped to curb mortality and reduce it to low levels. The great sanitary awakening began in England during the 1850s, when sewage was still running through the streets, with cholera and typhoid being major problems. The sanitory reform movement resulted in such concrete measures as public refuse removal, sewer systems which helped to combat water-carried diseases, and the provision of purified and disinfected water supplies which drastically reduced the incidence of typhoid fever. The filtering and purification of drinking water occurred between 1900 and 1914 in most Western cities. New habits of personal hygiene were also adopted. With piped-in water, cheap soap and a better understanding of the relationship between disease and filth, personal cleanliness standards improved drastically. Easy-to-wash underwear replaced woollen undergarments. The personal and public health revolutions were accompanied by a drastic change in preventive and curative medicine. The eighteenth century had already witnessed the founding of some hospitals and the emergence of apothecaries which prescribed and produced medicines. Edward Jenner discovered a preventive serum for smallpox (1798) which had been a major killer. In the late nineteenth century Pasteur's work and Koch's bacteriological investigations prepared the ground for modern bacteriology and the science of immunization. At the same time antiseptic surgery revolutionized clinical practices, saving countless lives. Diagnostic techniques improved also. Generally, medical discoveries began to accelerate after 1900. Advances were also made in chemotherapy especially when the sulfonamides and the antibiotics were discovered. Last but not least, the development of insecticides such as D.D.T. permitted a massive attack on insect-borne diseases such as malaria. At present, most infectious diseases have virtually disappeared in the more developed countries, and medical science now makes it possible for ever increasing numbers to live out their natural life span.

## *Contemporary Mortality in Developed Countries*

A few observations with regard to current mortality in the more developed countries are now in order. As stated before, the modernized nations have now achieved low mortality levels with stabilized crude death rates of below 13‰ and infant mortality rates ranging from about 13 - 30‰. The drop in mortality has been specifically to the advantage of the 0 - 20 age groups and females in the reproductive ages because of the susceptibility of these groups to infectious and deficiency diseases. The point is now being reached when most people either die early in life from congenital malformations, specific childbirth problems, or from degenerative diseases due to a deterioration or stoppage of one of the components of the body. Occasionally, people die from viral infections against which modern medicine is still relatively impotent. It seems unlikely that the developed countries will experience further spectacular declines in mortality levels. The general situation with regard to the degenerative causes of death is unlikely to change rapidly. The human life span can only be increased if radical improvements in the understanding of the ageing process occur and new biochemical discoveries are made.

Moreover, new subtle killers may be emerging because of the environmental hazards created by the increased production and use of chemical compounds. Health in the more developed nations may now be threatened by the production of industrial chemicals, such as PCBs (Polychlorinated biphenyls), which now invisibly float through air and water. The pesticides, herbicides and fungicides, which increase productivity on the farm, find their way to the human body. Their side-effects will only be known a few decades from now. Thousands of chemicals are added to food to improve appearance, taste, vitamin content, to extend their shelf-life and so on. Even if each chemical is harmless by itself, what are the effects of all these substances combined? Each second some 7000 pills are being swallowed in a country like the U.S.A. Little is known about the long-term side effects of all these drugs. The list could be extended but space is short. It could well be, however, that the future will either witness new diseases or a spread of known diseases such as cancer which bar a further lengthening of the expectation of life.

## *Mortality in Transitional Societies*

Mortality in the developing nations is a different story. First, the decline in mortality started much later than in the modernized countries. The colonizing nations helped to reduce mortality in Asian and African colonies by suppressing local wars and quarrels, improving of the transportation systems and introducing of some discoveries in the fields of public health and medicine. It was, however, after 1945, when most colonized areas gained independence, that an intensive process of importing life-saving techniques from the Western nations began, often with the assistance of international agencies such as the World Health Organization. Secondly, the decline in mortality was much faster than in the West. What took the more developed countries some 200 years to accomplish was done in some 50 years in the low-income countries. Third, in the developing nations the rapid decline in mortality has often not been a by-product of internally generated socio-economic and scientific developments. It resulted from a rapid and effective transplantation of public health devices and medical techniques, drug therapies and pesticides. All these facilities made possible a highly successful battle against infectious and parasitic diseases.

Because the mortality decline in the less developed countries was largely dissociated from endogenous socioeconomic progress it is possible that they now have reached a threshold which will be difficult to cross. With an average life expectancy of some 54 years and an infant mortality of some 140 per thousand, further declines in mortality in the developing nations may well be dependent on fresh socioeconomic advances resulting in higher incomes. Further disease control now depends on such factors as better balanced diets, improved housing conditions, adequate waste disposal systems and sewerage facilities, the provision of purified drinking water and an increased supply of hospitals and physicians. Low economic living standards impede the above-mentioned ameliorations and therefore hold back more rapid progress in mortality control.

## Bibliography

Brown, H., "Increase in Life Expectance Due to Modern Medicine," *Population in Perspective,* L.B. Young, New York: Oxford University Press, 1968.

Carr-Saunders, A.M., *World Population,* London: Cass & Co, 1964.

Goldscheider, C., *Population, Modernization and Social Structure,* Boston: Little Brown & Co, 1971.

Mitchell, B.R., *European Historical Statistics 1750 - 1970,* London: MacMillan, 1975.

Omran, A.R., "The Epidemiologic Transition," *Milbank Memorial Fund Quarterly,* Vol. XLIX, No. 4, October, 1971.

Palmore, J.A., *Measuring Mortality: a Self-Teaching Guide to Elementary Measures,* Honolulu: East-West Population Institute, 1975.

Tranter, N., *Population since the Industrial Revolution,* London: Croom-Helm, 1973.

## Chapter 7

# *Fertility*

## A. A Note on Nuptiality

The term nuptiality implies a number of things, such as marriage, divorce, widowhood and remarriage. Since most people marry before they reproduce, nuptiality is an important determinant of fertility. The crude marriage rate (C.M.R.) is given by the quotient:

$$\frac{\text{No. of Marriages in a Given Year in a Given Area}}{\text{Midyear Population in that Year in the Same Area}} \times 1000 = \frac{M}{P} \cdot k$$

where M = total number of marriages among residents in a given area during the year

P = average number of persons living in that area during the year

k = 1,000

The C.M.R. for the Canadian population in 1971 was $\frac{191,324}{21,568,310} \times 1,000 = 8.9‰$. The 1973 C.M.R. for Iraq (not Iran) was 14.7‰.

Several phenomena have an important impact on the C.M.R. Such phenomena include a nation's economic conditions, e.g., employment levels, and demographic factors, e.g., the age composition of the population, the latter being a major determinant of the supply of marriageable persons. Religion is also an important influence. Certain religions emphasize marriage more than others. Christianity, especially the Roman Catholic version of it, has always tended to stress celibacy and continence. But a celibate clergy or celibate religious orders are nonexistent in Islam. Moslem doctrine moreover holds that permanent celibacy is abnormal for men and unthinkable for women. Moselm belief therefore encourages universal marriage and high C.M.R.s.

Compared to other traditional preindustrial societies, fertility was low in premodern Western Europe. Age at marriage was relatively high and often many years beyond the biological minimum age. Another feature of premodern Western Europe was the relatively high proportion of people who did not marry at all. Again religion was an important conditioning factor.

Another difference between premodern Western Europe and other preindustrial societies was the virtual absence of the extended family system or kinship-family structure as it existed in Africa and Asia. Under the extended family system the burdens and costs of reproduction are often shared by other family members while the prestige involved in having children is enjoyed by the parents alone. Easy and universal marriage is thus encouraged. The buffering of the direct burdens of procreation also favours high birth rates. In Western Europe such arrangements were never found in the same way they are still found in many contemporary societies. The care for the children rested mainly upon wife and husband, and marriage implied, therefore, the setting up of a separate household involving considerable economic cost. In some areas the law supplemented existing customs by forcing couples to defer marriage until they were able to face the burdens involved. Even in the middle of the nineteenth century there still existed a law in Bavaria (Germany) dating from 1616 stating that marriage was authorized only to those individuals who could demonstrate proof of a regular guaranteed income. It was perhaps for this reason that at that time Bavaria had one of the lowest marriage rates in Europe (12.8‰). When the law was abolished in 1868, the marriage rate nearly doubled.

While marriage was often deferred or avoided because of the non-existence of the extended family and its pronatal incentives, economic circumstances such as harvest conditions, the price of wheat and employment opportunities also had their impact. In premodern agricultural Europe the number of marriages was often inversely correlated to the price of wheat. During the modernization process the link between agricultural phenomena and the number of marriages was definitely broken, but a weak relationship between the level of economic activity and the number of weddings still persists.

In the year 1973, 199,064 marriages were solemnized in Canada. The C.M.R. was 9%. The following tables gives an overview of the marriage rate from 1921 onwards.

TABLE 23. Marriage Rates for Selected Years, Canada: 1921-1974*

| Year | 1921 | 1931 | 1941 | 1951 | 1961 | 1971 | 1972 | 1973 | 1974 |
|---|---|---|---|---|---|---|---|---|---|
| Rate per 1,000 population | 8.0 | 6.4 | 10.6 | 9.2 | 7.0 | 8.9 | 9.2 | 9 | 8.9 |

***Sources:** Ministry of Industry, Trade and Commerce, *Canada Yearbook, 1974* . . ., p. 182.
Ministry of Industry, Trade and Commerce, *Canada Yearbook,* 1975 . . ., p. 185.
Ministry of Industry, Trade and Commerce, *Canada Yearbook, 1976-77* . . ., p. 198.
Kalbach, McVey, *The Demographic Bases of Canadian Society* (Toronto: McGraw-Hill, 1971), p. 267.

The marriage rate during the 1920s was high. Good economic conditions and high employment levels during the period provide the explanation. The low figure of 1931 is due to the economic depression which involved widespread unemployment.

Canada's involvement in the Second World War increased the rate of job creation. After the end of the hostilities many marriages which had been postponed took place. Employment conditions were favorable as well. Naturally this boosted the marriage rate. During the 1960s, however, the relatively small cohorts born during the economic depression came of age which implied a reduction of the supply of marriageable individuals. The high marriage rate of the early 1970s was obviously due to the increase in the proportion of young men and women in the population. A large fraction of the post-war baby boom reached the prime marrying age during this period. The peak in the marriage rate was apparently reached in 1972. The upward trend was reversed in 1973 when the marriage rate ranked 2% below the figure of the previous year.

It would seem that the marriage rates in modernized societies do not fluctuate very widely as the following figures for the United States and the Netherlands again show.

TABLE 24. Marriage Rate in the U.S.A. and the Netherlands, 1920-1975*

| Year | 1920 | 1930 | 1940 | 1950 | 1960 | 1970 | 1975 |
|---|---|---|---|---|---|---|---|
| Rate U.S.A. | 12 | 9.2 | 12.1 | 11.1 | 8.5 | 10.6 | 10.1 |
| Rate Netherlands | 9.6 | 8.0 | 7.6 | 8.2 | 7.8 | 9.5 | 7.4 |

***Sources:** U.S. Bureau of the Census, *Statistical Abstract of the United States 1977,* (98th edition) (Washington, D.C., 1977), p. 76.

U.S. Bureau of the Census, *Historical Statistics of the United States, Colonial Times to 1970* (Bicentennial Edition, Part 2) (Washington, D.C., 1975), p. 64.

Centraal Bureau voor de Statistiek, *75 Jaar Statistiek . . .*, pp. 13, 14.

Netherlands Central Bureau of Statistics, *Statistical Yearbook of the Netherlands, 1976* (The Hague: Staatsuitgeverij, 1977), p. 18.

As in Canada the Dutch C.M.R. seems to be declining again. It dropped from 9.5‰ in 1970 to 7.4‰ in 1975. The behavior of the American C.M.R. is quite similar to that of Canada although the American rate is consistently higher. In Canada as well as in the U.S.A. the comparatively high C.M.R.s of the late sixties and early seventies was a consequence of the relative increase in young people in the prime marrying ages. Figure 7 makes the relationship between the marriage boom which followed the baby boom, with a lag of some eighteen to twenty years, plainly visible.

Returning to the Canadian case, it seems that if we consider only the population of 15 years of age and over it would appear that between 1911 and 1961 the proportion of married people in Canada has increased from 54.2 percent to 66.6 percent. Since 1961, however, the proportion of married persons of 15 years and over has shown a slight drop whereas the proportion of single persons has increased. Table 25 shows this trend.

While the increase of persons of 15 years of age and above was 13.1% during the 1966-1971 period, the number of single persons increased by 14 percent. The percentage rise of divorced people also stands out, although numerically speaking the divorced category is still small. The percentage increase between 1966

FIGURE 7: Marriage and Birth Rates in the United States, 1925-1973*

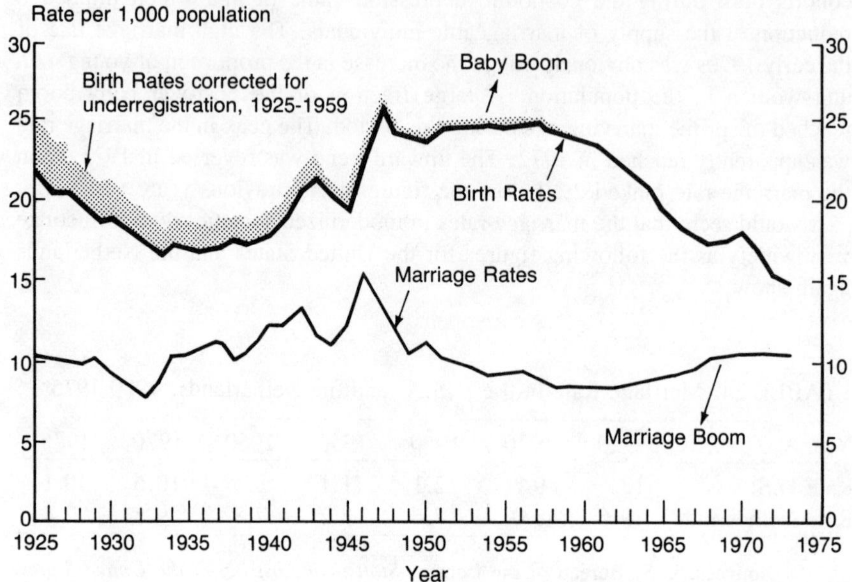


***Source:** U.S. Bureau of the Census, *Statistical Abstract* . . ., p. 52.

and 1971 was 170%. This, however, was mostly due to the 1968 changes in divorce legislation.

## *The Divorce Rate*

The divorce rate defines the frequency with which marriages are dissolved by the courts. The formula is:

$$\frac{\text{Number of Divorces in an Area in a Given Year}}{\text{Mid-year Population in that Area}} \times 1{,}000 = \frac{D}{P} \cdot k$$

where D = total number of divorces among residents in a given area
P = mid-year population
k = 1,000

Thus for Canada in 1971 we can compute $\frac{29{,}627}{21{,}568{,}311} \times 1{,}000 = 1.38‰$.[1]

The divorce rate in Canada increased from 0.39 per thousand in the 1951-1955 period to 1.48 per thousand in 1972. In the U.S.A. the rate rose from 2.6‰ in 1950 to 4.0‰ in 1972. In 1910 the American divorce rate was only 0.9‰. Some official documents calculate the divorce rate per 1,000 married women of

[1]Some statistical publications prefer to present the frequency of divorce per 10,000 or even per 100,000 population.

TABLE 25. Distribution by Marital Status, Canadian Population 15 Years of Age and Over, 1961, 1966, 1971*

| Marital Status | Numerical Distribution | | | Percentage Distribution | | |
|---|---|---|---|---|---|---|
| Population 15 | 1961 | 1966 | 1971 | 1961 | 1966 | 1971 |
| and over | 12,046,325 | 13,423,123 | 15,187,410 | 100.0 | 100.0 | 100.0 |
| Single | 3,191,206 | 3,764,833 | 4,290,675 | 26.5 | 28.0 | 28.3 |
| Married | 8,024,304 | 8,723,217 | 9,777,605 | 66.6 | 65.0 | 64.4 |
| Widowed | 778,223 | 870,297 | 944,020 | 6.5 | 6.5 | 6.2 |
| Divorced | 52,592 | 64,776 | 175,110 | 0.4 | 0.5 | 1.2 |

***Source:** Ministry of Industry, Trade and Commerce, *Canada, 1974* (Ottawa: Statistics Canada 1974), p. 11.

15 years and over. Many other more refined measures exist. One can relate the number of marriages in a given year to the number of divorces and legal separations in the same year and then obtain the so-called *marriage-divorce ratio*. Finally, one can simply compute the number of divorces per 1,000 married couples.

## B. Basic Measures of Fertility

When we analyse fertility we should first distinguish this concept from fecundity. Fertility denotes the actual reproductive performance of couples or women whereas fecundity implies the physiological capacity to reproduce. For the French Canadians this may be confusing because the French word "fertilité" means fecundity whereas "fécondité" denotes fertility.

### *The Child-Woman Ratio*

A first measure of fertility is the so-called child-woman ratio. It is computed as follows:

$$\frac{\text{Number of Children Under 5 Years of Age in a Population}}{\text{Number of Women in the Reproductive Period (15-49)}} \times 1{,}000$$

or $\dfrac{P_{0\text{-}4}}{P_{f\ 15\text{-}49}} \cdot k$

where $P_{0\text{-}4}$ = population under 5 years old

$P_{f\ 15\text{-}49}$ = number of women aged 15-49 years

$k$ = 1,000

Some demographers prefer to use the 15 to 44 period instead of the 15 to 49 period because the number of births occurring during those last 5 years is usually insignificant. In conclusion, the numerator of the child-woman ratio denotes the surviving children born during the last five years. The denominator comprises those women which are most likely to be their mothers. The ratio, therefore, shows the number of children under age 5 per thousand women of childbearing age.

A problem with this ratio is that it actually underestimates current fertility levels because children who have died are not included. The ratio only deals with the survivors of births during the last five years. In some less developed countries infant and childhood mortality are still considerable and the number of children actually born may substantially exceed the number of survivors. The ratio is often computed in countries where data for ordinary births are poor. A sample survey of age and sex composition in a country with defective birth registration is all that is needed to compute the ratio. Imperfect as it is, some index is better than none.

If we take the Canadian figures of 1971, we find the following child-woman ratio: $\frac{1,816,155}{5,281,715} \times 1,000 = 0.344$ children per woman or 344 children under 5 per thousand women. In 1966 for instance the Canadian C.W.R. still stood at the relatively high level of 468.3. By 1974 it had dropped to 311.8. For a typical developing country like Iran we find in 1973: $\frac{5,583,000}{6,679,000} \times 1,000 = 0.836$ children per woman or 836 children per thousand women.

The following chart will compare the evolution of the Canadian and American child-woman ratios between 1850 and 1970. The particular child-woman ratio used here is the number of children under 5 years per thousand women between exact ages 20-44.

FIGURE 8. Child-Woman Ratio for Canada (1851-1971) and the United States (1850-1970)*

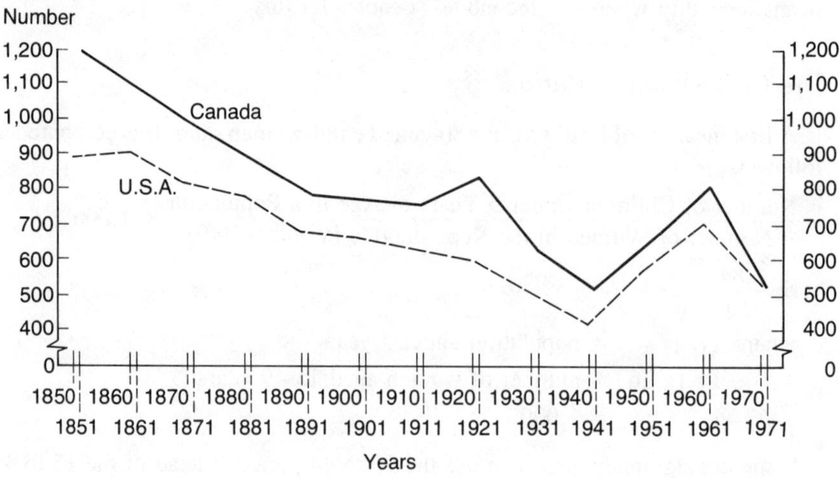


***Source:** Statistics Canada, *1971 Census of Canada, Profile Studies, Fertility in Canada* Vol. V, Part I, (Ottawa: 1976), p. 5.

Although this is not shown in the graph, the C.W.R. in the U.S.A. was higher for black women than for whites. For example, in 1850 the adjusted C.W.R. for white women was 892; that for black women stood at 1,087. In 1970 the two figures were respectively 507 and 689.

## *The Crude Birth Rate*

A second widely used index of fertility is the crude birth rate (C.B.R.) It is computed as follows:

$$\frac{\text{Number of Recorded Live Births in an Area During the Year}}{\text{Midyear Population in that Area}} \times 1{,}000 = \frac{B}{P} \cdot k$$

where B = total number of births in a given area in a given year
P = midyear population
k = 1,000

In 1971 Canada had an estimated population of 21,568,310. The total number of live births in that year added up to 362,187. Hence the C.B.R. for that year was: $\frac{362{,}187}{21{,}568{,}310} \times 1{,}000 = 16.8‰$.

The birth rate shows the relative frequency of births per thousand population. Useful as it is, this rate may easily distort actual fertility measurement because of the inclusion of non-producers of children. As a result of this the impact of the age distribution on the C.B.R. becomes very important. A population with a high proportion of adults between 18 and 40 years will, other things being equal, show a birth rate well above a more normally distributed population. At present (1977) many of the Western nations do have large proportions of young adults in their populations which tends to push the C.B.R. upwards. Table 26 gives some estimates of birth rates for major world areas. On average, the crude birth rates in the developing countries are about twice as high as those in the advanced nations.

The relatively low C.B.R. of East Asia is to be explained by the fact that it includes the low Japaneses birth rate while in Singapore, South Korea and Formosa fertility has dropped as well. The C.B.R. for Iran is very high, i.e., 42.7‰ (1972). That of Iraq stood at 42.6‰ for the year 1973. Such high figures are quite typical for the Middle East.

It is worth noting that in premodern northwestern Europe birth rates were considerably lower than in those Asian, African and Latin American nations which are now embarking on the modernization process. In 1750, for example, Norway had a C.B.R. of 30.6‰. The Danish birth rate ranked at 29.9‰ in 1800. France scored a birth rate of 27.7‰ in 1801. In 1850 the birth rate of England and Wales stood at 33.4‰; that of Belgium, at 30‰. The rates of other northwestern European nations were comparable. In all these nations fertility remained far removed from the biological maximum. Part of the explanation is to be found in the prevailing habit of deferring marriage or avoiding it altogether. This typically European phenomenon never prevailed in old Quebec. As a result its nineteenth century C.B.R. happens to be the highest recorded in the Western

TABLE 26. Estimated Annual Births for Different Major Areas of the World 1970 - 1975 (Per Thousand Population)*

| Area | Crude Birth Rate |
|---|---|
| World Total | 31.8 |
| More Developed Nations | 17.2 |
| Less Developed Nations | 39.2 |
| Europe | 16.1 |
| USSR | 17.8 |
| Northern America | 16.5 |
| Oceania | 24.7 |
| South Asia | 42.7 |
| East Asia | 26.0 |
| Africa | 46.5 |
| Latin America | 36.7 |

***Source:** United Nations, Department of Economic and Social Affairs, *Concise Report* . . ., p. 11.

world. In 1867 the birth rate in French Canada was as high as 43‰ while in 1920 it still stood at 37.6‰.

In 1959 Quebec's C.B.R. of 28.3‰ was still above the Canadian average of 27.4‰. After 1959, however, the fertility pattern in Quebec began to converge with that of the general population. In 1972 Quebec's C.B.R. had declined to about half the 1959 level. Its birth rate of 13.8‰ was now below the national average of 15.9‰. The following chart shows the rapid decline in fertility after 1958.

FIGURE 9. Crude Birth Rate, Quebec: 1958-1972*

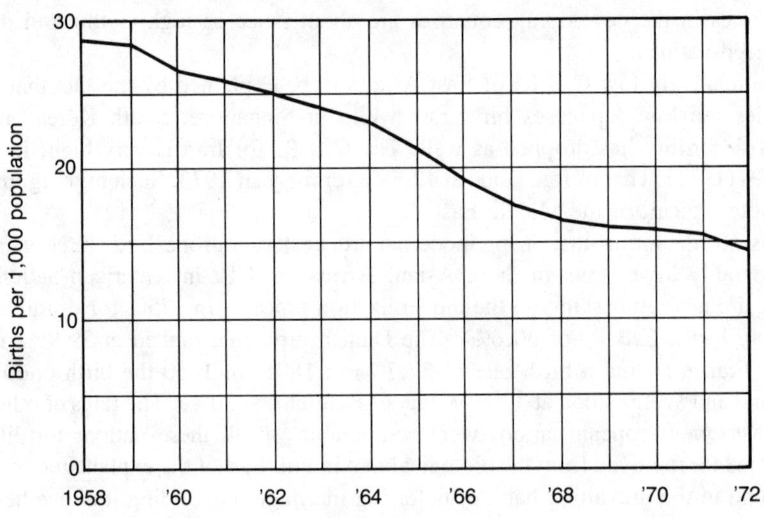


***Source:** Ministère de l'Industrie et du Commerce, *Annuaire du Quebec 1974* (Quebec Bureau de la Statistiques-Statistiques du Quebec, 1975), p. 312.

The total Canadian birth rate has, until recently, always been well below that of French Canada. The evolution of the national average over the last hundred years shows a secular decline although important fluctuations did occur. The most important one was the so-called "baby boom" which lasted from 1940-41 until the early 1960s. This temporary reversal of the long-term downward trend was also observed in other Western nations.

TABLE 27. Birth Rate in Canada, 1870-1974*

| Year | Births per Thousand Population |
|---|---|
| 1870 | 33.7 |
| 1890 | 28.6 |
| 1910 | 30.4 |
| 1920 | 29.2 |
| 1930 | 23.9 |
| 1940 | 21.5 |
| 1950 | 27.1 |
| 1960 | 26.8 |
| 1970 | 17.5 |
| 1974 | 15.4 |

***Sources:** O. J. Firestone, *Canada's Economic Development, 1867-1953* (London: Bowes & Bowes, 1958), p. 44.
Urquhart, Buckley, *Historical Statistics of Canada . . .*, p. 38.
Ministry of Industry, Trade and Commerce, *Canada Yearbook, 1976-77*, p. 198.

Figure 10 illustrates the drop in fertility which took place in the 1930s followed by the rather spectacular surge of births. Nowadays, however, the C.B.R. is even lower than in the interwar period.

The behaviour of the C.B.R. in the United States reveals a certain similarity with that of Canada as the following table shows. Birth rates in Canada, however, always tend to be a little bit above those of the U.S. or Western Europe.

## *The Crude Rate of Natural Increase*

Now that we are familiar with death and birth rates we can also find the difference between the two, i.e,. the crude rate of natural increase (C.R.N.I.). It is usually given as a percentage figure.[2] Its computation is as follows:

$$\frac{\text{No. of Births} - \text{No. of Deaths in a Given Year}}{\text{Midyear Population}} \times 100 = \frac{B - D}{P} \cdot k$$

[2]See also Chapter 3, Table 3. The crude rate of increase is different from the rate of population growth in that the latter takes net migration into account.

FIGURE 10. Crude Birth Rate Canada: 1921-1971*

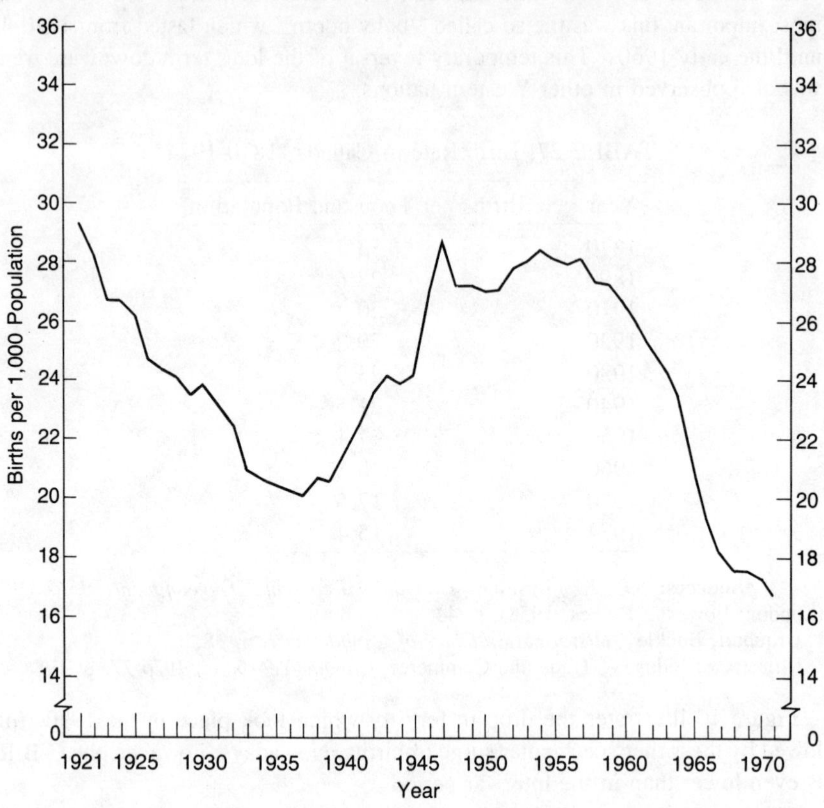


***Source:** Statistics Canada, *1971 Census of Canada, Profile Studies* . . . p. 7.

TABLE 28. Birth Rates in the U.S.A., 1910-1975 (per 1000 population)*

| Year | C.B.R. |
|---|---|
| 1910 | 30.1 |
| 1920 | 27.7 |
| 1930 | 21.3 |
| 1940 | 19.4 |
| 1950 | 24.1 |
| 1960 | 23.7 |
| 1970 | 18.4 |
| 1975 | 14.8 |

***Source:** U.S. Bureau of the Census, *Statistical Abstract of the United States, 1977* . . ., p. 55.
U.S. Bureau of the Census, *Historical Statistics of* . . ., p. 49.

To obtain the C.R.N.I. one can simply subtract the death rate from the birth rate.[3] Usually the annual number of births in an area exceeds the yearly number of deaths but if deaths were to be in excess of births the rate of increase would become negative. One might then more appropriately term it "rate of decrease".

In the 1851-61 period the Canadian rate of increase was still very high, i.e., 2.3%. It had descended to 1.4% during the 1891-1901 period. Because of the rapid decline in fertility and a more gradual drop in the death rate, the rate of increase plunged to very low levels during the interwar period. An all-time low of 0.97% was reached in 1937. During and after World War II the birth rate rose again while the death rate continued to drop gently. As a result the rate of increase mounted until it just exceeded the 2% figure in 1954. After that year the rate subsided again, mainly because the death rate began to stabilize at a low level of about 8‰ while the birth rate began to fall, first almost imperceptibly, later more visibly. In 1971 the rate of increase fell below the one percent figure while in 1973 it attained a low of 0.81%.

## *The General Fertility Rate*

Another important measure of natality is the general fertility rate (G.F.R.). Compared to the crude birth rate it is a refined measure because instead of relating births to the total population we now attribute all births to the women exposed to the risk of childbearing, i.e., the women 15-49 years of age. It is rare for a child to be born outside this age category of women. The G.F.R. can be written as follows:

$$\frac{\text{Number of Live Births During a Year in a Given Area}}{\text{Midyear Population of Women Between Ages 15-49}} \times 1{,}000 = \frac{B}{F_{15\text{-}49}} \cdot k$$

where B $=$ live births in one year

$F_{15\text{-}49}$ $=$ females of childbearing age 15-49

k $= 1{,}000$

The general fertility rate like the birth rate tends to fluctuate from year to year. For the year 1971 we find the value: $\frac{362{,}187}{5{,}281{,}715} \times 1{,}000 = 68.57‰$. Thus in 1971 in Canada, a thousand women in the childbearing years would give birth to 68.57 children.

For a country like Iran we observe a much higher figure. The situation for this country in 1973 was as follows: $\frac{1{,}212{,}000}{6{,}679{,}000} \times 1{,}000 = 181.46‰$. The figure for Iraq was even higher, i.e., 198.1‰ for the same year. The figure for Iran, however, does not quite give the full picture. Because many parents fail to register, registered births are lower than total births. The following table pictures the behavior of the Canadian and American G.F.R. between 1966 and 1974.

---

[3]The outcome, however, should be divided by the figure 10 because the C.R.N.I. is customarily expressed as a percentage amount.

TABLE 29. General Fertility Rate in Canada and the U.S.A. for 1966-1974*

| Year | Canada | U.S.A. |
|---|---|---|
| 1966 | 82.6 | 79.2 |
| 1967 | 76.8 | 76.1 |
| 1968 | 73.4 | 74.4 |
| 1969 | 72.7 | 75.2 |
| 1970 | 71.3 | 76.3 |
| 1971 | 68.6 | 71.5 |
| 1972 | 64.4 | 64.4 |
| 1973 | 62.3 | 60.9 |
| 1974 | 61.0 | 60.4 |

***Source:** United Nations, Department of Economic and Social Affairs, *1975 Demographic Yearbook,* (ST/ESA/STAT/SER.R./4), New York: 1976, p. 521.

Although the figures for the two countries differ, the trend is obviously the same. Actually, fertility trends in the Western World as a whole have been quite comparable at least since 1945. Although the G.F.R. permits a more realistic approach to fertility than the simple C.B.R., it does not distinguish between the fertility of the various age groups within the range 15-49 years. Obviously the frequency of childbirth is bound to vary a great deal with age.

## *The Age-Specific Fertility Rate*

A more refined analysis of fertility consists of computing the number of births per year to 1,000 women of a particular age. Such rates can only be calculated in countries where the age of the mother is recorded at the birth of each child. Usually, five year age groups are used, although an A.S.F.R. can be computed for each single year of age within the age range of 15-49 years. The A.S.F.R. is calculated as follows:

$$\frac{\text{Number of Live Births to Women in Age Group i in an Area in a Year}}{\text{Midyear Female Population in Age Group i, same Area, same Year}}$$

$$\times 1{,}000 = \frac{B_i}{W_i} \times k$$

where $B_i$ = number of births to women of age interval "i" in a given year in a given area

$W_i$ = number of women in age interval "i" during the same year

$k$ = 1,000

The typical curve showing the behavior of age-specific fertility first climbs very sharply while declining gently thereafter. The shape of the curve indicates that in most countries, if not all, women are most reproductive in their twenties.

The following chart shows the pattern of age-specific fertility in Canada for the years 1937, 1959 and 1968. The high fertility of the baby boom is visible in the 1959 curve.

Figure 11. Age-Specific Fertility Rates for Canada 1937, 1959 and 1968*

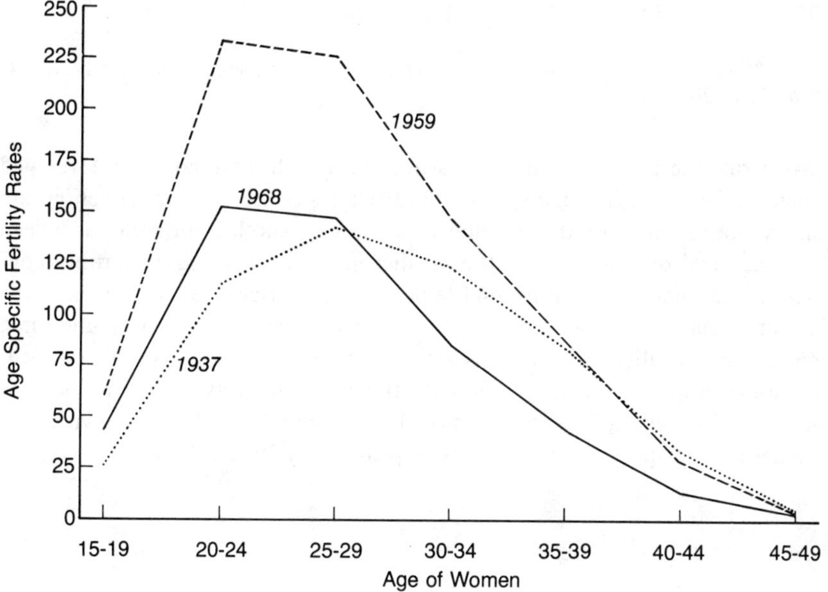


***Source:** Ministry of Industry, Trade and Commerce, *Canada Yearbook, 1971,* (Ottawa: Dominion Bureau of Statistics), 1971, p. 216.

Typically the A.S.F.R. is low in the 15-19 age groups. Peak fertility is reached between twenty and twenty nine. For women in their thirties fertility is usually quite moderate while it tends to drop to very low levels in the 40-49 age group. The following table also shows clearly that the modern Canadian woman is less and less inclined to have children after age 30.

TABLE 30. Age Specific Fertility Rates for Canada: 1926-1974*

| Year | Age Group | | | | | | |
|---|---|---|---|---|---|---|---|
| | 15-19 | 20-24 | 25-29 | 30-34 | 35-39 | 40-44 | 45-49 |
| 1926 | 29.0 | 139.9 | 177.4 | 153.8 | 114.6 | 50.7 | 6.0 |
| 1931 | 29.9 | 137.1 | 175.1 | 145.3 | 103.1 | 44.0 | 5.5 |
| 1936 | 25.7 | 112.1 | 144.3 | 126.5 | 90.0 | 36.3 | 4.4 |
| 1941 | 30.7 | 138.4 | 159.8 | 122.3 | 80.0 | 31.6 | 3.7 |
| 1946 | 36.5 | 169.6 | 191.4 | 146.0 | 93.1 | 34.5 | 3.8 |

| | | | | | | | |
|---|---|---|---|---|---|---|---|
| 1951 | 48.1 | 188.7 | 198.8 | 144.5 | 86.5 | 30.9 | 3.1 |
| 1956 | 55.9 | 222.2 | 220.1 | 150.3 | 89.6 | 30.8 | 2.9 |
| 1961 | 58.2 | 233.6 | 219.2 | 144.9 | 81.1 | 28.5 | 2.4 |
| 1966 | 48.2 | 169.1 | 163.5 | 103.3 | 57.5 | 19.1 | 1.7 |
| 1971 | 40.1 | 134.4 | 142.0 | 77.3 | 33.6 | 9.4 | 0.6 |
| 1972 | 38.5 | 119.8 | 137.1 | 72.1 | 28.9 | 7.8 | 0.6 |
| 1973 | 37.2 | 117.7 | 131.6 | 67.1 | 25.7 | 6.4 | 0.4 |
| 1974 | 35.3 | 113.1 | 131.1 | 66.6 | 23.0 | 5.5 | 0.4 |

***Source:** Ministry of Industry, Trade and Commerce, *Canada Yearbook, 1976-77*, p. 201.

As a rule the pattern is not too dissimilar for both more and less developed countries. However, the age specific fertility rates of the developing nations are usually above those of the developed countries. Another difference between developed and developing countries is that in the latter category fertility continues to be relatively high beyond female age 35.[4] Because the women in the developed nations know better how to protect themselves against undesired pregnancies, fertility drops sharply once the more advanced ages are reached. Hence the drop of the age-specific fertility curve often sets in later in the low-income nations and it falls less sharply. These features are clearly shown by the Indonesian age-specific fertility rates as pictured by Figure 12.

## *The Total Fertility Rate*

Once we find the age-specific fertility rates we can also compute the total fertility rate (T.F.R.), which is the sum of all age-specific fertility rates of women at each age within the range of 15 - 49 years multiplied by the interval (usually of five years) into which the ages are grouped. Obviously there are only 7 five-year intervals between 15 and 49. The total fertility rate has the advantage of being free from the effect of the variations in the age compositions between women in the childbearing period. The total fertility rates are sometimes expressed as rates per woman or else per thousand women. Stating it differently, the T.F.R. if referred to as a rate per 1,000 reveals the average number of children which a cohort of 1,000 women would have in their lifetime if throughout their entire reproductive period they experienced the A.S.F.R.s occurring in a specific year. Its computation is:

$$\text{T.F.R.} = n \sum_{i=1}^{i=7} \left(\frac{B_i}{W_i}\right) k$$

[4]When the author of this book first arrived in Iran he often mistook the children's parents for their grandparents.

where n = the width of the age intervals used (in our case 5 years)
$\Sigma$ = summation
i = age group (here we have 7 of these)
$B_i$ = number of births to women of age interval (i) in a year
$W_i$ = number of women in age interval (i) during the same year
k = 1,000

FIGURE 12. Age-Specific Fertility Rates for Java, Other Islands and all Indonesia: Average: 1966 - 1970*

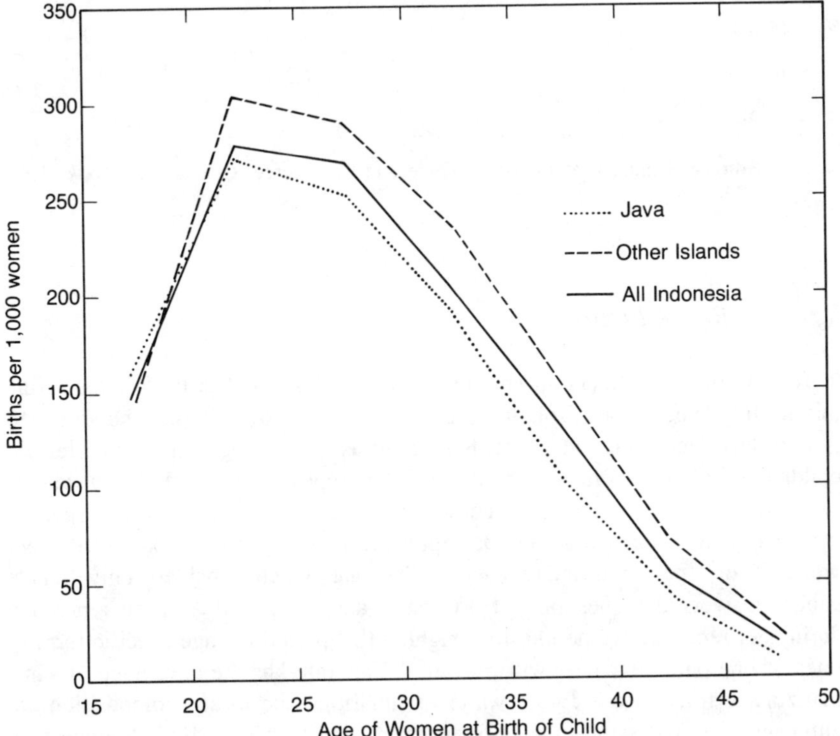


***Source:** G.McNicoll, Si Gde Made Mamas, *The Demographic Situation in Indonesia* (Honolulu: Papers of the East-West Population Institute, 1973), p. 21.

The assumption is that female mortality is zero until the end of the childbearing period. If the T.F.R. is two, the parents are close to replacing themselves and the rate of increase should be near the zero level. The following table reproduces the age-specific fertility rates and the total fertility rates of the Canadian population in the years 1956, 1966 and 1974. Between the first and the last date the T.F.R. was more than cut in half.

The pattern displayed by the American rates was not too different. From a high of 3,768 in 1957 it had declined to a low of 1,799 in 1975. In developing countries the T.F.R. reaches high levels. The 1973 T.F.R. for Iraq was 7,021.

TABLE 31. Age-Specific Fertility Rates and Total Fertility Rates of the Canadian Population, 1956, 1966, 1974 (per 1,000 women)*

| Age Group | 1956 | 1966 | 1974 |
|---|---|---|---|
| 1) 15-19 | 55.9 | 48.2 | 35.3 |
| 2) 20-24 | 222.2 | 169.1 | 113.1 |
| 3) 25-29 | 220.1 | 163.5 | 131.1 |
| 4) 30-34 | 150.3 | 103.3 | 66.6 |
| 5) 35-39 | 89.6 | 57.5 | 23.0 |
| 6) 40-44 | 30.8 | 19.1 | 5.5 |
| 7) 45-49 | 2.9 | 1.7 | 0.4 |
| Sum | 771.8 | 562.4 | 375 |
| 5 × Sum = T.F.R.: | 3,859 | 2,812 | 1,875 |

***Source:** Ministry of Industry, Trade and Commerce, *Canada Yearbook, 1975* . . ., p. 177.

## *Rates of Reproduction*

Total fertility considers all children born i.e., boys and girls. We can refine this fertility measure by isolating the girls. This is how we find the so-called gross rate of reproduction which is defined as the average number of female children born to a woman who survives her reproductive period and who is exposed at each age to the age-specific fertility rates prevailing during a specific calendar year. The gross rate of reproduction can also be expressed "per woman" or "per thousand women". The rate which considers only female babies answers the question: "How many daughters will a woman produce during her reproductive period if throughout that period the age-specific fertility rates of one particular year will prevail?" This rate has the advantage of summarizing fertility in one figure while irregularities due to age composition are eliminated. At the same time differences in fertility caused by belonging to a particular age category are also removed. The computation of the G.R.R. closely follows that of the T.F.R.

$$\text{G.R.R.} = n \sum_{i=1}^{i=7} \left(\frac{B^f_i}{W_i}\right) k$$

where $n$ = the width of the age intervals used
$\Sigma$ = summation
$i$ = age group
$F^f_i$ = number of *female* births to women of age interval (i) in a year
$W_i$ = number of women in age interval (i) during the same year
$k$ = 1,000

The gross reproduction rate (G.R.R.) then is a reproductivity formula. We find the number of daughters available to replace their mothers. Hence it is the sum of age-specific fertility rates (from ages 15-49) calculated for female births only. A simple way of finding the G.R.R. is the following:

$$\text{G.R.R.} = \text{Total Fertility Rate} \times \frac{\text{Female Births}}{\text{Total Births}} = \text{T.F.R.} \times \frac{B_f}{B_t}$$

The total fertility rate, in other words, is multiplied by the proportion of females at birth.[5] For a country like Canada, for instance, about 48.5% of all children born are females (of 1,000 births, 485 are girls). If we multiply the T.F.R. per woman for 1974, i.e., 1.88 by 485 we obtain 911 which is the number of daughters replacing one thousand women if age-specific fertility rates of that year continued. In other words, if a hypothetical cohort of 1,000 newborn female Canadian infants were throughout their entire reproductive period exposed to age-specific fertility rates of 1974, they would produce 911 daughters. An important assumption is that no woman would die before age 50.

The G.R.R. assumes that for a cohort of women under consideration mortality will be zero between birth and the end of the reproductive period. As the following tables and graphs will show, in Canada (and some other Western nations) the G.R.R. has fallen below one. Yet populations keep increasing because the birth rate exceeds the death rate. The age composition of the Canadian population, however, contains a large proportion of young adults, itself a consequence of the 1944-1961 baby boom. As a result, birth rates are higher than death rates even if one thousand mothers produce fewer than one thousand daughters to replace them. Table 32 reproduces in Canadian T.F.R. and G.R.R. for certain selected years. Since the G.R.R. is concerned only with female children it must be about half the size of the T.F.R.

The long-term implication of the 1974 schedule of fertility rates is that the Canadian population would no longer reproduce itself. A country like Iran which scored a G.R.R. of 3,350 in 1973 does not have to worry about this particular problem.

Table 32 confirms, however, our knowledge that T.F.R.'s and G.R.R.'s vary over a period of time. The G.R.R. neglects the mortality to which the females of a hypothetical cohort would be subjected. The net reproduction rate (N.R.R.) allows for that mortality from the time of their birth. Hence the hypothetical cohort of women would be exposed to the age-specific mortality rates *and* the age-specific fertility rates of a given year. Thus it shows the level of replacement of a hypothetical cohort. It gives a clear picture of the size of a generation in relation to the generation which anteceded it. As Tables 33 and 34 show, the

---

[5]The proportion of females to the total population is expressed as $\frac{\text{Females}}{\text{Total Population}}$ while the proportion of females at birth is written $\frac{\text{Female Births}}{\text{Total Births}}$. It is common that male births exceed female births by a small margin.

TABLE 32. Total Fertility Rate and Gross Reproduction Rate for Canada, Selected Years (per thousand women)*

| Year | T.F.R. | G.R.R. |
|---|---|---|
| 1931 | 3,200 | 1,555 |
| 1941 | 2,832 | 1,377 |
| 1951 | 3,503 | 1,701 |
| 1961 | 3,840 | 1,868 |
| 1971 | 2,190 | 1,061 |
| 1972 | 2,024 | 982 |
| 1973 | 1,931 | 937 |
| 1974 | 1,875 | 911 |

***Source:** Ministry of Industry, Trade and Commerce, *Canada Yearbook, 1976-77* . . ., p. 201.

figure for the N.N.R. always lies below that of the G.R.R. although the steady decline of mortality of women has helped to narrow the gap between the two figures. In countries such as Iran, where female mortality is still considerable, the gap between G.R.R. and N.R.R. is also significant, i.e., 3,350 and 2,470.

TABLE 33. G.R.R. and N.N.R. for Canada, 1970-1973*

| Year | G.R.R. | N.N.R. |
|---|---|---|
| 1970 | 1.122 | 1.085 |
| 1971 | 1.061 | 1.026 |
| 1972 | 0.982 | 0.955 |
| 1973 | 0.937 | 0.911 |

***Source:** United Nations, Department of Economic and Social Affairs, *1975 Demographic Yearbook* . . ., p. 520.

The American reproduction rates between 1930 and 1970 show the same cyclical behavior as the Canadian ones. They were low during the 1930s, rose during and after World War II but fell after the late 1950s.

TABLE 34. G.R.R. and N.N.R. for the U.S.A., 1930-1974*

| Year | G.R.R. | N.N.R. |
|---|---|---|
| 1930-1935 | 1.108 | 984 |
| 1940 | 1.121 | 1.027 |
| 1950 | 1.505 | 1.435 |
| 1960 | 1.783 | 1.715 |
| 1970 | 1.207 | 1.168 |
| 1974 | 0.904 | 0.879 |

***Source:** United Nations, . . ., *1975 Demographic Yearbook* . . ., p. 521.
U.S. Bureau of the Census, *Historical Statistics of the United States, Colonial Times to 1970* . . ., p. 53.

FIGURE 13. Gross and Net Reproduction Rates, Netherlands: 1930-1972*

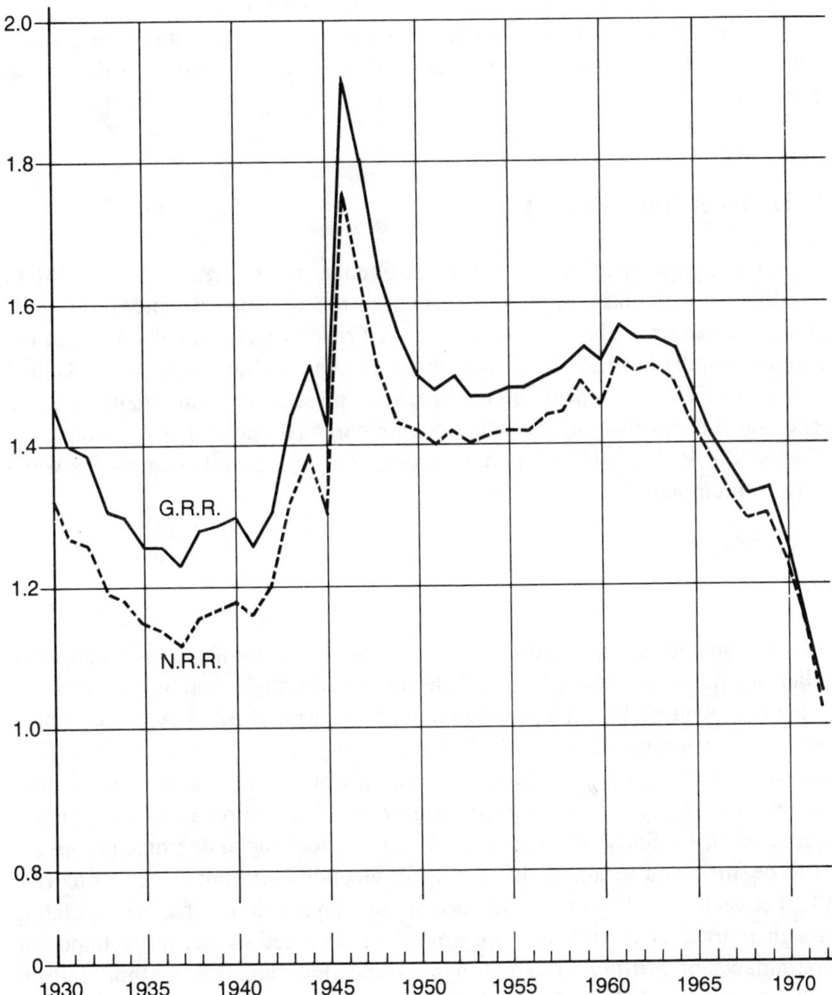


***Source:** Centraal Bureau voor de Statistiek, *75 Jaar Statistiek van Nederland* . . ., p. 16.

We noted before that the N.N.R. assumes that the age-specific fertility and mortality rates of a particular year will continue to prevail during the entire 0-50 age period of a particular cohort of women. It is especially the age-specific fertility rates which tend to fluctuate over time. The N.N.R. therefore cannot be used to make forecasts about future population change. During the inter-war period demographers did in fact use the N.N.R., which was then a relatively new tool, for such long-term prognoses. One might for example have argued in the 1930-35 period that with an N.N.R. of 948 the American population was doomed to die out in the long run. During and after World War II, however, birth rates rose and the pessimistic forecasts of the 1930s were completely upset. Figure 13 pictures the substantial fluctuations or the reproduction rates in the Netherlands. The narrowing of the gap between G.R.R. and N.N.R. is also clearly visible.

## C. Differential Fertility

Aggregate fertility in such countries as Canada, the U.S.A. or France differs according to race, class, religion, occupation, income and residence. It is well-known, for example, that for a long time the French Canadian component of the Canadian population had birth rates above the national average. In the United States the black component of the American population traditionally has had higher fertility levels than the white counterpart. To cite just one example, in 1974 the T.F.R. for the black population stood at 2,322 while that for the white population amounted to 1,708.

### *Race*

Race is sometimes an important determinant of fertility levels. As mentioned earlier, the nonwhites in the United States have traditionally had birth rates above those of the whites. The first generation of Mexicans in the U.S.A. tends to have about twice the number of children of the average native American family. In Canada the fertility of the Indians and Eskimos birth rate is above the national average. In 1970 the Eskimo birth rate was 55‰ compared to the national average of 18‰. Such differences in fertility between racial or ethnic groups are not to be attributed to innate differences in fecundity. Fecundity seems to vary little between racial groups. Socioeconomic and cultural factors operating through individual motivations are nowadays accepted as the more important determinants of fertility. The willingness and determination to limit fertility deliberately depends largely on whether an individual or couple is sufficiently motivated or not.

### *Religion*

Religion is a second factor determining fertility. A positive relationship has often been ascertained between commitment to church doctrine and completed fertility. In many countries such as Canada, the United States, Switzerland and the Netherlands, where Protestants and Catholics have lived side by side, Catholics have been observed to have larger families than Protestants. This has been partly due to the fact that the Catholic Church has until now opposed the use of contraceptives while larger families were favored. During the last decade however, the differential fertility between Catholics and Protestants has been disappearing rapidly because the younger Catholics increasingly disregard the official tenets of the Church regarding contraception and birth control. This is especially true for the Western nations, much less so for the Latin American countries.

## *Urban-Rural Residence*

Fertility differentials between rural and urban areas have long attracted the attention of scientific observers. As a rule, fertility has been found to be higher in rural than in urban communities. Cultural, psychological and economic reasons explain this. The grip of traditional social customs is stronger on the rural dweller than on the urban resident. The relatively low level of instruction and education in combination with geographical isolation tend to delay acceptance of the small family ideal. Economic factors are also important. It is easier to raise a child in the countryside than in the city and on the farm children may have value as productive agents and often contribute to the family income. In a number of developing nations, parents still rely on their children especially their sons to take care of them when they are old or ill.

## *Occupation*

A comparison of the fertility of different occupational groups in countries like Canada reveals a nonperfect inverse relationship between fertility and occupational status. This feature has long been a characteristic of Western civilization and probably of other cultures as well.[6] Generally speaking, farmers and agricultural workers are the most fertile. The least fertile groups are the members of what is called the lower middle class, which consists of white collar workers, clerical workers, semi-professional people and small businessmen. A possible explanation for this low fertility is that it is in the lower middle class that the tension between income and perceived needs is the greatest. The stronger the desire to improve one's position in society, the lower one's fertility tends to be. The fertility of the upper middle class, which consists of professionals, managers and proprietors, tends to be a little higher than that of the lower middle class but well below that of farm laborers and farmers.

## *Income*

The relationship between income and fertility also tends to be inverse. As

---

[6]It should be admitted, however, that several research studies have found a positive relationship between economic status and fertility. See for example: D.E. Driver, *Differential Fertility in Central India,* Princeton: Princeton University Press, 1963.

income and educational achievement tend to be closely connected, the association between education and fertility is also broadly negative. The exception to the rule is that the average family size of the very highest income groups tends to be above that of the income groups just below them. The inverse correlation between income and fertility also holds between regions and nations. Relatively wealthy northern Italy has had much lower fertility levels than the poorer south. Rich Ontario had a 1974 birth rate of 15.3% while the birth rate of not-so-rich New Brunswick stood at 17.3%. Between rich and poor nations a comparison of birth rates is also instructive. The contrast is sharp and still widening, it seems. The estimated birth rate of the more developed countries for the 1970-1975 period is 17.2%. That of the less developed regions for the same time period is 37.8%. The developing nations are obviously caught in a vicious circle: poverty is associated with high fertility which itself dampens economic progress and retards improvements in living standards.

The low fertility levels of the higher income groups, the urban and the better educated is, as stated earlier, not related to differential fecundity but to more effective family planning. In order to plan a family properly, spouses must be motivated to space their children. They must discuss together the desired family size. Understanding male and female anatomy is important, and contraceptive information must be sought. All in all, uninhibited, active, constructive and open attitudes are required. It is among the lower income groups that training and the habit of coping with problems is likely to be inferior. Among this group also attitudes of passive resignation to whatever fate will bring are more frequently found and higher fertility is often the result. The history of the Western nations has shown that family planning started among the educated, urban upper middle and middle classes and spread from there to the other sections of society.

## D. Trends in Fertility

### *Fertility in the Past*

In traditional preindustrial societies fertility was bound to be high. The elevated level of fertility can be seen as a logical adjustment to the prevailing high uncontrolled death rate. A mere survival of the premodern community demanded constant mobilization of all available reproductive powers. Consequently, traditional values and institutions always tended to favor early and universal marriage and large families. Young people were put under considerable pressure to marry early and have children. In many premodern societies the extended family was a dominant feature. These groups of families which cover several generations and degrees of relationship accommodate high fertility patterns very well. While the procreating parents receive all the prestige and status associated with numerous offspring, the extended family takes on part of the burden of raising them. In such a kinship dominated system there are no real social or personal gains to be achieved if couples reduce the size of their offspring. And this is precisely the way the system wants it to be.

## *Premodern Europe*

It should be noted, however, that premodern northwest Europe differed from many other traditional societies in the sense that marriage was often tied to the setting up of a separate household, thus imposing the full burden of procreation on the parents. The extended family as it existed and still exists in many areas in Africa and Asia was unknown. As a result Western Europeans tended to marry comparatively late while a considerable proportion of people avoided marriage altogether. Thus premodern Europe knew ''marriage control'', which is different from ''birth control'' but they both tend to reduce overall fertility levels.

The guild systems, consisting of associations of craftsmen and merchants, which arose after 1000 A.D., often restricted the conditions of entry and the training period of apprentices was long, sometimes many years. Once the training period was over the young adult had to work as a journeyman in other towns to acquire experience. Marriage could not be contracted until the end of the training period.

It should also be noted that the emphasis on celibacy and chastity by the Roman Catholic Church introduced an element in European society which tended to countervail possible social and cultural pressures to get married and procreate. In any event the fact is that in northwest Europe a tradition of relatively late marriage has prevailed for centuries while numerous people kept away from marriage altogether. In a society where birth control within marriage is not practiced, marriage patterns are a major determinant of fertility. Marriage control did help to avoid extreme densities of population but could not prevent temporary imbalances between numbers and resources. In premodern Europe birth rates could for long periods of time be above the death rates with a low rate of increase the result. In preindustrial England the rate of increase stood perhaps at 0.4% towards the end of the seventeenth century. Numbers would grow. Yet the environment would, beyond a certain point, resist such growth. Time and again the death rate would rise, perhaps because of a set of bad harvests, an epidemic or the like. More children and adults would die directly or indirectly from hunger, malnutrition or disease. The survivorship of women in their productive ages was lowered and more marriages were interrupted by death. Potential marriage partners would defer marriage and thereby the births these marriages could have produced. Still others would avoid marriage altogether. The incidence of induced abortion would probably also rise. Over time the relationship between food and population would improve again and per capita food supplies would increase, partly because the crisis had eliminated a fraction of the population, in part because fertility had been reduced for a number of years. Slowly improving agricultural techniques would then ensure an expanding food basis and the death rates would fall again. Deferred marriages would now be contracted and the mean age of marriage might move downward. This was in part because those young people who survived the crises could succeed earlier to the agricultural holding, enterprise or workshop belonging to the family or relatives. Because of the demographic depletion during the crisis, employment opportunities and wages would be favorable. Thus the damage done by food scarcity, epidemics or war would be repaired in time and population would continue its upward course until the next turn of the tide.

## *The Industrial Revolution and its Aftermath*

Some countries such as England witnessed an increase in the rate of population growth towards the end of the eighteenth century. It seems that in England this rate peaked between 1780 and 1820. Several factors explain this. The agricultural revolution of the 18th century mildly improved the quality and quantity of the available food supplies, while better transport facilities (canals had been dug, etc.) eliminated local food shortages. Mortality dropped a little because more and improved hospitals were built, while widespread vaccination against small pox reduced the incidence of the dreaded disease. At the same time no major epidemic occurred in Europe. The Industrial Revolution, which occurred in this period, implied a greatly increased demand for labor both adult and child.

Domestic as well as factory industry employed increasing quantities of labor. The widespread prevalence of child labor reduced the costs of raising them, whereas the employed, money-earning women now became more attractive marriage partners. The mean age of marriage fell and marital fertility increased. It has also been suggested that the rural-urban migration and the accumulation of a growing proportion of the population in cities tended to weaken the prudential restraints practised in the countryside.

Especially after 1850 the downward trend in mortality became firmly established in the Western World. Smallpox was increasingly controlled by vaccination. The practice of midwifery grew better. The available range of drugs widened and medical science in general greatly advanced. Infectious diseases became better understood, which facilitated their repression. Public health also made rapid strides. The water supplies improved in quality while sanitary sewage and garbage disposal became more common. Cotton clothes and underwear began to replace their woollen equivalents and a better understanding of the elementary principles of personal hygiene (use of soap, etc.) began to penetrate. Food supplies also grew more abundant. The development of the Western Hemisphere added a granary of enormous size and potential to the existing food sources. Perfected transport, especially by railway and steamship, brought rich harvests in no time to other parts of the world, mainly Europe of course.

While mortality continuously dropped, fertility remained relatively high at least until about the late 1870s. Although this period coincides with the discovery and spread of upgraded contraceptives (pessaries and condoms), the decline in fertility was certainly not caused by these findings. Yet effective contraceptive techniques break the link between nuptiality and fertility because marital fertility can be reduced without postponement or avoidance of the wedding bond. In fact, after the 1870s the small family ideal was increasingly adopted by married couples who consciously limited the number of children within marriage. Many hypotheses have been offered about the reasons for this. The following explanations have been generally accepted by most population specialists.

Towards the end of the 19th century infant and child mortality had begun to decline conclusively. Earlier, a large proportion of all children born had not lived long enough to become much of an economic burden on the parents. With higher survival rates, however, parents were prompted to pay serious attention to the number of children they could support until adolescence. The improved chances for survival for children also meant that fewer births were required to secure a given number of surviving children. A second reason for the drop in fertility was that by the end of the 19th century child labor in Europe had been abolished while primary education had become compulsory. Youngsters therefore were no longer able to contribute to the family income and thus earn their own upkeep, if not more. Again, this new piece of legislation increased the burden of added children especially for the low-income groups. At that time a growing proportion of the population in such countries as England had become urbanized. Raising children in an urban environment involves relatively high material and psychic costs. The supervision of children is more difficult in the city than on the farm, while more has to be spent on clothes, shoes and the like when children live in an urban environment. These increased costs exerted pressure toward having a small family.

In the course of modernization, industrialization and urbanization, new occupations and opportunities to move up the social ladder are constantly created. In order to be able to take full advantage of the possibilities for social advancement, a great deal of money and time must be invested in training and retraining, the latter sometimes in evening hours and on weekends. At the same time spatial mobility or migration is sometimes a step towards advancement because the best opportunities may be outside one's area of residence. A large family size conflicts clearly with the aspirations and life styles of such an environment. It reduced a man's mobility while making less time available for career-oriented activities.

The emancipation and improved education which accompanied socioeconomic progress and the widening range of gainful occupations available to them caused women to question increasingly the traditional assumption that marriage and motherhood were the only roles open to them. During and after World War I married women began to join the labor force in large numbers. Children tie the mother to the home and the increased involvement of women in outside activities tend to reduce desired family size.

The transformation of societies undergoing modernization and industrialization furthers the breakdown of traditional family relationships. Many of the functions of the family are taken over by other social institutions. In the premodern society parents often relied on children for financial help in old age. Children were then a kind of investment requiring initial outlays but yielding a return afterwards. Enough children had to be brought into the world to secure at least a few surviving sons. In the more developed society the family loses the mutual assistance function. Collective private programs and state controlled welfare systems provide for the aged while it becomes customary not to turn to one's children for economic help.

Industrialization and socioeconomic progress tend to be accompanied by a spirit of rationalism and calculation which pervade nearly all spheres and replace custom and tradition. The latter have nearly always been pro-natalist in their implications for reasons explained earlier in this text. The decline of tradition and religion-bound attitudes and values and the rise and adoption of more rational attitudes in general prompt a decrease in desired family size.

The greater availability of contraceptive knowledge and effective low-cost contraceptives is a last factor to be mentioned here. A drastic decline in fertility implies that effective techniques of fertility reduction are available and known. The spouses must also be able to communicate on the subject. In fact, it was towards the end of the nineteenth century that better contraceptives became available while contraceptive information circulated more widely. In 1880 Walter John Rendall, a London chemist experimented successfully with a pessary containing quinine. The rubber condom was also improved. Higher literacy levels allowed more people to learn about existing contraceptive technology.

France happened to be the first country experiencing a decline in fertility. Throughout the second half of the 19th century, the other northwestern European nations, the United States and Canada followed.

## The Historical Present

The secular decline in fertility in the Western World continued unchecked until World War II. In the 1930s birth rates had already reached the low levels one might expect in a modernized environment. Rates of reproduction were close to unity and had fallen below that level in some nations including the U.S.A. The temporary reversal of the long-term trend usually called the "baby boom" which started in the 1940s was a somewhat abnormal phenomenon and petered out in the 1960s. The baby boom has been attributed to a number of causes, of which only a few will be mentioned here. Because of the economic crisis of the 1930s a number of couples had either postponed marriage and/or childbearing. With improved employment opportunities in the 1940s more marriages were contracted and some of the deferred births were recouped. Marriage became more frequent again and the mean age of first marriages dropped. The mean age of childbearing also declined while the number of desired children definitely rose. Childlessness among married couples virtually disappeared. Contraception was still far from perfect while husband-wife communication on sexual and marital matters also left much to be desired in a number of cases. With a lower mean age of marriage, exposure to wanted and unwanted pregnancies was obviously lengthened while continuous medical progress ensured regular improvements in survival. In the 1960s, new and more effective contraceptives such as "the pill" and the I.U.D. made their appearance and public discussion of sex and family related matters became more open. In Canada the mean age of marriage has crept up since 1961 while the proportion of unmarried is also slightly on the rise. This may perhaps be due to such factors as the increased proportions of young adults going to universities and the reduction in unplanned marriages, the latter being due to the greater availability of contraceptive information and effective means of birth planning. Nuptiality, however, has not been the chief factor in the recent decline of fertility. It has been estimated that the marriage factor accounted for only 9% of the fertility decline between 1961 and 1967. The remainder of the drop in fertility is to be attributed to such factors as postponement of births by young married couples and a decline in the desired family size. Baby boom cohorts may easily be supposed to opt for relatively small families confronted as they are with deficient employment opportunities and high housing prices. As a rule baby boom cohorts unfortunately tend to experience relative deprivation when they move into adulthood. Their sheer numbers tend to put the labor market and housing market under high pressure. With the new contraceptives, postponement and avoidance of births has become a great deal easier. If the small family norm of not more than three children is increasingly accepted among younger couples, the new contraceptives facilitate the attainment of this standard. One of the astounding facts in recent demographic history is the similarity of fertility patterns in all modernized nations while the reasons for modifications in these patterns are almost always identical.

### *Fertility in the Developing Countries*

The low-income countries have experienced an entirely different demographic pattern. Mortality has dropped very sharply since the 1940s because public health improvements, medical discoveries and scientific contributions of all sorts, such as chemotherapy, have been and still are transmitted from the more to the less developed nations. Often enough those death control techniques are superimposed on traditional peasant societies where a basic modernization process has hardly started and where drastic declines in fertility are not to be expected soon. In many an Asian or African country the extended family still prevails and, as was stated earlier, kinship dominated systems are conducive to high fertility patterns. It is of course hoped that the low-income nations will soon enter the transition from high to low fertility. Some of the smaller nations such as Singapore, Hongkong, South Korea and Taiwan have in fact done so. However, it will take a long time before both mortality and fertility will be lowered in the majority of the developing nations. In the meantime huge increments in their populations must be expected.

## E. The Theory of the Demographic Transition

The foregoing historical considerations can be schematically presented by the so-called ''demographic transition model'' of which Figure 7 below is a stylized example. The demographic transition (D.T.) refers to the change-over from the high birth and death rate equilibrium which characterizes premodern societies to the low birth and death rate equilibrium of the contemporary industrialized and urbanized societies. Depending on the author, between three and five stages are distinguished.

FIGURE 14. The Demographic Transition Model in Four Stages

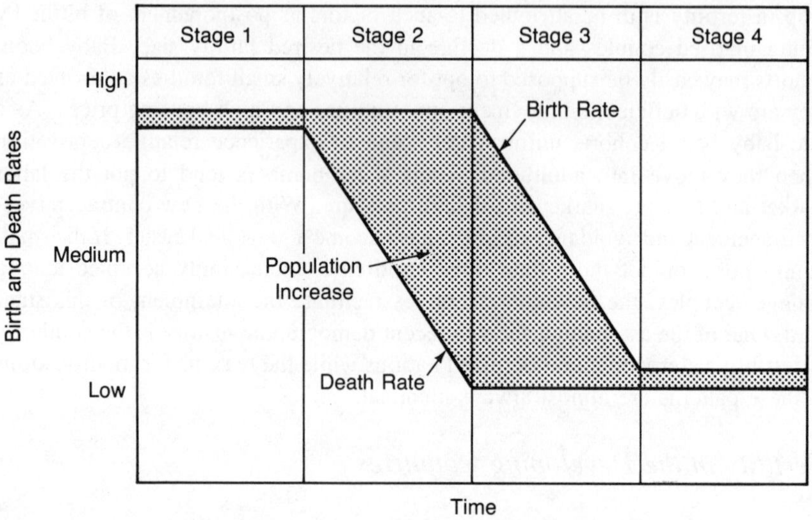

Stage one corresponds to a society where both birth and death rates are out of control. Both vital rates are in the 30-50‰ range. The birth rate is usually a little above the death rate. Expectation of life at birth is perhaps as low as 25 years and even less during years of famine and epidemics. The second stage might be called ''early expanding interval''. Death rates begin to drop but birth rates remain high. They may even rise. Improved health conditions which depress mortality also better the survivorship of women in the reproductive ages. The healthier women also carry more babies to term. Such conditions easily make for slightly higher fertility levels. The expectation of life may rise to some 50 years.

The following period might be called the ''late expanding phase''. The death rate keeps declining but the birth rate starts dropping as well. This is no longer due to postponement and avoidance of marriage but to a fall in marital fertility. Couples want and plan for smaller families. At the same time, medical progress and advances in public health guarantee a continuous descent of mortality levels. If we base ourselves on the Western European experience, life expectancy at birth keeps rising steadily. The fourth interval has been termed ''low quasi-stationary phase''. The death rate keeps falling gently until it reaches a level of about 8-12‰. The birth rates also keep sliding down to a plane between 15 and

20 per thousand. Life expectancy at birth rises to approximately 70 years. Fluctuations in fertility are wider than in mortality. The baby boom in the West occurred during this phase. A fifth phase would imply that birth and death rates are about equal with zero population growth as a result. In many Western nations the death rate is bound to rise somewhat, perhaps to a level of about 12-13.5‰ because of the growing proportion of older, high-mortality risk people in their populations.[7] Expectation of life at birth may rise to approximately 76-77 years. As the following chart shows, it seems that Belgium is rapidly approaching zero population growth with both vital rates being close to the 12‰ figure. The economically advanced nations are either in stage four or about to enter stage five.

FIGURE 15. Crude Birth and Death Rates, Belgium: 1900-1974

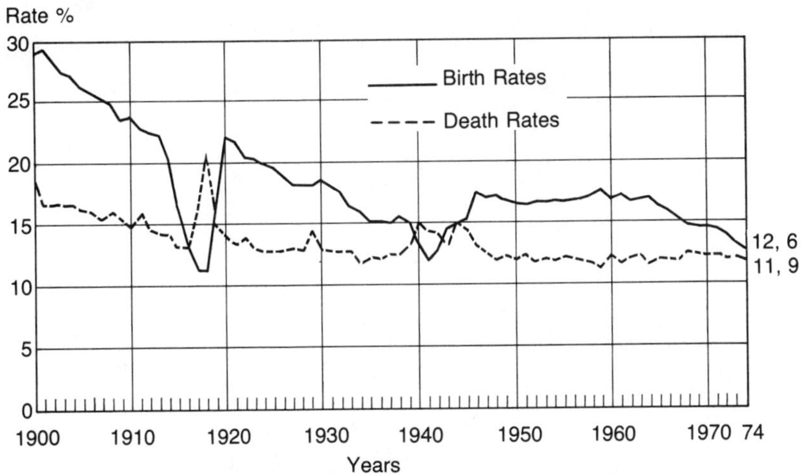


***Source:** Ministère des Affaires Economiques, Institut National de Statistique, *Annuaire Statistique de la Belgique*, Vol. 95, (Bruxelles: 1975), p. 51.[8]

About two thirds of the world population has not yet gone through the transition and experiences falling death rates in combination with high fertility levels. As a result the population of the developing countries will increase from about 2.5 billion in 1970 to approximately 5 billion in the year 2000. The only sign of hope is that some of the latecomers in this transitional process such as Germany, Italy, some Eastern European countries and also Japan have moved more rapidly through the demographic transition than such countries as France and England which started it first. There is therefore some hope (but no certainty) that the developing countries will also experience an accelerated transition.

---

[7]Chapter 11 will explain the ageing process of population in greater detail.

[8]The transition model for Belgium shows that this country suffered heavily from both world wars.

## Bibliography

Coale, A.J., "The History of the Human Population", *The Human Population*. A Scientific American Book, San Francisco: W.H. Freeman & Co., 1974.

Habakkuk, H.J., *Population Growth and Economic Development Since 1750,* Bath: Pitman Press, 1972.

Kirk, D., "A New Demographic Transition?", *Rapid Population Growth* ed., Study Committee of the Office of the Foreign Secretary, National Academy of Sciences, Baltimore: The John Hopkins Press, 1971.

Matras, J., *Population and Societies,* New Jersey: Prentice-Hall, *1973*.

Palmore, J.A., *Measuring Fertility and Natural Increase: A Self-Teaching Guide to Elementary Measures,* Honolulu: East-West Population Institute, 1975.

Stolnitz, G.J., "The Demographic Transition: From High to Low Birth Rates and Death Rates", *The Vital Revolution,* ed. R. Freedman, New York: Anchor Books, 1964.

Wrigley, E.A., *Population and History,* New York: McGraw-Hill, 1969.

Chapter 8

# *Migration*

## A. Basic Concepts and Measures of Migration

Man is not the only species capable of adopting, either temporarily or permanently, a new country or climate. For as long as we know, a number of animal species, especially birds, have displaced themselves seasonally or for good, searching for food and shelter. Migration of people is not new either. Migration over short and long distances has played a continuing part in the adjustment of man to his environment.

After mortality and fertility, migration constitutes the third population process. Like mortality and fertility, migration has a direct impact upon the size of the population. Fertility and immigration affect a population upwards while mortality and emigration involve a decline in numbers. Demographically speaking, migration implies a change of residence from one clearly defined geographical unit to another. Sociologically speaking, migration entails a significant change in community ties and conditions of life.

Migration then, refers to the movement of people in space. It involves a change in the usual place of residence. A migrant, therefore, changes his permanent place of residence for a long period of time and crosses political or administrative boundaries in the process. The latter qualification distinguishes him from a simple mover who moves from one house to another but who does not cross administrative or political frontiers. It is customary to subdivide the field of migration into two areas: internal and international migration. Internal migrants move within the nation's frontiers. International migrants cross international boundaries. Internal migration streams tend to accompany economic and social changes and are usually of a larger magnitude than their international counterparts.

The terms in- and out-migration which are usually used with reference to internal migration refer to the arrival into an area of destination and the departure from an area of origin during a migration interval. The interval itself may be one year, five years or ten years. The equivalent terms immigration and emigration are commonly used with reference to international migration.

Net migration is the number of migrants coming in, minus the migrants the same area loses to other regions. The net balance is termed "net migration" and may be positive or negative. In Canada the net balance is usually positive although this country tends to lose large numbers to the United States. The sum total of people leaving an area and entering into it during a given period is defined as "gross migration" or "population turnover".

Fertility and mortality have their crude rates. The same applies to migration. Migration measures are usually referred to as rates. A migration rate is the ratio of migrants observed or estimated to the exposed population during a given interval of time. Normally, the exposed population or the population at risk consists of the initial population in the case of out-migration and the terminal population in the case of in-migration.

Effacing for a moment the difference between internal and external movements we can distinguish four commonly used migration rates:

Crude in-migration rate: $\frac{I}{P} \cdot k$

Crude out-migration rate: $\frac{O}{P} \cdot k$

Crude net-migration rate: $\frac{I - O}{P} \cdot k$

Crude gross-migration rate: $\frac{I + O}{P} \cdot k$

where I = the number of in-migrants to an area
O = the number of out-migrants from an area
P = the exposed mid-year or average population of an area
k = a constant; in this case 1,000

The following table shows some migration rates between 1870 and 1975 in Canada.

TABLE 35. Immigration, Emigration and Net Migration per thousand of Population, Canada, Selected Years, 1870-1975*

| Year | Immigration Rate | Emigration Rate | Net Migration Rate |
|---|---|---|---|
| 1870 | 6.8 | 6.0 | 0.8 |
| 1890 | 15.6 | 16.0 | −0.4 |
| 1910 | 40.3 | 28.6 | 11.7 |
| 1930 | 10.2 | 6.4 | 3.8 |
| 1950 | 5.3 | 2.7 | 2.6 |
| 1970 | 7.3 | 1.3 | 6.0 |
| 1975 | 8.2 | 0.5 | 7.7 |

***Sources:** O. J. Firestone, *Canada's Economic Development* (London: Bowes & Bowes, 1958), p. 44.
Ministry of Industry, Trade and Commerce, *Canada Yearbook, 1976-77,* pp. 212, 217.

## B. Data Sources and Functions of Migration

Countries such as the Netherlands and Denmark, which maintain individual registers recording all vital events including individual movements, are faced with an ideal situation. All migratory movements of each individual are registered and all data pertinent to internal migration are known. Countries such as Canada which do not possess such registers must rely on census counts and surveys. When a census is taken the inhabitants of a country can be asked where they were residing during a certain time span (say 5 years ago). The past place of residence is then compared to the current one. It is also possible to compare the place of birth with the current place of residence. In the 1971 Census such questions were in fact included. The result, however, will not reveal how many times the citizen moved between his birth and the moment of enumeration. Sample surveys consist of holding interviews or sending questionnaires to be filled out to representative samples of the population. Such surveys are the third major method of collecting migration data.

Data on international migration streams are in certain instances obtained from port statistics. The custom officers are provided with lists of passengers which normally distinguish between outward bound passengers who are emigrants and those who are not. Land frontier statistics and passport statistics are equally important sources of information on migration.

## *Objectives of Migration*

Migration obviously plays an important role in modern society. Some of its more important functions are the following. First, migration redistributes population. In a modern community or a society which is moving through the development/modernization process, constant redistribution of population is a prime necessity. Areas such as Alberta, where new resources are being discovered or developed, need extra manpower. Industrial cities such as Hamilton need considerable amounts of unskilled and skilled workers. The local residents may not be able to supply those in sufficient numbers. The manpower reserves of other areas must be tapped. The local supply of administrators and experts in Ottawa may be insufficient to staff all government agencies. They must be recruited from somewhere else. Other examples abound.

Migration also maintains equilibrium between the various regions of a country, be they provinces or simply rural and urban areas. Fertility differs from area to area and so do economic opportunities. Without migration people would pile up in certain areas while other regions would face acute manpower shortages. In the early industrial towns of the eighteenth and nineteenth century age-specific mortality rates were higher than in rural places. Without constant rural-urban migration the towns and cities could never have grown the way they did.

Migration equally permits a more optimal use of specific skills and talents. Specialists of all sorts may abound in one area and may be short in another. Normally, income and opportunity differentials reflect relative scarcity and abundance. Migration streams tend to close the gap between areas which have a relative abundance of skills and areas which are in short supply.

On the individual level migration helps people to cope with specific regional or national problems. Droughts, harvest failures, soil erosion, the exhaustion of raw materials, racial and religious persecution, social oppression, to name the most obvious sources of individual distress, can all, to some extent, be met by voluntary migration to other areas.

## C. Types of Migration

A first distinction one could draw is between *traditional* and *modern* migration. *Modern* migration consists of those human movements on the surface of the globe which occur once the modernization process has started. *Traditional* migration embodies spatial movements which take place in the premodern traditional society. The latter type of spatial displacement consists mainly of (a) group movements such as the journeys of nomads and tribes, and (b) erratic displacements of individuals. Among the most common reasons for such migratory movements are (1) changes in season and therefore in the availability of food, water and pasturage, (2) ecological factors such as lasting changes in climate and the various forms of ecological collapse, (3) political factors such as war and the threat of conquest, and (4) social factors such as exogamous rules forcing individuals to select marriage partners outside the community of residence.

In traditional societies the rate of migration is usually low. Such societies are relatively unchanging, social mobility is absent and the rewards of migration are usually negative. The migrant is usually regarded as undependable and untrustworthy in his community of origin, whereas he would be hardly welcome in the area of destination.

A somewhat analogous classification has been made by Dollot.[1] He draws a distinction between *continuous* and *terminal* migration. *Continuous* migration is basically premodern with nomadism being the best example. Usually nomadism implies a close relationship between man and his cattle, between the shepherd and his flock. A major underlying cause of nomadism is the lack of water and the resulting absence of vegetation. In Iran, for instance, a large part of the country is outside the limit of pluvial agriculture. Without irrigation most crops cannot be grown. With the exception of the Caspian Sea area and the foothills of the mountains in the North and West, vegetation is sparse. Nomadism can be considered to be a logical adjustment to the barrenness of the land. For centuries nomadism has been a predominant factor in Iranian life and today it is still very much alive. In the spring the nomads and their animals (mostly goats and sheep) move to the north. In the fall they return to the south, always following exactly the same roads.

*Terminal* migration is the most common type of migration. It implies a once and for all move. Migration from rural to urban areas would be a prime example of terminal migration.

---

[1]L. Dallot, *Les Migrations Humaines,* Paris: Presses Universitaires de France, 1976 pp. 29, 40.

A third classification which is basically geographical is that between *internal* and *international* migration. We defined the two concepts in an earlier section. *Internal* migrations occur within the limits of a nation or a given geographical area. Usually they are either seasonal or terminal. *International* migration can be analysed according to the underlying motivations. The French author P. George differentiates between political and economic reasons for international migration.[2] *Political* migrations mostly occur because of the breakdown of those societal mechanisms which hitherto guaranteed peaceful coexistence between different religions, cultural, social or ethnic groups. The breakdown results in war, revolution, racial or religious persecution. Although the Christian and Moslem communities had lived peacefully together for many decades, the status quo in Lebanon broke down in 1976. Another case of breakdown is Northern Ireland in the mid-seventies. When the Weimar Republic of Germany collapsed in the early 1930s the Jews had to suffer racial persecution once the Nazis had taken over. *Economic* international migrations can be considered as a kind of corrective action to individual or collective poverty. The causes of the poverty are often social, economic, demographic, or ecological in origin. At present the largest inflows of immigrants into the United States are from Mexico and the Philippines, two countries which are unable to cope with their respective demographic explosions. Canada also receives an increasing percentage of its immigrants from Asia and Africa. The decision to migrate is usually taken by individuals. The main motive for departure, it is remembered, is the desire to improve one's socioeconomic position.

Professor W. Peterson in his well-known textbook distinguishes between *primitive* migration, *impelled* and *forced* migration, *free* migration, *group* and *mass* migration.[3] *Primitive* migration occurs when people are unable to cope with natural or ecological forces. The environment is no longer able to sustain all the inhabitants. It may be that soil erosion sets in. Perhaps a series of droughts destroys part of the area's economic basis. It is possible that demographic growth has resulted in a permanent imbalance between resources and numbers.

*Impelled* and *forced* migration usually result from political pressures. Migration is *impelled* when the persons involved can decide for themselves whether to stay or to leave. The liberally minded Jamaicans who in 1977 were leaving their country in anticipation of the Marxist police state which seemed to be in the making did have the option to stay. They were not (not yet?) discriminated against. But when Algeria became independent in 1962, the French Algerians could not stay. Their migration back to France and some other places was *forced*. The partition of India (1947) into basically Muslim and Hindu states resulted in a massive forced displacement of some 11 million people.

With *free*, voluntary, or sometimes called "pioneer", migration the will and intent of the migrant are the decisive elements. Free migration consists of migra-

---

[2]P. George, *Les Migrations Internationales*, Paris: P.U.F. 1976, p. 23.

[3]W. Peterson, *Population*, 3rd ed., New York: MacMillan, 1975, pp. 321-326.

tion of people who act on their own initiative and responsibility. They move with their families or individually. The migrant is not put under any kind of heavy pressure. Such individuals are strongly oriented towards novelty, economic improvement or both. At the start migration can be free but as the word gets around and the free migrants are successful in the area of destination, free migration may develop into group migration as it has done in Ireland, Sweden and Italy. *Group* migration refers to the movement of people in clusters larger than the family. When a clan, a tribe or any other social group moves as a unit under the leadership of a religious or social head or ruler we are faced with group migration. Group migration may evolve into *mass* migration as it has done in certain communities. People in a certain area are now so intensely exposed to migration that each eligible individual must make a conscious decision either to move out or to stay.

## D. Differentials and Selectivity of Migration

This section emphasizes the fact that some groups are more migratory than others. As with deaths and births migratory movements are associated with such characteristics as sex, age, occupation and geographical region.

The search for universally valid migration differentials has not been too successful. The reason is that migratory streams reflect profound social and economic mutations under way. Such transformations vary from time to time and place to place.

It must be admitted, however, that the age differential has withstood the test of time. In the past as well as in the present the highest rates of migration and mobility are to be found with late adolescents and young adults. In both internal and international migration streams, persons in the young adult age groups prevail. In 1961 for instance 65% of the post-war immigrants then living in Canada were in the age range 15-44[4]. For the native-born only 41.1% was in that age group. Between 1945 and 1960 the average immigrant was fifteen years younger than the average Canadian. In the United States during the 1970-1974 interval 59.6% of the immigrants belonged to the 16-44 age interval. Some 12.4% exceeded age 45 while 27.7% were under 16 years. The immigration figures for any randomly chosen year, say 1975, reveal the same pattern.

One important reason for the high propensity to migrate of the young is that after age fifteen large numbers complete their education and the time comes to seek a first or new job. Commitments to the surroundings are usually weak for the young and a move is often necessary to find suitable employment. Many of them will try their chance in the large cities either at home or abroad. This accounts for the fact that cities receive so many newcomers between age twenty and twenty-nine. The stream of migrants which moves out of the cities and into

---

[4]W. E. Kalbach, *The Impact of Immigration on Canada's Population* (Ottawa: Dominion Bureau of Statistics, 1970), p. 170.

TABLE 36. Immigration Arrivals by 5-Year Age Groups, Canada: 1975*

| Age Group | Arrivals |
|---|---|
| 0 - 4 | 16,625 |
| 5 - 9 | 19,269 |
| 10 - 14 | 15,228 |
| 15 - 19 | 14,519 |
| 20 - 24 | 27,568 |
| 25 - 29 | 32,840 |
| 30 - 34 | 19,657 |
| 35 - 39 | 11,978 |
| 40 - 44 | 6,835 |
| 45 - 49 | 4,654 |
| 50 - 54 | 3,998 |
| 55 - 59 | 3,426 |
| 60 - 64 | 4,623 |
| 65 - 69 | 3,192 |
| 70 + | 3,469 |

***Source:** Ministry of Industry, Trade and Commerce, *Canada Yearbook 1976-77*, p. 214.

the suburbs is also young, yet older than the previously discussed current. Prevailing in this stream are the young parents between twenty-five and thirty-five. Their families are growing and thus they are looking for a suitable house in a more quiet environment.

Depending on the circumstances, migration can also be selective by sex. In the second half of the nineteenth century a large stream of younger females left the countryside in England in order to work as domestic servants in urban middle class families. In England this particular stream of migrants belongs to the past, but the pattern repeats itself in a number of Latin American countries such as Chile. If a generalization with regard to sex can be made, most observers seem to agree that males tend to dominate when distances are long and when migration has an innovative and/or pioneering character. Females seem to preponderate in short distance, low-risk and well-established migratory currents. This generalization, however, does not have the same power as the one regarding age. The great movement of immigration into Canada which coincided with the development of the Canadian West brought an excess of men into the country. Since this was a pioneer type of immigration, the composition of the migration stream was as one would expect. While before 1931 adult male immigrants exceeded females in number, the case was reversed between 1931 and 1947. The changing character of Canadian society brought in more females while in 1945 and 1946 the war brides of Canadian service men entered. From 1947 to 1957 adult male immigrants outnumbered the females once more. Since then it has changed from year to year with both sexes running a close race. The predominance of males during the 1947-1957 period is probably related to the fact that a considerable proportion of those immigrants intended to work in the agricultural sector.

A last question to be raised here is how selective is migration of education and occupational characteristics. As might be expected the data are mixed. The situation changes from country to country and it all depends in what stage of socioeconomic development a nation happens to be. When a country like Canada still had a frontier, its immigrants consisted largely of farmers, loggers, fishermen, hunters, trappers, miners and the like. Modern Canada of the 1970s appeals to very different categories. In 1973 for instance, the largest occupational groups among the foreign immigrants were manufacturing and mechanical workers (22.8%), professionals (20.7%), clerical workers (14.6%) and people employed in the service sector (12.9%). In the 1946-1950 period 29.1% of the immigrants still intended to work in the agricultural sector. In 1973 this percentage had declined to 0.2%.

Professor Caldwell who studied migration patterns in Ghana (Africa) concludes that in this country schooling turns people towards town life.[5] One problem in many a less developed country is that the education which was brought to rural areas was in fact urban in character. The subjects taught were often not very relevant for rural people. It frequently alienated young people from their own culture and seemed rather about a foreign way of life, more frequently found in towns and cities. No wonder that such education accentuates the flight to cities. It seems that in developed countries such as Canada and the United States schooling also tends to make people more migration prone. Persons with a college education and professional as well as semi-professional workers are among the most mobile fractions of the population.

## E. Motivation and Migration Decision

A large number of theoretical observations in explanation of migration have been made. We will only survey a few here. An exhaustive treatment would require another full-length monograph.

Neoclassical economic theory looks at the migration process as follows.[6] Assuming that labor is homogeneous and that no obstacles exist between countries and regions, migration simply flows from areas with low to regions with high earnings. The high and low earnings reflect respectively high and low productivity levels. As migration continues the disparity in wages and productivity between the two regions narrows and ultimately disappears. The assumptions of homogeneous labor, lack of geographical and administrative obstacles and the absence of migration costs do not reflect reality quite faithfully but the model is a useful point of departure. It also seems that in spite of migration local differences

---

[5]J. C. Caldwell, *African Rural-Urban Migration,* New York: Columbia University Press, 1969, pp. 60-61.

[6]See for example: J. Isaac, *Economics of Migration,* London: Kegan Paul, 1947. A. Winsemius, *Economische Aspecten der Internationale Migratie,* Haarlem: Bohn, 1939.

in wages and productivity are not always ironed out. The example of the Maritimes on the one hand and Ontario on the other immediately comes to mind.

Another theory which has been highlighted in a study published by the International Labor Office identifies two kinds of pressures, one inducing people to leave the area of origin and another drawing people into the area of destination.[7] The two pressures have been denominated "push" and "pull". Among push factors we note the pressure of rural poverty, low wages and incomes, few or declining employment opportunities, a decreased demand for the commodities produced by local industries, the absence of facilities or amenities, poor educational facilities and the like. Pull factors are such advantages as free or cheap farm land, attractive opportunities for employment and perhaps promotion, relatively good salaries, the availability of schools, hospitals, entertainment facilities and so on. It is quite obvious that many forms of migration to be found in the real world result from some combination of both pull and push factors. The tragic experience of the Irish potato famine in 1846-47 is an illustration of an extremely powerful push factor. For many a peasant the choice was between moving or death. The so-called "brain drain" or the flow of scientists and engineers which occurred in the 1950s and 1960s and which had the U.S.A. as its main area of destination is an exemplification of a strong pull factor. The salaries of scientists and engineers in the U.S.A. were well above those offered by other nations.

An interesting approach to the determinants and motives of migration can be found in an article written by the demographer E.S. Lee.[8] According to Lee the components of the decision to migrate are the following:

1. Positive and negative factors with regard to place of origin.
2. Positive and negative factors with regard to the area of destination.
3. Intervening obstacles standing between place of origin and destination.
4. Personal factors.

The positive and negative factors in both the area of origin and destination will either attract or repel the potential migrant. The intervening obstacles can be physical, such as distance; they may consist of restrictive migration laws or simply the costs of moving. The fourth and last factor allows for individual differences in the perception and assessment of the remaining other elements.

Another relatively recent approach to migration can be found in the works of two economists by the names of Theodore Schultz and Larry Sjaastad.[9] The argument is presented within the framework of investment in humans, generally defined as the human capital approach. Migration, then, is seen as a decision which entails costs as well as benefits. There are disadvantages which are associated with it but the move will often yield returns too. As such, the decision to

---

[7] International Labor Office; *Why Labor Leaves the Land*, Studies and Reports, New Series, No. 59, Geneva: Tribune de Geneve, 1960, p.17.

[8] E. S. Lee, "A Theory of Migration" *Demography*, Voll. III, No. 1, pp. 47-59.

[9] T. W. Schultz, "Reflections on Investment in Man", *Journal of Political Economy*, Vol. LXX, Supplement (Oct. 1962), pp. 1-8. L. A. Sjaastad, "The Costs and Returns of Human Migration", *ibid.*, pp. 80-93.

migrate can be compared with an investment in any other direction such as education. A person will migrate when the perceived benefits exceed the costs. If they do not he will stay home. The costs can be divided into direct money costs such as the costs of moving and the indirect or opportunity costs. The latter mainly consist of the foregone earnings while travelling, searching for and learning a new job. Sjaastad also recognizes the existence of psychic costs to migrants. They include the discomfort and sorrow (''disutility'', in economists' jargon) associated with leaving home, family and friends. The fact of being placed in a new and unfamiliar environment is also upsetting while building up a new routine also requires flexibility and adjustment capacity. The costs of migration are incurred as soon as the decision to migrate has been taken or very shortly thereafter. This is not the case for the benefits which are farther off and must therefore be discounted.[10] The model presented by Sjaastad and Schultz has many implications. If, as been observed, the migratory flow tends to be inversely related to distance it is because the greater the distance the higher the direct cash costs of travelling and moving. The psychic costs also increase with distance because the separation from the previous environment becomes more radical. It is a known fact that younger people have a higher propensity to migrate than the old. This makes sense according to the model presented by Sjaastad and Schultz. The opportunity costs increase with age while the remaining lifespan over which an increased income might be earned is reduced.

The model presented by Sjaastad and Schultz does not explain, however, why in a number of developing countries people are moving at increasing rates to the urban areas while unemployment rates in towns and cities are high and the chances of finding a job are often slim. In response to this problem the American economist M. P. Todaro has observed that apart from existing rural-urban income differentials we must consider also the ''*anticipated* income differential''.[11] It is not unreasonable to assume, says Todaro, that the migrant thinks in terms of the long run. He may disregard the fact that initially he becomes worse off by moving to the city. In the long run, however, he anticipates being better off. He hopes to make rewarding contacts, learn about existing employment opportunities and expects to find a rewarding job ultimately. This new position will compensate him for initial losses. As long as the present value of the net flow of expected urban income exceeds that of the anticipated rural income the rural worker will move. No doubt, the Todarian amendment of the Schultz/Sjaastad model is ingenious and has in fact been recognized as such.

In conclusion we may perhaps say that, apart from purely political migrations and Malthusian evacuations due to a collapse of the environment or overcrowd-

---

[10] A given sum or income due in the future or ''deferred'' has a present value of less than that sum, and the more distant the deferred sum or income the lower its present value. The present value of something which is only available in the future or deferred is known as a ''discounted'' value.

[11] M. P. Todaro, ''Income Expectations, Rural-Urban Migration and Employment in Africa'', *International Labour Review,* Vol. CIV No. 5 (November, 1971), p. 387-413.

ing, the economic factor seems to predominate in the decision to move. Much migration occurs because individuals expect that the migratory move will permit him or her to improve his (or her) economic status, if not immediately at least eventually. Migration and redistribution of people also occurs in response to changing economic opportunities which emerge in the course of economic development. Areas which offer relatively attractive employment opportunities and relatively high wages and salaries will tend to pull in people. Areas characterized by unemployment or underemployment tend to lose their residents, at least as long as better alternatives are available. Thus in Canada the Atlantic provinces are the losers of people while Ontario, Alberta and British Columbia are the gainers. Finally, migrants tend to flock to areas of comparatively high average incomes and this sometimes irrespective of immediate employment opportunities. In the light of the foregoing it is not surprising that migration, especially international migration, is sensitive to fluctuations in the trade cycle. Immigration to Canada has remained very responsive to fluctuations in the level of economic activity, and this in spite of government regulations. When employment levels rise immigration increases and vice versa. Immigration into the United States has not displayed the same degree of responsiveness to cyclical movements.

## F. Consequences of Migration

Although the consequences of internal and international migration are comparable, the implications of migrations between nations have been better studied. Our discussion, therefore, will be mainly limited to the latter type. The consequences of migration are demographic, economic and social, and we will start this section with a discussion of the demographic impact.

### *Demographic Effects*

Migration first has an impact on total numbers. Immigration increases the population of the countries of destination by a certain number of units while a corresponding decrease takes place in the countries of origin. Table 37 gives an impression of the additions to the Canadian population by immigration.

Canada, however, also loses people through out-migration. The fact is that while inflows into Canada are large so are the outflows. Emigrants mainly go to the United States. Table 38 compares immigration with emigration. The relatively small net migration figures which are also shown indicate Canada's relatively low retention rate.

A second demographic effect of migration is that on the growth potential of both the sending and receiving nations. Because of the sex-age selectivity of migration, a flow of people from one area to the next tends to change the existing

TABLE 37. Immigrant Arrivals to Canada by Calendar Year, 1852-1973*

| Year | Arr. | Year | Arr. | Year | Arr. | Year | Arr. |
|---|---|---|---|---|---|---|---|
| 1852 | 29,307 | 1882 | 112,458 | 1912 | 375,756 | 1942 | 7,576 |
| 1853 | 29,464 | 1883 | 133,624 | 1913 | 400,870 | 1943 | 8,504 |
| 1854 | 37,263 | 1884 | 103,824 | 1914 | 150,484 | 1944 | 12,801 |
| 1855 | 25,296 | 1885 | 79,169 | 1915 | 36,665 | 1945 | 22,722 |
| 1856 | 22,544 | 1886 | 69,152 | 1916 | 55,914 | 1946 | 71,719 |
| 1857 | 33,854 | 1887 | 84,526 | 1917 | 72,910 | 1947 | 64,127 |
| 1858 | 12,339 | 1888 | 88,766 | 1918 | 41,845 | 1948 | 125,414 |
| 1859 | 6,300 | 1889 | 91,600 | 1919 | 107,698 | 1949 | 95,217 |
| 1860 | 6,276 | 1890 | 75,067 | 1920 | 138,824 | 1950 | 73,912 |
| 1861 | 13,589 | 1891 | 82,165 | 1921 | 91,728 | 1951 | 194,391 |
| 1862 | 18,294 | 1892 | 30,996 | 1922 | 64,224 | 1952 | 164,498 |
| 1863 | 21,000 | 1893 | 29,633 | 1923 | 133,729 | 1953 | 168,868 |
| 1864 | 24,779 | 1894 | 20,829 | 1924 | 124,164 | 1954 | 154,227 |
| 1865 | 18,958 | 1895 | 18,790 | 1925 | 84,907 | 1955 | 109,946 |
| 1866 | 11,427 | 1896 | 16,835 | 1926 | 135,982 | 1956 | 164,857 |
| 1867 | 10,666 | 1897 | 21,716 | 1927 | 158,886 | 1957 | 282,164 |
| 1868 | 12,765 | 1898 | 31,900 | 1928 | 166,783 | 1958 | 124,851 |
| 1869 | 18,630 | 1899 | 44,543 | 1929 | 164,993 | 1959 | 106,928 |
| 1870 | 24,706 | 1900 | 41,681 | 1930 | 104,806 | 1960 | 104,111 |
| 1871 | 27,773 | 1901 | 55,747 | 1931 | 27,530 | 1961 | 71,689 |
| 1872 | 36,578 | 1902 | 89,102 | 1932 | 20,591 | 1962 | 74,586 |
| 1873 | 50,050 | 1903 | 138,660 | 1933 | 14,382 | 1963 | 93,151 |
| 1874 | 39,373 | 1904 | 131,252 | 1934 | 12,476 | 1964 | 112,606 |
| 1875 | 27,382 | 1905 | 141,465 | 1935 | 11,277 | 1965 | 146,758 |
| 1876 | 25,633 | 1906 | 211,653 | 1936 | 11,643 | 1966 | 194,743 |
| 1877 | 27,082 | 1907 | 272,409 | 1937 | 15,101 | 1967 | 222,876 |
| 1878 | 29,807 | 1908 | 143,326 | 1938 | 17,244 | 1968 | 183,974 |
| 1879 | 40,492 | 1909 | 173,694 | 1939 | 16,994 | 1969 | 161,531 |
| 1880 | 38,505 | 1910 | 286,839 | 1940 | 11,324 | 1970 | 147,713 |
| 1881 | 47,991 | 1911 | 331,288 | 1941 | 9,329 | 1971 | 121,900 |
| | | | | | | 1972 | 122,006 |
| | | | | | | 1973 | 184,200 |
| | | | | | | 1974 | 218,465 |
| | | | | | | 1975 | 187,881 |

***Sources:** L. O. Stone, *et al.*, *The Population of Canada* . . ., p. 7.
Ministry of Industry, Trade and Commerce, *Canada Yearbook, 1976-77,* p. 212.

age-sex composition in both home country and area of destination. As we observed earlier, migrant streams contain high proportions of young adults, that is, persons in the earlier part of their reproductive period. Birth rates among such persons tend to be high, death rates low. To the extent that the migratory stream contains married couples, emigration deprives the homeland of births which

TABLE 38. Migration to and from Canada 1861-1971 by Decade (Thousands of Persons)*

| Decade | Arrivals | Departure | Net Migration |
|---|---|---|---|
| 1861-71 | 183 | 375 | - 192 |
| 1871-81 | 353 | 440 | - 87 |
| 1881-91 | 903 | 1,109 | - 206 |
| 1891-01 | 326 | 506 | - 180 |
| 1901-11 | 1,759 | 1,043 | - 716 |
| 1911-21 | 1,612 | 1,381 | 231 |
| 1921-31 | 1,203 | 974 | 229 |
| 1931-41 | 150 | 242 | - 92 |
| 1941-51 | 548 | 379 | 169 |
| 1951-61 | 1,543 | 462 | 1,081 |
| 1961-71 | 1,429 | 802 | 627 |

***Source:** Manpower and Immigration, *Immigration and Population Statistics* (Ottawa: Information Canada 1974), p. 8. The above figures are only estimates.

would have occurred in that area, had they stayed. Such births now take place in the country of destination which, other things being equal, face a higher demographic growth rate. To the extent that migration exists of single persons, the sex distribution changes in both area of origin and destination. If, for example, the migration stream is characterized by a small excess of males, the women in the country of reception have improved chances of getting married. The marriage rate may accordingly rise in the area of destination and drop in the home country. A modification of the marriage rate will ultimately change the birth rates and growth potentials as well. In such traditional areas of emigration as Ireland and Southern Italy the heavy outflow of males has resulted in an unbalanced sex composition prevailing those regions. The decline in birth rates which those areas have experienced may in part be due to this phenomenon. The areas of origin which witness an outflow of young people may also experience an increased death rate as the older, high-mortality risk people stay behind. The proportion of such people in the total population automatically increases when the young ones leave so that the overall mortality figure which that community experiences is modified.

The third demographic effect of migration is on the age and sex structure of the population in both the country of destination and the area of origin. Migration streams often consist mainly of young adults with males dominating when distances are long. Hence, in areas of origin the quantity of youthful individuals (who are at least potentially economically active) declines while their number increases in areas of reception. Migrations consisting of political refugees are the exception to this rule because the motivation for departure is different. The usual impact of predominantly economic migration, therefore, is to raise the median age in the country of origin and to lower it in the country of destination. If males predominate, the sex ratio (i.e., the number of males in the population per 100 females) must drop in the home country and rise in the receiving nation. The intensity of these effects will vary according to the volume of net migration as compared to the size of the sending and receiving population. Taking Canada as an example, some 35% of all immigrants arriving between 1946 and 1957 were in the 20-30 age group which had a rejuvenating effect on the entire Canadian population. The table below compares the age distribution of the native and immigrant population in the period immediately following World War II.

TABLE 39. Age Distribution of the Canadian Native Population in 1951 and Immigrants during the Period 1946-1957 (in %)*

| Age Group | Canadian Population 1951 (P.C.) | Immigrants 1946-1951 (P.C.) |
|---|---|---|
| 0 - 15 | 30.3 | 21.9 |
| 15 - 20 | 7.6 | 7.2 |
| 20 - 30 | 15.9 | 35.5 |
| 30 - 40 | 14.6 | 19.8 |
| 40 - 50 | 11.4 | 9.4 |
| 50 + | 20.2 | 6.2 |

***Source:** International Labor Office, *International Migration 1945-1957* (Geneva: La Tribune de Geneve, 1959), p. 320.

During the fifteen years following World War II most immigrants entering Canada had travelled long distances. As could be expected they were predominantly male. The year 1946 was an exception because of the entry of war brides and fiancees. After 1946, however, the predominance of male immigration resumed. Table 40 shows the sex ratios of the major ethnic groups which made up the resident post-war immigrant population living in Canada in 1961.

## *Economic Effects*

The economic effects of migration are partially associated with the demographic consequences. This is especially true for the so-called "labor force effect" of migration. Migrants who move for non-political reasons are usually young and economically active. Moreover, migrants commonly move in order to improve their material well-being. Consequently, they often display a higher participation rate in the labor force than the receiving and sending populations as a whole. Normally, about forty percent of the population is economically active or potentially so. Among migrants the percentage figure may vary from fifty to one hundred.

The first economic effect of immigration, therefore, is to increase the ratio of the economically active to the total population in the country of destination. Immigration produces a greater percentage increase in the labor force than in the

TABLE 40. Distribution of Resident Post-War Immigrant Population of Selected Ethnic Origins in Canada by Sex (1961)*

| Ethnic Origin | Sex Ratio |
|---|---|
| Asiatic | 110.9 |
| British Isles | 89.0 |
| French | 103.0 |
| German | 101.9 |
| Hungarian | 138.3 |
| Italian | 120.3 |
| Jewish | 104.7 |
| Netherlands | 112.3 |
| Other European | 127.7 |
| Other Central European | 114.1 |
| Other Eastern European | 108.1 |
| Polish | 127.9 |
| Russian | 93.8 |
| Scandinavian | 124.7 |
| Ukrainian | 139.2 |

***Source:** W.E. Kalbach, *The Impact of Immigration on Canada's Population* (Ottawa: Dominion Bureau of Statistics, 1970), p. 178.

total population. The reverse happens in the area of origin.

The post-war immigration in Canada increased the labor force to a proportionally greater extent than the total population. Between 1950 and 1960, for instance, immigration accounted for almost half of the total labor force increase. In 1961, 64.9% of the post-war immigrants of 15 years and over, participated in the labor force as compared to 53.7% of the native Canadian population of the same age category.

Normally, about 50% of the immigrants intend to participate immediately in the labor force. In 1950, some 51.3% of the arriving immigrants wanted to join the labor force. In 1973 we find a figure of 50.1%. Those not intending to look for gainful employment are usually the dependents of immigrants or close relatives sponsored by Canadian residents or citizens.

The second economic effect of migration is on incomes and economic growth. The impact of immigration on the country of destination depends a great deal on the conditions prevailing in that nation. In Canada, for instance, the overall impact of post-war immigration was probably beneficial. This country possessed ample landed resources while investible funds were also relatively abundant. The nation as a whole probably enjoyed increasing returns. The steady arrival of immigrants made a better division of labor possible while the expanding market stimulated the launching of new ventures. The immigrants supplied the country with new skills, while many newcomers entered key sectors, such as agriculture, mining, metallurgy and construction, filling vacancies. The skills which the migrants brought with them possibly removed some bottlenecks due to the existing shortage of various types of expertness and proficiency thus allowing for fuller employment in the sectors concerned. Inevitable overhead expenses, moreover, could be spread out over a larger number of tax-paying citizens. Besides, the Canadian economy had no difficulty in providing the infrastructural outlays which the added numbers required.

The effects of immigration on an economy beset with a chronic oversupply of labor and/or scarcity of landed resources and capital are of course wholly different. Therefore, the effects of an inflow of people differ sharply from area to area. The same type of argument can be applied to the countries of origin. The departure of people produces a beneficial effect if out-migration siphons off unemployed persons or employed individuals who will be replaced by previously unemployed workers.[12]

If however, an economy runs at full employment or comes near to it, departures may create bottlenecks causing some currently employed workers to lose their jobs as well.

## *Social Effects*

Our discussion of the social effects of migration will be limited to the societal adaptation process in the country of destination.

Generally speaking the immigrant moves through three stages: settlement, adaptation and assimilation. Settlement is completed when the migrant has found

---

[12]If in the country of origin emigration reduces the supply of labor, while immigration makes it more abundant in the area of destination, conventional economic theory would suggest that wages will adjust to this situation by rising in the country of departure and falling in the country of arrival. Figure 1 shows a demand curve (DD) and quantity of labor is shown on the horizontal x axis of the diagram, while wages are measured on the vertical y axis. The demand schedule (DD) shows that as the price of labor (wages) falls some employers will hire more workers, while rising wages force some employers to release laborers. In other words, the price of labor and the quantity demanded are inversely associated.

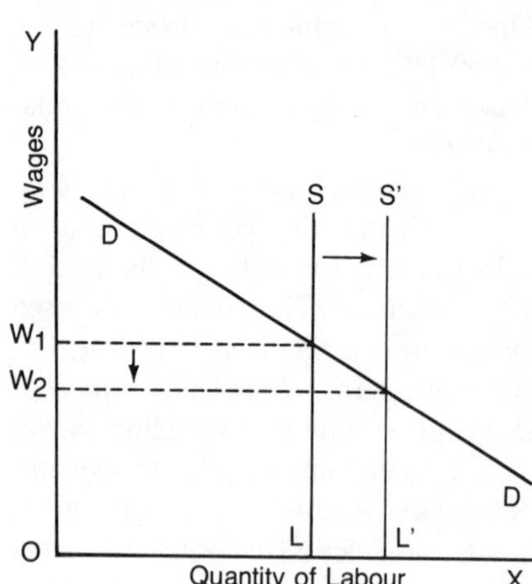


Suppose now that we consider a small island with a fixed labor supply (LS). A ship brings in a load of workers LL' eager to work under the same conditions as the islanders. *Ceteris paribus,* the supply curve will shift to the right and the wage level falls from $W_1$ to $W_2$. In the area of origin the reverse happens. In reality economic conditions differ from country to country, which makes a more subtle analysis necessary.

a place to live and a job permitting him to take care of his basic needs. Adaptation comes next. The individual inserts himself into the new environment, learns the language, gets used to the climate and generally adjusts to his new surroundings by following the example of the local native population. Adaptation is sometimes achieved by partly recreating the original surroundings. Canadians are familiar with the partially separate ethnic neighborhoods in such cities as Toronto and Vancouver. Americans are informed about residential segregation on an ethnic basis in such cities as New York and Boston. Living amongst one's own ethnic group in a foreign country may speed up the adjustment process but it can also delay complete integration into the society of destination. Assimilation is the third and most difficult step. An assimilated individual really has become part of the new community. He now resembles the natives of his new country on a number of essential points. In the process of assimilation both the immigrant and the native population undergo changes. The immigrants which entered Canada after 1945 altered the dominant culture by becoming themselves "Canadized". Often enough, assimilation is not achieved by the first generation unless the migrants were very young when they left the area of origin. A number of factors facilitate adjustment and assimilation. Rapid economic absorption seems a prerequisite, although other factors are required as well. A flexible social structure with political equality and equal opportunities for socioeconomic advancement definitely fosters social integration. Available research seems to show that "among those expressing the highest degree of satisfaction with life in Canada and the most inclined to become naturalized were those who had experienced some initial decline in occupational status, but who subsequently recovered or improved their former position".[13] The absence of ethnic or racial prejudice should also be noted as an important element in social integration as well as sameness or close similitude of language, religion, social and cultural traditions. Richmond reports that immigrants from Great Britain are more frequently members of Canadian clubs and associations than immigrants from continental Europe.[14] This may perhaps be interpreted as an indication that the relative similarity of language and culture speeds up adjustment and integration. The nonexistence of obvious differences in physical appearance is the last factor which helps to bring together migrants and natives.

Those who fail to adjust and to integrate themselves into the new society are likely to be subject to stressful circumstances. Some will perhaps return to the home country and thus join the return flow which inevitably results from any major migratory stream. Others may display various symptoms of anti-social behavior such as delinquency or crime. Still others may become the victim of some form of mental disorder or of some psychosomatic disease.[15]

---

[13]A.H. Richmond, "Immigration and Pluralism in Canada," *The International Migration Review,* Vol. IV Fall 1969, p. 18.

[14]*Ibid.*, p. 19.

[15]For bibliographical references the reader is referred to the end of the next two chapters.

Chapter 9

# *Internal Migration*

## A. Characteristics

Internal migration represents the dynamic aspect of population distribution. As we noted earlier, internal migrants flow towards those parts of the country where incomes are relatively high and where the variety of job openings is the greatest. Migrants also clearly prefer areas where educational facilities, health services and recreational opportunities are the most appealing.

In Canada and the U.S.A. most movers are actually not migrants. Most people who change place move within short distances. Between 1951 and 1961, 42.4% of the 1961 Canadian population of 5 years and over (6.5 million people) had changed residence. Of all movers, about 60% shifted place within the same municipality, 32% moved within the province and 8% moved between provinces. The picture was not very different in 1971. The Census revealed that 47.4% of the total population of 5 years and over were in 1971 living in a different dwelling than 5 years earlier. About half that number, i.e., 23.5% of the total population, had moved within the same municipality. The other half (23.9% of the total population) consisted of migrants, who can be divided into three categories: the largest share, 14% (of the total population), changed place within the same province, 4.3% moved from one province to another while 4.2% moved in from abroad.

## B. Interprovincial Migration

Although in the twentieth century Canada has had one of the highest net immigration rates in the world, the net internal movement still exceeded it. What the findings about interprovincial migration confirm is that the provinces of the West are more affected by it than those of the East. The initial settlement pattern was to the advantage of the Maritime provinces, Quebec and Ontario. The latter two have been able to maintain their dominant position throughout the period 1861-1971. The Maritime provinces, however, have experienced net outmigration since 1881 with Prince Edward Island being the largest loser and Nova Scotia (the most industrialized) the lesser victim of the three. The Maritimes have behaved in a way which is quite typical for lesser developed areas. The rate of natural increase was high, but most of the surplus migrated to other areas. In the State of Hawaii, for instance, such islands as Hawaii, Maoi and Kauai have for decades experienced a positive net rate of increase, yet their populations did not grow. The surplus siphoned off to the island of Oahu with its capital Honolulu where most economic, political and cultural activities are concentrated.

Quebec has been the most stable province of Canada, which is perhaps due to its cultural and linguistic isolation. This province behaves like an independent demographic unit, absorbing a large majority of its own internal migrants. At the same time, it receives some migrants from the Maritimes and other provinces plus considerable numbers of foreigners. It tends to lose people to Ontario and the West.

Ontario occupies a key position on the Canadian scene. It has attracted and still pulls in many migrants because of its industrial wealth and high level of socioeconomic development. Yet it also loses considerable numbers to the Western provinces. Between 1881 and 1901 Ontario actually experienced net outmigration. Since then arrivals have exceeded departures. In recent decades Ontario has behaved like a typical highly developed area. Its own rate of natural increase has been very low while experiencing high net immigration. During the 1966-1971 period Ontario was the most favored province by internal as well as foreign migrants.

The Prairie provinces yield a mixed picture. When the railways were built and the West was opened up, farmers rushed to the cheap lands and population grew fast. The 1901-1911 period in particular boosted the population of that area. Since 1921, however, the picture has changed. During the depression decade the outflow exceeded the inflow. Manitoba and Saskatchewan have in recent decades behaved like "the East of the West". Like the Maritimes these provinces are net losers. Many of their residents tend to move to Alberta and British Columbia.

Alberta has experienced a net inflow since the 1940s, which is due to its magnificent resources (oil, gas, etc.), which in turn stimulate industrialization and urbanization.

British Columbia, for a long time separated from the remainder of Canada by the Rocky Mountains, has now become a great favorite of the interprovincial migrants. Until the late 1920s the Prairies absorbed most of the "Western" immigrants. Once the Prairie provinces became settled and saturated, British Columbia turned into a magnet. With Ontario, Quebec and Alberta, this province is one of the most preferred destinations of foreign as well as internal migrants. Her own natural rate of increase is low, like that of Ontario.

Now that B.C. is filling up too, the Yukon and the Northwest territories are getting *their* chance. During the 1961-1971 period the N.W. Territories were among the few to gain from net migration. Table 41 pictures interprovincial migration between 1921 and 1971.

## C. Rural/Urban Migration

Much of the interprovincial migration discussed in the previous section con-

TABLE 41. Rates of Net Migration by Decades for Provinces, Canada: 1921-1971 (per thousand)*

| Province | 1921-31 | 1931-41 | 1941-51 | 1951-61 | 1961-71 |
|---|---|---|---|---|---|
| Newfoundland | - | - | - | - 29 | - 90 |
| Prince Edward Island | -103 | - 28 | - 86 | - 96 | - 62 |
| Nova Scotia | -120 | 10 | - 72 | - 46 | - 59 |
| New Brunswick | - 93 | - 18 | - 64 | - 49 | - 85 |
| Quebec | 6 | 8 | 2 | 36 | 4 |
| Ontario | 49 | 27 | 76 | 123 | 86 |
| Manitoba | - 14 | - 53 | - 54 | - | - 55 |
| Saskatchewan | 13 | -155 | -181 | - 80 | -136 |
| Alberta | 66 | - 47 | 26 | 109 | 38 |
| British Col. | 200 | 118 | 236 | 160 | 190 |
| Yukon and Northwest Terr. | | 99 | 177 | 96 | 46 |

***Sources:** W. Kalbach, *The Demographic Bases* . . . p. 88.
L.O. Stone, *et al., The Population of Canada* . . . p. 76.

sisted in fact of migration out of rural regions into urban areas. From a predominantly rural background Canada has emerged as one of the world's most urbanized nations. This transition reflects of course the development of the industrial and service sector and the associated economic opportunities which have mainly occurred in urban areas. This transition from agricultural to other economic activities required a redistribution of the population.

Rural/urban migration then is often the most important current of internal migration. Rural/urban net migration is not new. It existed in ancient times as well as during the Greek and Roman empires. However, the size of the movement was small. Landed property was an important barrier to large-scale rural/urban migration. Ownership of land, the prospect of inheriting it and customary rights to cultivate certain areas tied individuals to their places of residence. A second reason was the low productivity per man and per acre in agriculture. Farming was cumbersome and the tools were clumsy. With low productivity levels the agricultural surplus was small. In ancient times between 50 and 90 farmers were required to sustain one person in the city. Cities, therefore, had to be small and people remained tied to the land.

The empires of Greece and Rome saw larger cities and more rural-urban migration, yet the proportion of their populations living in urban areas remained small. It was in Western Europe that the limitations on city growth and the concommitant redistribution of population were overcome. The point is that agricultural and non-agricultural technology kept improving once the Middle Ages were over. As farming became increasingly rationalized, automatized and mechanized, fewer and fewer people were needed on the land. At the same time technological inventions first permitted a highly organized handicraft and ultimately a new form of production which took place in urban-located factories, first driven by steam power and later by electricity. As the countryside pushed people out, the cities pulled them in.

At present about 39% of the world population has become urban. There is no indication that the rate of urbanization for the world as a whole is slackening. Between 1970 and 1975 some 106 million people transferred their residence from rural to urban places. The net rural to urban population flow in the less developed areas amounted to 73 million and to 33 million in the more developed nations. If the rate or urban growth as revealed by the 1971 Census continues, nine out of ten Canadians will live in towns and cities before the end of the century.

At the moment Ontario and Quebec are the most urbanized provinces. Some 82.4% of Ontario's population is urban; in Quebec the figure is 80.6%. The most rural province is Prince Edward Island with only 38.3% of its population urban. A spectacular change has taken place in Alberta between 1951 and 1971. In 1951 only 47.6% of its population was urban. This figure had increased to 73.5% in 1971. The expansion of oil, gas and other resources fostered industrialization and the associated urbanization. Much of the net foreign immigration is probably also rural-to-urban. Although precise figures are not available, it is quite probable that many foreigners have also come from rural areas. Upon their arrival they establish themselves in cities. An identical phenomenon has taken place in the U.S.A.

In the developing countries rural/urban migration is proceeding quickly as well. In Iran, for instance, 47.1% of the total population was classified as urban in the year 1977; the remaining 53.9% lived in rural places. Between 1966 and 1976 the urban population rose by nearly six million compared to just under two million in rural areas which implies a ration of three to one. What these figures suggest is that much of the rural population growth was absorbed by the cities via the rual/urban migration process.

For the world as a whole we cannot expect any slowing down of the rate of urbanization. However, this rate is bound to slacken in the economically mature countries as most of the inhabitants already live in urban places. In Canada, therefore, urbanization will continue at a diminished rate. In a number of developing countries this rate will still rise.

## D. Metropolization

As we stated in the previous section, beyond a certain threshold the rate of urbanization slows down and rural/urban migration starts tapering off. When the farm population begins to have lower fertility levels and the rural population has become a relatively small part of the total population, rural/urban migration declines, to be replaced by interurban migration. It is certainly no exaggeration to state that in the post industrial-revolution societies most migration is between urban regions. This process in combination with rural/urban and foreign migration has resulted in the emergence of ever more numerous big cities. Their sizes, moreover, have increased to dimensions hitherto unknown in history.

The metropolis can perhaps be defined as a large and complex city which exercises an integrating influence on the socioeconomic activities of a large expanse of territory. Hence, the metropolis consists of a central city and a surrounding area with which it is intimately interconnected. The central city is typically divided into specialized districts which go in for specific activities such as finance, retail trade, industry and the like. Around the metropolitan centre we find satellite towns, dormitory towns, manufacturing cities and so on.

The emergence of large urban areas surrounded by satellite communities has occurred since the beginning of the twentieth century. In 1901 Canada counted already two such centers, Montreal and Toronto, each containing about 200,000 people. Quebec City, Ottawa and Hamilton with populations exceeding already 50,000 inhabitants began to emerge as metropolitan areas. Since that period the growth of metropolitan areas has continued unabated. In 1971 the number of metropolitan areas as defined by Statistics Canada had increased to 22 with Toronto and Montreal being the two biggest and Saint-John the smallest.[1] Between 1971 and 1976 one more metropolitan area, namely Oshawa (Ontario) was added to the existing total. It also appeared that in the 1971-76 period, Calgary showed the highest rate of growth at 16.5 per cent. The province of Ontario now contains ten of the twenty-three metropolitan regions, five are in the Prairies, three in Quebec, three in the Atlantic Provinces and two in British Columbia.[2]

To return to our subject, migration, it appears that between 1966 and 1971 the metropolitan areas were the major areas of origin as well as destination of migrants. By locality of origin, 44.6% of the people who migrated to metropolitan areas in the 1966-1971 period also resided in metropolitan areas in 1966, 15.2% of the migrants came from other urban localities, 9.7% from rural areas and 24.3% from abroad. The majority of migrants from abroad also move to the metropolitan regions. Montreal, Toronto and Vancouver are increasingly preferred by internal as well as foreign migrants. The biggest cities are apparently bound to get even bigger. It should be noted also that in recent times the population of the fringe and satellite areas of the metropolitan centers has increased faster than the population of the city centers. At some point the central

[1]The 1971 Census Metropolitan Areas and their population were the following:

| | | | |
|---|---|---|---|
| Montreal | 2,743,208 | London | 286,011 |
| Toronto | 2,628,043 | Windsor | 258,643 |
| Vancouver | 1,082,352 | Kitchener | 226,846 |
| Ottawa-Hull | 602,510 | Halifax | 222,637 |
| Ontario (part) | 453,280 | Victoria | 195,800 |
| Quebec (part) | 149,230 | Sudbury | 155,424 |
| Winnipeg | 540,262 | Regina | 140,734 |
| Hamilton | 498,523 | Chicoutimi-Jonquière | 133,703 |
| Edmonton | 495,702 | St. John's, Nfld. | 131,814 |
| Quebec | 480,502 | Saskatoon | 126,449 |
| Calgary | 403,319 | Thunder Bay | 112,093 |
| St. Catharines-Niagara | 303,429 | Saint John, NB. | 106,744 |

[2]According to the latest (1976) definition a metropolitan area contains the principal labour market for a continuous built-up area having a population of 100,000 or more.

city runs out of space whereafter the process of metropolitan dispersion is accelerated. Surrounding areas are gobbled up, and with land being cheaper, industries and people are attracted by the periphery provided that roads are good, communications easy and the necessary infrastructural services (energy, water, sewage, etc.) available.

In the developing countries the biggest cities are also the ones with the highest growth rate. Taking the example of Teheran, it grew form 200,000 inhabitants in 1900 to just under 4.5 million people in 1976. It is not impossible according to one source that by 1986 about one fourth of the entire Iranian population will be living in this city.[3]

There are a number of reasons why in the developing nations the metropolitan center is the natural attraction for business firms and industries. Most workers have a very low level of training and instruction. As a result one must have a large quantity to choose from. In the smaller cities and towns public services are too often inadequate. Blackouts are frequent, the water may be polluted, roads are low-grade, telephone services difficult, delivery of inbound materials is slow, hotels for guests, salesmen and the like are often of poor quality, schools for children of managers and engineers may be third-rate or nonexistent, houses may be in short supply, cultural life and entertainment facilities are perhaps close to zero and so forth and so on. As a result corporations and firms settle in the metropolitan areas which do have the best facilities and local people naturally flock to those regions where employment opportunities are unmatched.

## Bibliography

Elias, C. E. et al., *Metropolis, Values in Conflict,* Belmont: Wadsworth, 1966.

Dollot, L., *Les Migrations Humaines,* Paris: Presses Universitaires de France, 1976.

George, M. V. *Internal Migration in Canada,* Ottawa: Dominion Bureau of Statistics, 1970.

Sauvy, A., *General Theory of Population,* London: Weidenfeld and Nicolson, 1969.

Siegfried, A., *Canada,* London: Alden Press, 1937.

Thompson, W. S., D. T. Lewis, *Population Problems,* New York: McGraw-Hill, 1965.

Veyret, P. *La Population du Canada,* Paris: Presses Universitaires de France, 1953.

---

[3]D. Behnam, M. Amani, *La Population de L'Iran* (Paris: Committee for International Coordination of National Research in Demography, 1974), p. 40.

# Chapter 10

# *International Migration*

## A. A Short History of Canadian and American Immigration

### *The Canadian Case*

There is little doubt about the enormous importance of immigration on Canadian demographic history. As many as six, if not eight, periods can be distinguished between the genesis of this country and the 1970s.

### *From Origins to 1763*

From 1605, when the first French colonists arrived in Canada, to 1783, Canada's population history was almost exclusively French-Canadian. Between 1600 and 1750 some 10,000 immigrants arrived from France amounting to a yearly average of about 65 persons. Since the French colonists kept civil and ecclesiastical records we have rather precise information about their numbers. In 1666 they even conducted a first complete modern style census of the French-speaking population. It appears that in that year 3,215 people lived in New France. This number grew to 40,000 in 1736. From 1700 onwards emigration from France had virtually stopped. The French government, acting faithfully according to mercantilist teachings, believed that the national interest required a growing population at home. Emigration was merely seen as a "dead loss" of people.[1] When in 1763 the Treaty of Paris was concluded between France and England the French-speaking population had increased to about 65,000, most of their ancestors originating from France's western departments. Intercourse with France was cut off. Yet the treaty guaranteed protection with regard to language, religion and land tenure arrangements. Between 1763 and 1783 arrivals were few.

---

[1]For details on mercantilism see: J. Overbeek, *History of Population Theories*, Rotterdam: Rotterdam University Press, 1974, ch. 4.

## *From American Independence to Canadian Confederation*

In 1783 the American colonies of Great Britain won their independence and a new nation was created. Uncertainty about America's future and loyalty to the British Crown induced over 30,000 American settlers to leave for Canada. The newcomers established themselves in Ontario, that is, between Quebec and the Prairies. It isolated the French-speaking part of Canada and put the English speaking group in an ideal position to expand westwards. The English governors now ruling Canada attempted to encourage immigration from the British Isles in order to transform Canada into a genuinely English-speaking colony. From 1815 onwards large-scale immigration from Great Britain began. Between 1815 and 1830, for instance, Canada received an annual average of some 23,000 people from the British Isles.

## *The 1867 - 1900 Interval*

In 1867 Quebec, Ontario, New Brunswick and Nova Scotia formed the Canadian Confederation, and Canada was now protected from absorption by the United States. During the second half of the nineteenth century, however, immigration was very moderate. Most emigrants from Europe headed for the United States. The American "West" was being opened up and developed. This area now provided the most attractive opportunities. The Canadian "West", however, was still not organized to receive migrants in large numbers. Nevertheless, Canada did attract a considerable influx, but many newcomers left again for the superior opportunities that lay across the border.

## *The Great Wave, 1900-1914*

Although between 1900 and 1902 immigration was still relatively modest it rose sharply after that date. Railways now linked the Atlantic with the Pacific Ocean and arable land in the Prairies was easily available and cheap, whereas in the U.S.A. most virgin lands were gone. Canada now had the "last best West". The urbanization of Eastern Canada pulled in factory hands and skilled workers not interested in seeking employment in the farming sector. Between 1900 and 1915 just under three million people entered.

Until the end of the 19th century the British element had dominated the immigration flow. In the 1900-1914 period Slavs and Latins joined the stream. The same happened in the U.S.A. Germans and Scandinavians also became more actively involved. In southern and eastern Europe powerful push factors existed. Population pressure resulting in continuous subdivsion of the land, archaic landholding systems, low wages, heavy taxes, political discontent, and residential restrictions (on Jews) drove thousands out of their countries. With the outbreak of Word War I this period of lusty immigration came to an end.

## *From War to Depression*

Between the end of World War I and the Economic Depression a fairly important revival of immigration occurred. It often exceeded 100,000 per annum. What made Canada relatively attractive was the fact that the U.S.A. had barred the gates in the early 1920s. Between 1880 and 1914 America's power to assimilate had been stretched to the breaking point by the massive arrival of southern and eastern Europeans. From 1921 onwards the U.S.A. imposed quotas mainly aimed at Latins and Slavs.

## *The 1930s*

The Great Crash of the 1930s swelled the stream of return migrants. The totalitarian countries (the Soviet Union, Italy, Germany) began to curb emigration thus reducing the supply of potential movers. In order to cope with the massive unemployment resulting from the crisis, migration controls in Canada were tightened to the point that immigration virtually ceased to exist. Taking the 1851-1941 period as a whole, out-migration (6.3 million) practically matched immigration (6.7 million). Without continuous immigration Canada would almost have emptied itself into the U.S.A.

## *After World War II*

The post-war era falls into distinct periods: the first lasting from 1945 to about 1955; the second from 1955 to the 1970s. During the entire period from 1945 to 1970, Canada received some 3 million immigrants out of which 2 million stayed. The other million returned home or went to the U.S.A. This new wave was due to a concurrence of circumstances. Because of the World War and its settlement, numerous refugees and displaced persons found themselves without a home. With the humanitarian desire to assist such persons, Canada generously met the demands of a wartime era. Since 1945 some 350,000 refugees have been admitted. Canadian soldiers who had fought overseas brought home their fiancees, wives and children. The upturn of the Canadian economy during and after World War II increased the demand for labor, skilled and unskilled. The Canadian government also deliberately encouraged immigration especially from Europe. In addition, the rapid industrialization of the post-war period fostered the inflow of professional and skilled people to meet Canada's skilled manpower needs. Between 1946 and 1968 Britain and Italy turned out to be the most important suppliers of prospective Canadians. During the period, Britain sent some 827,567 migrants while Italy forwarded just about half that number (409,414). Britain sent out large numbers of managerial, professional and highly skilled workers. Socialism in England and its trail of high taxes, government interference and a devitalized economy apparently provided the push factor. Lower taxes, a less stifling environment for entrepreneurs and managers, a more dynamic economy, and higher wages and salaries constituted the pull factors in Canada. The Italian flow contained a large component of unskilled laborers. Italy gave Canada the ''bone and senew'' her growing industry needed. The influx of people with valuable skills constituted an immense saving in the national outlay on education, vocational and professional training. While other countries had born the costs, Canada obtained the benefits. An essential difference between the 1945-1955 period and the following time span was that in the first era the migration current still contained substantial numbers of farmers, fishermen, loggers, trappers and miners. As Canada urbanized and industrialized, witnessing also a fast growth of her service sector, the character of immigration changed with professional and technical people, mechanics, machinists, repairmen and white-collar workers becoming the largest categories. Table I compares the composition of immigration during the entire 1946-1973 period. The decline of the flow of farm workers paired with the rise of people with special skills and factory laborers is clearly visible.

In the 1960s Canada participated actively in what came to be known as the ''brain drain''. This term refers to a transfer of highly trained and middle-level personnel to a few major developed countries. In the medical field, for instance, Indian and Pakistani medical doctors migrated to the United Kingdom in order to occupy positions left vacant by doctors who had headed for Canada. A number of Canadian physicians, in their turn, crossed the southern frontier. The flow was set into motion by such factors as salary differentials and the expansion of research programs and universities in North America. In the 1960s Canada received regularly over 100,000 immigrants a year, losing some 40,000 to the United States. This current out of Canada did in fact contain a relatively large proportion of highly trained manpower. However, the ''brain drain'' to the United States was more than compensated for by the ''brain gain'' from Europe. Canada also benefited from a considerable influx of university professors from its southern neighbour. As a matter of fact there has been a great deal of movement in both directions. Among those who moved back and forth, there were many members of that growing group of people which is very mobile and which has easily saleable skills and qualifications. Such persons do not necessarily intend to settle permanently when they come to a country like Canada.

## *Some Characteristics of Contemporary Immigration*

In recent years the sex distribution of the immigrants has been quite regular. Now that the days of pioneering are over, that is what one would expect. Between 1968 and 1972, for instance, 37.2% of all immigrants consisted of adult males. The percentage of adult females was 37.9% while 24.9% of the arrivals consisted of children under 18.

In 1973, moreover, of the total immigration of persons 15 years of age and over, 34.6% were single, 39.6% were married, while 4.6% were widowed, divorced or separated. We mentioned earlier that immigrants tend to be young;

TABLE 42. Intended Occupation of Immigrants Destined to the Labor Force, Percentage Distribution by Occupational Groups, 1946-1973*

| Occupation Group | 1946-50 | 1951-57 | 1958-62 | 1963 | 1964 | 1965 | 1966 | 1967 | 1968 | 1969 | 1970 | 1971 | 1972 | 1973 |
|---|---|---|---|---|---|---|---|---|---|---|---|---|---|---|
| Managerial[1] | | 1.0 | 1.9 | 2.5 | 2.2 | 2.3 | 2.3 | 2.5 | 2.5 | 3.0 | 4.0 | 5.7 | 7.4 | 5.9 |
| Professional | 4.4 | 9.1 | 15.2 | 21.0 | 21.3 | 22.4 | 23.8 | 25.8 | 30.6 | 31.9 | 28.8 | 26.6 | 25.7 | 20.7 |
| Clerical | 7.6 | 8.5 | 11.3 | 13.5 | 14.1 | 13.4 | 13.3 | 13.9 | 13.2 | 14.5 | 15.6 | 16.2 | 14.4 | 14.6 |
| Transportaion | | 1.9 | 1.4 | 1.0 | 1.0 | 1.3 | 1.3 | 1.1 | 1.0 | .8 | .8 | 1.0 | 1.1 | 1.1 |
| Communications[2] | 3.2 | .5 | .5 | .4 | .4 | .4 | .5 | .4 | .4 | .3 | .3 | .2 | .2 | .2 |
| Commercial[3] | 5.5 | 3.5 | 3.4 | 3.0 | 3.4 | 3.4 | 3.1 | 2.5 | 2.8 | 3.2 | 3.3 | 3.4 | 3.5 | 3.4 |
| Financial | | .2 | .3 | .3 | .1 | .2 | .3 | .3 | .6 | .7 | .6 | .6 | .7 | .6 |
| Service | 9.3 | 12.1 | 17.5 | 13.3 | 11.4 | 10.2 | 8.7 | 9.0 | 9.7 | 10.7 | 10.1 | 10.4 | 11.1 | 12.9 |
| Farmers | 29.1 | 14.4 | 8.1 | 5.2 | 4.0 | 3.2 | 3.2 | 2.7 | 3.3 | 2.7 | 2.7 | 3.6 | 3.6 | 3.3 |
| Loggers | | | | .1 | .1 | .2 | .2 | .2 | .1 | .1 | .1 | .1 | .1 | .2 |
| Fishermen, hunters & trappers[4] | 2.9 | 1.2 | .3 | — | — | — | .1 | .1 | — | — | — | — | — | .1 |
| Miners | 2.5 | 1.2 | .5 | .3 | .2 | .3 | .3 | .3 | .5 | .5 | .4 | .4 | .2 | .2 |
| Construction | 7.0 | 9.4 | 7.9 | 8.4 | 8.5 | 8.9 | 9.6 | 8.9 | 8.1 | 7.1 | 7.7 | 6.5 | 6.4 | 5.8 |
| Manufacturing & Mechanical | 23.2 | 23.6 | 17.6 | 23.0 | 22.6 | 23.7 | 24.7 | 23.5 | 24.3 | 20.7 | 20.6 | 19.8 | 19.4 | 22.8 |
| Labourers | 2.9 | 12.6 | 13.6 | 7.8 | 10.2 | 9.6 | 7.7 | 7.4 | 2.8 | 2.4 | 2.1 | 2.2 | 2.0 | 3.0 |
| Not stated | 2.4 | .8 | .5 | .1 | .5 | .5 | .9 | 1.4 | .1 | 1.4 | 2.9 | 3.3 | 4.2 | 5.2 |
| Total workers | 100.0 | 100.0 | 100.0 | 100.0 | 100.0 | 100.0 | 100.0 | 100.0 | 100.0 | 100.0 | 100.0 | 100.0 | 100.0 | 100.0 |

1 No record of Managerial group available for period 1946 to 1952.
2 Includes Transportation for the period 1946-50.
3 Includes Financial for the period 1946-50.
4 Includes Loggers for the period 1946 to 1962.

***Source:** Manpower and Immigration: *Immigration and Population Statistics* (Ottawa: Information Canada, 1974), p. 71.

therefore many will move while still unmarried.

With regard to the destination of migrants, the most urbanized and industrialized provinces, Ontario, Quebec, British Columbia and Alberta, are the great favorites. Between 1970 and 1972 Ontario alone was preferred by 52.8% of all male immigrants and 53.8% of all moving females. It seems that the most desired destinations of internal and foreign migrants are the same.

A major change has taken place in the origin of the immigrants. The European countries are no longer the big suppliers of new Canadians as they used to be. Between 1946 and 1967 Great Britain and Italy were the two biggest providers of prospective Canadians. In the 1968-69 period, however, the U.S.A. replaced Italy as the second major source. In 1972, Canada's mighty neighbour even became source number one. Since then Great Britain and the U.S.A. have been running a close race. The fact that there was less racial violence and poverty in Canada made this country relatively attractive. As opposition to the war in Vietnam rose, Canada became a major recipient of draft evaders and deserters. The traditional gap between American and Canadian salaries and wages had also narrowed. The geographical proximity between the two nations and the close economic ties all facilitated and encouraged movement across the border.

Another new feature is the increasing inflow of Asians and people from the Caribbean nations. On October 1, 1967, Canada put an end to migratory discrimination by reason of race, color and religion. Canada now wanted bearers of valuable skills who could contribute to Canada's needs. Ethnic origin was to be disregarded. *De facto*, ethnic discrimination was replaced by professional and vocational discrimination. Since then, Asia, Africa, the Caribbean isles and Latin America have become growing sources of immigrants. The push factors in these areas have grown overwhelmingly strong. The distribution of immigrant arrivals by ethnic origin in 1975 shows this evolution clearly. It is almost certain that Canada's powers of assimilation will be put to a severe test. While the influx of immigrants from third world nations may contribute to the unemployment of certain sections of the receiving country's labor force, it may be added that the continuous flowing in of people whose ways of thinking, feeling and living are radically different is equivalent to injecting explosives into the domestic social fabric. Problems of maladjustment and social unrest will inevitably become more frequent, especially if the majority of immigrants heads for Toronto, Vancouver and Montreal.

## *The American Magnet*

Migratory flows to the U.S.A. before 1800 were very small, which is to be explained by the absence of cheap and rapid transport as well as the prevailing ignorance about conditions outside one's own country. The flow began to thicken after 1800 when a massive migratory movement from Europe to North America started. Although Canada received many thousands of Europeans the United States was to become by far the chief outlet for Europeans.

TABLE 43. Immigrant Arrivals by Selected Areas of Last Permanent Residence: Canada, 1975*

| Area of Last Permanent Residence | 1975 |
|---|---|
| *Europe* | 72,898 |
| British Isles | 34,978 |
| Portugal | 8,547 |
| Other Europe | 29,373 |
| *Africa* | 9,867 |
| *Asia* | 47,382 |
| Hong Kong | 11,132 |
| India | 10,144 |
| *North and Central America* | 39,638 |
| U.S.A. | 20,155 |
| Jamaica | 8,211 |
| *South America* | 13,270 |
| *Oceania* (Pacific Isles) | 2,652 |
| *Australasia* | 2,174 |

***Source:** Ministry of Industry, Trade and Commerce, *Canada Yearbook, 1976-77*, pp. 212-213.

Between the revolution and the 1870s the U.S.A. was basically a developing country heavily oriented towards agricultural pursuits. The frontier in the West kept moving and the nation needed pioneers knowing how to cultivate the land with current technology, how to raise cattle and also how to fight the Indians. Estimated gross immigration between 1790 and 1870 amounts to some 6.6 million.

Between 1870 and 1914 the situation changed radically. The U.S.A. was now becoming an industrialized country. At the same time it developed its infrastructure, embarked on heavy urban construction, extended its railway network linking the various regions of the nation together and was marked by a large scale expansion of its iron, coal and steel industry. The U.S. also began to flood other nations with cheap cereals. Europe invested heavily in the New World and immigration rose sharply. Between 1870 and 1914 some 25 million people entered the country. Hundreds of thousands went to America's cities, mines and mill towns. Traditionally most immigrants to the U.S. had come from the British Isles and north-western Europe. After 1870, however, southern and Eastern Europe came to the fore. Southern and Eastern Europe were then still basically rural and in the earlier stages of the demographic transition with death rates declining and birth rates still high. These immigrants supplied America with the manpower and skills the country needed in its expanding mines, factories and building industry.

After World War I, America sharply curtailed the inflow by the adoption of a restrictive quota system which stipulated that each country's allotment was to be two percent of the number of people originating from that country and residing in the United States in 1890. The choice of the year 1890 when Latins and Slavs still comprised a relatively small proportion of America's population operated in favor of the older stocks of immigrants (British and northwest European) while reducing the arrivals from southern and eastern Europe.

When the First World War was over the United States was no longer the land of opportunity it had been before. The best lands were taken, the gold mines were exhausted and on the farms technological advances resulted in a substitution of mechanical devices for men.

The economic crisis of the 1930s deterred immigration, but after 1945 the flow increased again. As in Canada, many of the newcomers consisted of displaced persons, refugees, orphans, war brides and the like. In 1952 the new Immigration and National Act (McCarran-Walter Act), although maintaining the country quota system expressed qualitative pre-occupations. Fifty percent of the visas granted to quota immigrants had to be reserved for people with special occupational qualifications. In 1965 the national origin basis was abolished and new preference categories were set up, making it easier for people with special skills and abilities to enter America. Presently the U.S.A. no longer receives the majority of its immigrants from its traditional European suppliers. Obviously it is in the developing countries that the push factors are extremely potent, providing the incentive to leave. As it turns out Mexico and the Philippines are sending the thickest flows to America. The following chart shows this.

FIGURE 16. Immigrants by Selected Country of Origin, U.S.A., 1975*

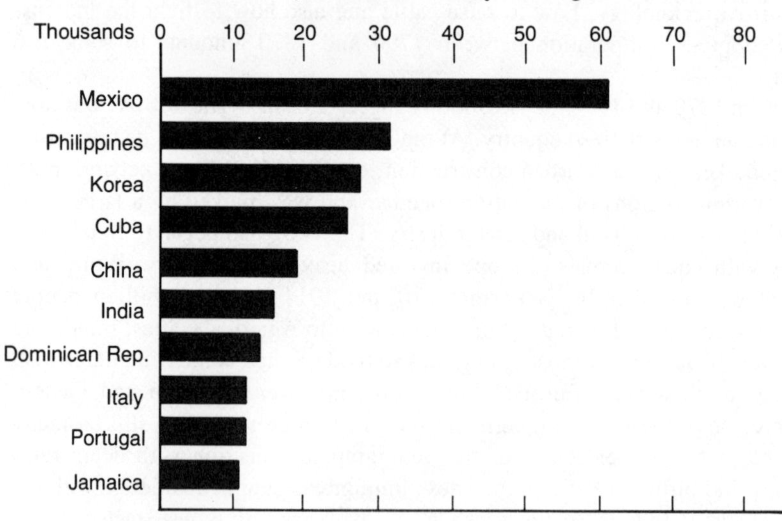


***Source:** U.S. Bureau of the Census, *Statistical Abstract of the United States, 1976,* 97th edition (Washington, D.C., 1975), p. 101.

The following table shows the total arrivals in the U.S.A. for ten-year periods from 1820 until 1970 and annually thereafter.

TABLE 44. Immigrant Arrivals to the United States 1820-1979*

| Period | Number (in thousands) |
|---|---|
| 1820 - 1830 | 152 |
| 1831 - 1840 | 599 |
| 1841 - 1850 | 1,713 |
| 1851 - 1860 | 2,598 |
| 1861 - 1870 | 2,315 |
| 1871 - 1880 | 2,812 |
| 1881 - 1890 | 5,247 |
| 1891 - 1900 | 3,688 |
| 1901 - 1910 | 8,795 |
| 1911 - 1920 | 5,736 |
| 1921 - 1930 | 4,106 |
| 1931 - 1940 | 528 |
| 1941 - 1950 | 1,035 |
| 1951 - 1960 | 2,515 |
| 1961 - 1970 | 3,322 |
| 1971 | 370 |
| 1972 | 385 |
| 1973 | 400 |
| 1974 | 395 |
| 1975 | 386 |

***Source:** U.S. Bureau of the Census, *Statistical Abstract of the United States, 1976* . . ., p. 102.

## B. Canadian Immigration Policy: Past and Present

The first attempt to regulate immigration in accordance with Canada's needs was made in 1869 with the adoption of the British North America Act. This act and subsequent legislation gave, in general, priority to the immigration of farmers, farm workers and domestic servants from the British Isles, the United States and Western Europe. Both the provinces and the federal government were given the power to legislate with regard to immigration.

The new Act of 1906 excluded from immigration such individuals as the feeble-minded, criminals or persons likely to become a public charge. In 1917 the newly established Department of Immigration and Colonization became responsible for immigration matters. A 1923 amendment specified that admission of Asians was restricted to *bona fide* farmers, farm hands and domestic servants. Each immigrant from Asia, moreover, was to possess $250 in order to qualify for admission. The idea was to restrict entry of Asians as much as possible while encouraging the inflow of British and American citizens. In 1930 the entry of Asians was further restricted to the wife or dependant child of a Canadian citizen.

Because of the depression, immigration was virtually suspended in 1931. Only certain categories of British and American subjects and legal dependants of Canadian subjects were still eligible for admission.

After World War II a radically new situation emerged. In 1947 Prime Minister Mackenzie King specified that in the long run immigration as well as natural increase were to build up the Canadian population. Although Canada did not want to alter the fundamental character of its population, this nation was to allow entrance of as many people as the economy could advantageously absorb. A whole range of regulations and amendments reflected the new government approach to immigration. The main idea was to foster the expansion of the Canadian population by selective immigration. Citizens from the British Isles, France, the U.S.A., Australia, New Zealand and South Africa were to enjoy priority. They could enter very easily provided that they met some minimum standards with regard to helath and character. They also had to be able to support themselves until they found a job. A second category, Europeans with useful skills, was also welcomed. Asian immigration was restricted to close relatives of Canadian resident citizens while from 1951 onwards a small number of people from India (300), Pakistan (100) and Ceylon (150) was also allowed to enter each year. Priority in other words was given to immigrants who were adaptable to Canadian life in terms of ethnic, social and political background. New skills which could stimulate the economy were also welcomed.

Another major change came in 1953 when a simplification of existing regulations had become necessary. British, French, American, Australian, South African citizens and inhabitants of New Zealand could still enter without further formalities if they had the means to support themselves until they had found work. Other European nationals could also enter provided they had the required qualifications. Canadian citizens and permanent residents could also bring in dependant children, spouses and close relatives from almost any part of the world provided that the sponsors had the will and the means to provide for the sponsored. Apart from the sponsored, the Asians were still being kept out.

In 1962 a major shift occurred in Canadian immigration policy. The 1962 amendment changed the existing regulations in the sense that discrimination against non-Europeans was abolished. Anyone, regardless of ethnic origin, color, citizenship, country of residence, or religious belief, was eligible to apply for admission, provided he or she had the education, training, skills or special qualifications Canada needed. The new admission policy in other words now used occupational skill and not country of origin as the main criterion for admittance. As Kalbach observed, the potential significance for changes in Canada's ethnic composition had now become very great indeed.[2] As we noted in an earlier section, the influx of Asians, Caribbeans and Latin Americans has greatly increased.

---

[2]W.E. Kalbach, *The Impact of Immigration on Canada's Population* (Ottawa: Dominion Bureau of Statistics, 1970), p. 24.

In 1966 a separate Department of Manpower and Immigration was established. The issue of immigrant entry was now separated from matters pertaining to citizenship. Alien admission was tied even more firmly to the economic needs of Canadian society. The selective recruiting function of Canadian immigration laws was again brought to the fore.

In 1967 the admission policy was modified once more. Three main categories of immigrants were distinguished, i.e., the independants, sponsored dependants (husbands, wives, and close relatives of Canadian citizens and residents) and nominated relatives. The latter category also consists of close relatives, but the sponsor must be willing to provide care, maintenance or provide him or her with a job or assist that person in finding one.

The independant immigrant is admitted solely on the basis of his or her potential adaptability to Canadian life and the economy. The new regulations were supplemented by a points assessment system. The independant applicant had to obtain at least 50 out of 100 points, which were to be awarded on the basis of education, training, qualifications, skills, occupational demand, personal qualities, language proficiency, age and adjustment potential. The nominated relatives have to go through the same assessment system but may receive between 15 and 30 points on account of their relationship to the sponsor. In this system the discretionary powers of the immigration official are very great indeed. He actually may give up to 15 points on the basis of the applicant's adjustment potential, of which he is the sole judge.

It seems in the 1970s that the 1967 policy regulations are no longer thought to be satisfactory. One problem is that the present non-discriminatory immigration policy (non-discrimination in terms of place of origin) gives rise to integration problems which are bad for the immigrant as well as for the host society. It also appears that manpower needs are no longer what they used to be in the 1960s when the economy boomed and skills were lacking. The 1970s have witnessed considerable unemployment especially among the younger age groups. In the mid-seventies there were at least six policy issues which a new immigration policy would have to face.

(1) How numerous do Canadians want their population to be towards the end of this century? Immigration in Canada has been and still is an important component of overall population growth. (2) Most immigrants prefer to settle in English-speaking areas and adopt the English language as their main vehicle of communication. The existing imbalance between the French-Speaking and Anglophone sectors of Canadian society is steadily worsening. (3) The fact that discrimination according to place of birth has been abolished does not suffice to guarantee a broad and reasonable representation in Canada's annual immigration current. Nations experiencing population explosions will tend to be overrepresented. Nations which are in the last stages of the demographic transition will send a few representatives. (4) In the 1960s Canada has made a major investment in schools, universities, vocational training institutes and the like. Besides, the members of the baby boom who were born between 1944 and the early 1960s have entered and are still entering the labor market. To what extent should

Canada now rely on foreign manpower? National labor shortages, moreover, seem to have disappeared. Regional labor deficiencies, however, are still a problem. (5) The distribution of immigrant settlement is unbalanced. Foreign immigrants prefer, obviously, Toronto, Montreal and Vancouver to other parts of Canada. Foreign immigrants do not always go to those places where local labor shortages are the greatest. (6) The principle of non-discrimination with regard to ethnic origin has given rise to ghetto formation, racial anxieties and conflict in the big cities.

In February of the year 1975 a government document usually referred to as the ''Green Paper'' was presented in the House of Commons. This Paper which voiced some anxiety with regard to Canada's future was supposed to initiate a national debate on immigration. The government hoped to get feedback from public and press which would facilitate the reshaping of Canadian immigration regulations in accordance with the national will. The Green Paper consisted of four volumes accompanied by eight supplementary studies. It has been observed that the document was somewhat disappointing since it has not really benefited from serious research. It was also cooly received by the press.

In April, 1978 a new ''Immigration Act'' came into effect. The Act gave the government broader powers to set immigration target levels. Actually the Candian government is now allowed to set *and* change its own demographic objectives with regard to distributions, size, rate of growth and structure of the population and admit accordingly the number of immigrants it judges appropriate. The limit on immigration will be set on a year to year basis by the Minister of Employment and Immigration after consulting with the provinces. Explicit numerical quotas were not set but in March, 1977 before the Act was passed by Parliament the Minister of Immigration mentioned an average annual number of some 140,000.

## Bibliography


Bouscaren, A.T., *International Migrations Since 1945,* New York: Praeger, 1963.

Boyd, M., ''Immigration Policies and Trends: A Comparison of Canada and the United States'', *Demography,* Vol. XIII, Feb., 1976.

Dollot, L., *Les Migrations Humaines,* Paris: P.U.F. 1976.

Hawkins, F., *Canada and Immigration, Public Policy and Public Concern,* Montreal: McGill-Queen's University Press, 1972.

________________''Immigration and Population: The Canadian Approach'', *Canadian Public Policy,* Summer 1975.

Kalbach, W.E., *The Impact of Immigration on Canada's Population,* Ottawa: Bureau of Statistics, 1970.

Keyfitz, N., ''Some Demographic Aspects of French-English Relations in Canada'', M. Wade, (ed.) *Canadian Dualism,* Toronto: University of Toronto Press, 1960.

Kraus, M., *Immigration, The American Mosaic,* New York: Nostrand, 1966.

Star, S., ''In Search of a Rational Immigration Policy'', *Canadian Public Policy,* Summer 1975.

Chapter 11

# *The Composition of Population*

## A. Sex and Age Structure

### *Definition of Population Composition*

The population processes – fertility, mortality and migration – are essentially movements. The population structure is a state of facts. The composition of population refers to the basic demographic characteristics by which the individuals who make up the population may be differentiatied. Some of these characteristics are more important to demographers than others. Of particular interst are sex, age, marital status, education, religion and profession. Sex and age, however, are the pivotal features and it is to these two traits that we shall devote our attention. The demographic processes and the population composition are intimately related. As we shall discover in a later section, fertility, mortality and migration condition the population structure while the existing composition of the population determines the processes, at least to a certain degree. Information about the structural components of a population such as the Canadian one is chiefly obtained from offical censuses and intercensal sample surveys.

### *Sex Composition*

The sex composition in a population is a most basic characteristic which has a direct impact on nuptiality and fertility. Sex constitutes one of the most readily observable components of population structure. People may misreport their age, but they are less likely to misstate their sex. The sex composition of a population is conventionally expressed by a summarizing device called the sex ratio or the masculinity ratio. It expresses the number of males per hundred females (see Chapter 5). As will be remembered, it is written as:

$$\frac{M}{F} \cdot k$$

M = total number of males in the population
F = total number of females in the same population
k = arbitrary factor of 100
Thus for Canada in 1971 we obtain $\dfrac{10{,}795{,}370 \text{ males}}{10{,}772{,}940 \text{ females}} \times 100 = 100.2$

In other words the sex composition in 1971 was almost perfectly balanced. In earlier times male dominant populations were typical for Canada. This was partly due to the composition of the immigration current which has tended to contain more males than females. In 1911 the high sex ratio figure of 113 was attained. Since then the figure has dropped gently in order to reach the virtually balanced sex composition of the early 1970s.

In most Western populations, Canada included, the sex ratio at birth is about 105 which means that for every one hundred girls about one hundred and five boys are born. In Canada the sex ratio at birth has remained between 105 and 107 since 1921. The sex ratio tends to decline progressively for each age group because of the excess male mortality.

Sex ratios below 94 and above 107 require an explanation. Sex ratios constitute an important piece of demographic knowledge. An unrecognized imbalance betwen the sexes can result in erroneous interpretations of statistics on marriages and births.

## *Determinants of Sex Ratio*

As stated earlier, sex ratios at birth hover around the 105 figure. This number applies mainly to Western countries such as Canada or France where women are generally in good health with prenatal losses being few. In low-income countries where prenatal losses are more frequent, sex ratios at birth are rather around the 102 figure. Since ordinarily more boys than girls are conceived, improved care for and better health of pregnant mothers must result in a higher sex ratio at birth.

The prevalence of female infanticide is another determinant of the sex ratio. In the past, in societies where boys were strongly preferred, with infanticide being practiced, more girls than boys were being put to death. This increased the sex ratio.

In a number of societies girls get inferior treatment and care. The boys get better food, more attention and the like. This relative neglect of female infants usually results in higher female mortality and ultimately higher sex ratios. It is probably for this reason that rather high sex ratios are found in such countries as Pakistan, India, Turkey and Iran. The latter country had a sex ratio of 107 in 1973.[1] Part of the explanation lies also in female underreporting at birth.

In advanced societies the mortality differential visibly favors females, as we observed in our chapter on mortality. This mortality differential tends to reduce the sex ratio. Especially when the proportion of aged people in population increases (a problem to be discussed in detail in later sections) the sex ratio is bound to decline because the proportion of surviving females steadily grows in such situations.

---

[1] Its computation was as follows:

$$\frac{16{,}328{,}000 \text{ Males}}{15{,}317{,}000 \text{ Females}} \times 100$$

$= 106.60 = 107$ males per 100 females

Wars which result in large numbers of male casualties also distort the sex ratio. It has been calculated that if the First World War had not occurred, the Germans' sex ratio in 1925 would have been 98.8 whereas in fact it stood at 93.9.

Migrations especially when they occur on a large scale will affect the sex ratio in the area of origin as well as in the area of destination. In Canada and the United States the sex ratio was considerably influenced by pre-World War I immigration, which was preponderantly male. In 1911 the Canadian sex ratio reached a peak of 113. In the U.S.A. the figure of 106 was attained in 1910. The American sex ratio had dropped below the 100 figure in 1950 and stood at 94.8 in 1970. The secular downward trend of the sex ratio in modernized societies is due to the fact that boy and girl babies and infants are now equally well cared for. As male mortality normally exceeds female mortality at all ages the initial preponderance of males is gradually reduced until between ages 40-50 the ratio reaches unity while at older ages females outnumber males in each cohort.

## *Trends in Sex Ratios*

As the following table shows, the general trend of the Canadian sex ratio since 1851 has displayed three features. Between 1861 and 1881 it declined in order to rise again thereafter. The peak was reached in 1911 after which the secular trend has been downwards again. This decline is likely to continue in the future, resulting in a slightly female-dominant population. Urban centers tend to have lower sex ratios than rural areas and the heavily urbanized provinces have lower while the more rural provinces have higher sex ratios. In 1971 the sex ratio for all urban areas taken together was 98. For all rural non-farm regions it stood at 107 while for rural farm areas the figure leveled at 116. The two provinces with the lowest sex ratio were Quebec and Ontario both with 99. Yukon and the Northwest Territories had the highest figures with respectively 117 and 111. Frontier areas in Canada, the U.S.A. and other immigrant countries have always been

TABLE 45. Sex Ratios for Canada, 1851-1971*

| Census Year | Sex Ratio | Census Year | Sex Ratio |
|---|---|---|---|
| 1851 | 105 | 1921 | 106 |
| 1861 | 106 | 1931 | 107 |
| 1871 | 103 | 1941 | 105 |
| 1881 | 103 | 1951 | 102 |
| 1891 | 104 | 1961 | 102 |
| 1901 | 105 | 1971 | 100 |
| 1911 | 113 | 1976 | 99 |

***Sources:** 1971 Census of Canada, *Profile Studies Demographic Characteristics*, The Age-Sex Structure of Canada's Population, Vol. V, Part 1 (Ottawa: Statistics Canada, 1976), p. 4.

1976 Census of Canada, *Population: Demographic Characteristics*, Five-Year Age Groups, Vol. II (Ottawa: Statistics Canada, 1978), p. 1.

characterized by high sex ratios because such areas attract male rather than female immigrants. The following short table shows the high masculinity ratios prevailing in the frontier areas at the beginning of this century.

TABLE 46. Sex Ratios for Certain Selected Canadian Frontier Areas: 1901*

| Region | Sex Ratio |
|---|---|
| N.W. Territories | 236 |
| British Columbia | 177 |
| Prairies | 120 |

***Source:** W.E. Kalbach, W.W. McVey, *The Demographic Bases . . .*, p. 116.

At present the sex ratios are higher in the less developed countries than in the more developed nations for reasons stated earlier. As the low income areas move through the modernization process their sex ratios are bound to fall as they have done in the industrialized nations.

## *Age Structure*

It is important for the social scientist to have precise information about the age composition of a population because the actions and reactions of a population differ according to the proportions of young, adults and aged. Familiarity with the age configuration of a population is also a necessary ingredient for sound demographic predictions.

## *Median Age*

A very simple way to describe the age distribution of a population is to use some sort of average. Although some authors use the mean or average age as a tool for analysis, the median age is more commonly employed. The median of a set of values is normally the central value in terms of magnitude. It is, in other words, the middle term when a group of figures is written in numerical order. Thus the median of 3,5,6,7,8, is 6. If we have an odd number of values such as in the example above, the median will be a whole number. If there is an even number of scores then there are two central values and the median is defined as their arithmetic mean. Thus, the median age of a population divides that population into two equal groups, one half being older and one half being younger.

Like individuals, populations can grow older but unlike them they can also grow younger. When a population ages, the median age rises; when a population is in the process of rejuvenating itself the median age falls. Demographers define populations with medians of less than twenty as ''young''. Populations with medians of twenty to twenty-nine are of ''intermediate age'' while those with medians of thirty or over are earmarked as ''old''. For modernized countries like Canada the long-term trend of the median age is upwards which reflects the aging or graying process, typical for all low fertility, modernized nations. The following table shows the evolution of the median age between 1851 and 1971.

TABLE 47. Median Age of the Population, Canada: 1851-1976*

| Year | Median Age | Year | Median Age |
|---|---|---|---|
| 1851 | 17.23 | 1921 | 23.97 |
| 1861 | 18.24 | 1931 | 24.75 |
| 1871 | 18.80 | 1941 | 27.08 |
| 1881 | 20.07 | 1951 | 27.68 |
| 1891 | 21.43 | 1961 | 26.29 |
| 1901 | 22.73 | 1971 | 26.26 |
| 1911 | 23.80 | 1976 | 27.80 |

***Sources:** 1971 Census of Canada, *Profile Studies* . . ., p. 22.
1976 Census of Canada, *Population: Demographic Characteristics* . . ., p. 2.

The largest increase in the median age occurred in the 1931-1941 period. This era corresponds to the decade of the Great Depression, characterized by low birth rates and equally low levels of immigration. The population of Canada was obviously graying quickly. The post-war rejuvenation of population reversed the trend in graying. Because of the drop in fertility which started in the early 1960s the long-term trend in ageing is bound to resume.

The developing countries have much lower median ages than the high-income countries. Iran, for instance, had a median age of 20.2 years in 1956 which sharply declined to 16.9 in 1966. As a general rule one can state that high birth rates are accompanied by low median ages and vice versa.

## *Age Composition and Age Pyramid*

Once the census data are known, age distribution is relatively easy to calculate. To present all known data in great detail may sometimes be confusing. To simplify matters the age structure of a population can be split into three main categories, i.e., the young (0-14 years), the adults (15-65 years) and the old (65 and above). The following table presents the % distribution by broad age groups for the years 1901, 1961 and 1971.

TABLE 48. Population of Canada, Distribution by Age, 1901, 1961, 1971, 1976*

| Age Group | Percent of Total Population | | | |
|---|---|---|---|---|
| | 1901 | 1961 | 1971 | 1976 |
| 0 - 14 | 34.4 | 34.0 | 29.5 | 25.6 |
| 15 - 64 | 60.6 | 58.5 | 63.3 | 65.6 |
| 65 + | 5.0 | 7.6 | 8.1 | 8.7 |

***Sources:** Kalbach, McVey, *The Demographic Bases* . . ., p. 127.
Ministry of Industry, Trade and Commerce, *Canada Yearbook, 1975,* p. 166.
1976 Census of Canada, *Population: Demographic Characteristics* . . ., pp. 1, 2.

A major feature of the above table is the visibility of the ageing process, which is shown in the increase of the proportion of sixty-five and above.[2]. At this point it may be interesting to compare the Canadian population with the Iranian one which, as the figures show, is a great deal younger.

TABLE 49. Age Groups of Population of Iran, 1972*

| Age Group | Percent of Total Population |
|---|---|
| | 1972 |
| 0 - 14 | 45.5 |
| 15 - 64 | 51.5 |
| 65 and above | 3.0 |

***Source:** Kayhan Research Associates, *Iran Yearbook, 1977* . . ., p. 41.

Obviously, the proportion of very young is extremely high in this population while the proportion of old is almost insignificant. The Iranian age structure is typical for many developing countries.

A slightly more advanced quantitative representation of the population is by five-year age groups. The following table is an example of such a distribution.

TABLE 50. Percentage Distribution of the Canadian and Dutch Population: 1975-1976*

| Age Group | Canada (1976) | Netherlands (1975) |
|---|---|---|
| 0 - 4 | 7.5 | 7.3 |
| 5 - 9 | 8.2 | 8.8 |
| 10 - 14 | 9.9 | 9.0 |
| 15 - 19 | 10.0 | 8.6 |
| 20 - 24 | 9.3 | 8.3 |
| 25 - 29 | 8.7 | 8.9 |
| 30 - 34 | 7.0 | 6.8 |
| 35 - 39 | 5.8 | 6.0 |
| 40 - 44 | 5.5 | 5.6 |
| 45 - 49 | 5.4 | 5.5 |
| 50 - 54 | 5.3 | 5.4 |
| 55 - 59 | 4.4 | 4.7 |
| 60 - 64 | 3.9 | 4.3 |
| 65 - 69 | 3.1 | 3.8 |
| 70 + | 5.6 | 7.1 |

***Sources:** 1976 Census of Canada, *Population: Demographic Characteristics*, pp. 1, 2.

Netherlands Central Bureau of Statistics, *Statistical Yearbook of the Netherlands, 1976,* The Hague: Staatsuitgeverij, 1976, p. 21.

---

[2]Aging is usually defined as an increase in the median age *or* an increase in the proportion of the old (65+).

We will now compare the Canadian and the Dutch populations of the years 1975-1976.

As the above figures suggest, the two populations have remarkably similar age distributions. A major difference between the two populations is that in 1975 the proportion of aged was slightly higher in the Dutch population.

Age and sex compositions can also be represented by a special type of bar graph called population pyramid or histogram. These population pyramids provide graphic statements of the current sex and age distribution of a population. They are static representations of a population which itself is always changing because of the action of fertility, mortality and migration. A histogram "freezes" this motion at a particular point of time.

The population pyramid itself consists simply of two bar graphs placed on their sides and put back to back. The bars, however, can be placed adjacent to each other without any space between them. This procedure helps to emphasize the continuity of the data. The length of each bar represents the number of percentage size of each age or age category (5-year age groups are commonly used). Males are usually placed at the left, females at the right side. The youngest ages are at the bottom, the oldest at the top. Since cohorts normally lose each year part of their number either through death or emigration, each bar is usually shorter than the previous one which conveys the impression of a pyramid. A vertical comparison of the bars shows us the relative proportions of each age group in the population while horizontal comparisons show the proportions of males and females at each age. The population pyramid can be based on absolute numbers or proportions. The latter type is the more common.

## *The Construction of the Pyramid*

In order to build a population pyramid we first draw a horizontal axis on which we plot the population either in millions (absolute figures) or percentages (relative figures; they are obtained by dividing the age group by the total population and multiplying the quotient by 100). Ages or age groups are shown straddling the vertical central axis. The size of each age group is represented by a horizontal bar from the central axis. The length of each bar or rectangle is proportional to the size of each age group. The width of the bar indicates the number of years of the age interval considered. The surface of the rectangle is now equal to the product of width and length or number of individuals times age interval. Supposing we would construct a population pyramid representing the population of Canada in absolute numbers at intervals of five years, we would probably start with the males taking the 0-4 age group first. In 1971 the total number of this age category was 905,800. The bar associated with this total should have a length equal to $\frac{905,800}{5}$ = 181,160. Hence, after this operation each of the single age groups 0,1,2,3,4 years has the same average number equal to one-fifth of the total five-year group or 0.4. Although in this manner the pyramid loses some precision, the general format of the group remains correct. The following representation of Canada's age structures superimposes the pyramids at two different periods of time. The pyramids are based on percentages.

FIGURE 17. Populations of Canada by Age and Sex: 1961, 1973*

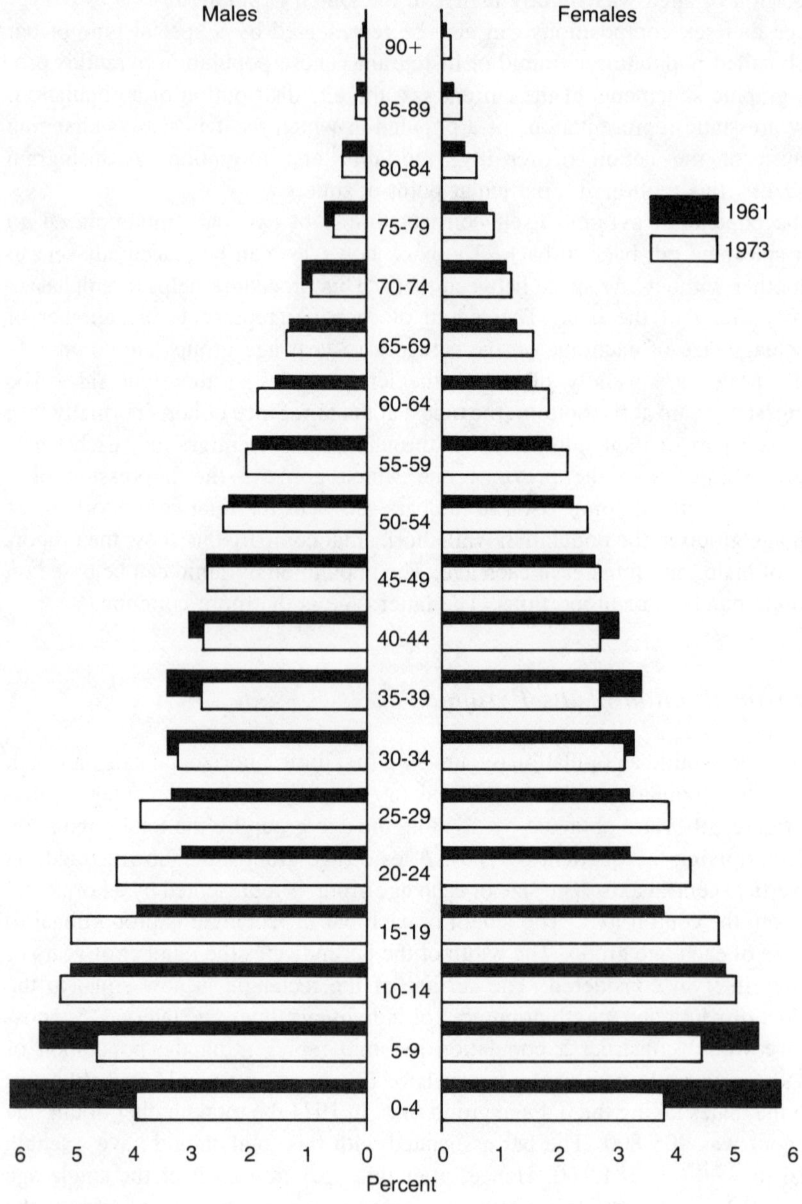


***Source:** Ministry of Industry, Trade and Commerce, *Canada Yearbook, 1974* . . . p. 143.

The 1973 pyramid shows all the events pictured in the 1961 pyramid advanced 12 years. Because the birth rates dropped after 1960, the 1973 pyramid has an indented base. The 1961 pyramid still has a very large foundation which reflects the post-war recovery of the birth rate. The relatively small number of those in their twenties and thirties pictured in the 1961 pyramid reflect the "empty" depression cohorts passing through the system. One can say that the population pyramid shows year-in, year-out the history of a population over the last hundred years including wars, waves of in- or out-migration, fluctuations in fertility, mortality and the like. Like the American population pyramid the Canadian sex and age distribution shows no marked irregularities, but the French histogram of say 1975 does.

FIGURE 18. Population Pyramid for France 1st of January 1975*

(a) Deficit of Births due to World War I (1914-1918)
(b) Deficit of Births due to World War II (1939-1945)

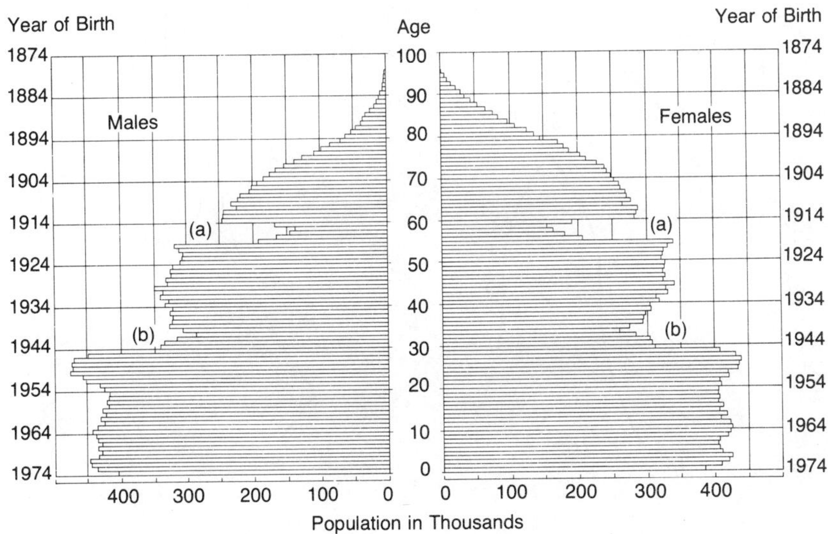


***Source:** Ministère de L'Economie et des Finances, Institut National de la Statistique et des Etudes Economiques, *Annuaire Statistique de la France 1976* (Paris: 1976), p. 713.

The very oldest age groups in the pyramid shown above show very low sex ratios which mirror the male war losses of World War I estimated at 1,400,000. The pyramid also shows clearly the deficient birth cohorts born during the two world wars as they move through the system. The two post-war recoveries (after W.W.I and W.W.II) are also visible as well as the more recent decline in fertility which occurred once the post Second World War baby boom was over. All these events have produced bulges and dents still clearly visible in the histogram of 1975.

## *Classification of Pyramids*

As shown below several types of population pyramids can be distinguished. We will limit ourselves to five cases.

FIGURE 19. Five most Frequent Forms of Age Pyramids

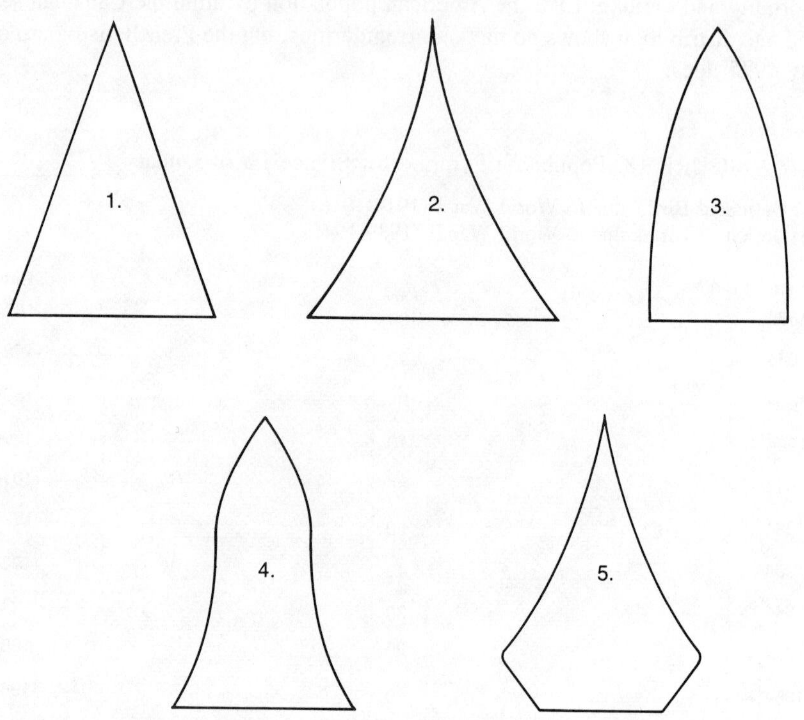


The first category of age pyramids looks like an ordinary triangle. It may be called the "primitive" type as it corresponds to premodern fertility and mortality conditions. Before 1800 all populations looked like this. At present there are still a few developing countries displaying this kind of age-sex profile. It reflects a population with high vital rates and a low median age. A second variety of pyramid has a broader base than the first category. The 0-14 age group is larger because this population is beginning to control mortality but not fertility. The most impressive gains in mortality reduction are made in the younger age groups. The steeply sloping sides reflect the large proportion of younger people and the small percentage of aged people. The population structure of Iran in 1974 fits this description perfectly as the following graphic illustration shows.

FIGURE 20. Age and Sex Discrimination of Iranian Population: 1974*

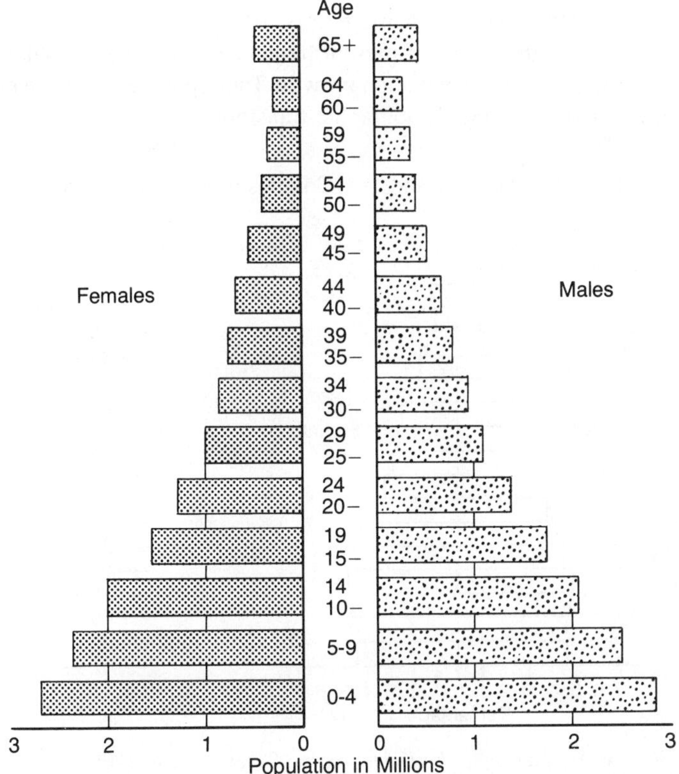


***Source:** Echo of Iran: *Iran Almanac 1977,* Tehran: Echo, 1977, p. 378.

It should be noted that in the pyramid shown above the males are now on the right side. The high sex ratio prevailing in Iran is visible. The chosen cutoff point is at 65 which is early for a developed nation but not for a developing country with relatively few inhabitants of sixty-five and above.

A third class of histograms looks like an old-fashioned beehive or a Chinese lantern. Both vital rates are relatively low, the median age is now higher and the proportion of aged has increased too. The Canadian population of 1941 as well as many west European populations of the same period fit this picture. The birth rate had fallen considerably during the 1930s and immigration into Canada had come to a standstill while mortality had continued its descent which started during the previous decades.

The fourth category of age and sex distributions is bell-shaped. It mirrors an older population in the process of rejuvenation. Canada, as well as other countries in the West, has experienced a post-war recovery in the birth rate after World War II. It lasted until the early sixties. In 1961 the Canadian pyramid had a broad base again reflecting the years of the baby boom. During the recovery of natality the median age dropped.

The last category of pyramids pictures populations which, after a period of rejuvenation and vigorous growth, experience a fertility decline again. The proportion of young falls and the median age rises. All Western populations as well as that of Japan are in this stage. If present trends continue these populations will ultimately experience zero population growth. These populations have obviously entered the last stage of the demographic transition.

FIGURE 21. Age and Sex Composition Canada: 1941*

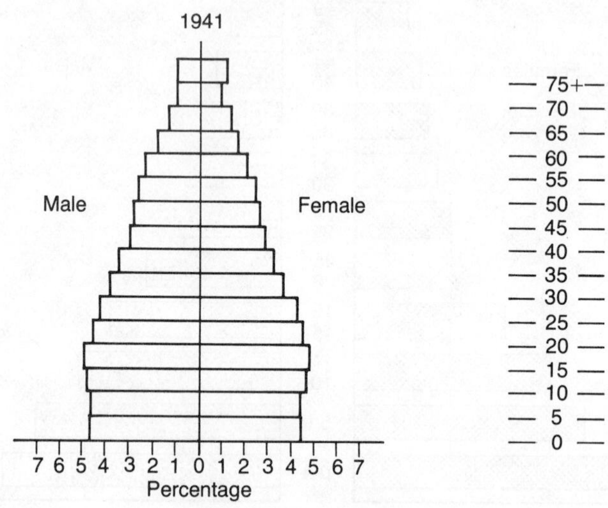


***Source:** W Kalbach, *The Demographic Bases* . . ., p. 120.

## B. Factors Affecting the Sex and Age Composition

Mortality, fertility, migration and exceptional circumstances such as war may be considered to be the main determinants of age composition.

Mortality, the first conditioning factor, has dramatically declined during the last two hundred years. In most Western nations such as Canada, however, the reduction was gradual which made the effects on the age-sex profile hard to see. Since about the 1950s the less developed countries have gone through a different evolution. As stated earlier, these countries have been able to import relatively quickly the death control techniques which the more advanced nations have developed over the last two centuries. This large scale transfer of health technology has resulted in disproportionately high reductions of death rates in the younger age groups. As a result, the base of their population pyramids became larger and larger as these countries were faced with an ever growing proportion of children and young teen-agers. In Iran, for instance, the proportion under 10 years of age grew from 32.6% in 1956 (first Census) to 34.1% in 1966 (second Census). The proportion under 20 years of age grew from 49.7% in 1956 to

54.6% in 1966. The Iranian population obviously became younger between the two censuses.

Fertility is the second determinant of age and sex structure. Again, if fertility changes are slow, the effects on the pyramid will hardly be perceptible. Spectacular swings, however, clearly show up. The low fertility years of the economic depression and the very first years of World War II, which were followed by a baby boom, have produced a clearly visible dent in the Canadian pyramid of 1961. The spectacular recovery of natality has resulted in a bulge which is clearly visible in the 1971 pyramid. Pyramids of comparable populations (U.S.A., etc.) show similar characteristics.

Migration is the third factor conducive to modifying the age-sex structure. Again depending on volume, immigration and emigration may produce bulges and dents in the pyramids of the receiving and sending countries. In both internal and international migration, adolescents and young adults tend to dominate, hence the modifications in the age structure produced by migration occur in certain age groups only. The age structure of countries like Ireland and Sweden was modified in the second half of the nineteenth century when millions left these countries heading for America and Canada. The outflow was large relative to the populations of these areas. The Canadian pyramid also changed moderately during the post-war period when immigration was heavy.

Special circumstances such as wars will again affect a country's pyramid. France suffered 1,400,000 casualties during World War I. The effects are still visible at the summit of the French pyramid. Such heavy casualties are bound to produce a shortage of eligible males, reduce the marriage rate and thereby the level of fertility. The low fertility level of the war-years produced a deep symmetrical dent in the pyramid which has remained visible because of the revival of fertility which occurred once the war was over. When the deficient birth cohorts born during World War I passed into the reproductive ages, natality declined again. The fertility of the cohorts born during the 1915-1919 period was further lowered by the separations due to World War II. Thus a second niche was created in the French histogram. A major war, therefore, can send ripples, if not waves, through the sex-age profile of several future generations.

## C. Demographic Consequences of Age Structure

It would be too strong a statement to make that a nation's age profile determines its institutions and way of life. However, any particular age distribution, no matter how it came about, establishes boundaries and limitations on a nation's institutions and potentialities as well as on short-term changes in its institutional and social life. If the cohorts in the reproductive period are depleted, fertility need not necessarily be low but clear boundaries are set on the potential number of children which can be born. In other words, the age structure of a population (and the sex structure too) is restrictive or permissive of social institutions without causing them to exist or disappear. As the table below shows, the more developed countries have older populations than the less developed nations. As a result their demographic (and other) potentialities are differently confined.

TABLE 51. Population of More and Less Developed Countries Distributed by Age, 1970 (percentage)*

| Region | Population by Age Groups | | | | | |
|---|---|---|---|---|---|---|
| | 0 - 4 | 5 - 14 | 15 - 24 | 25 - 44 | 45 - 64 | 65+ |
| MDC's | 8.5 | 18.2 | 16.7 | 26.9 | 20.0 | 9.6 |
| LDC's | 15.6 | 24.9 | 18.8 | 24.1 | 12.7 | 3.8 |

***Source:** Department of Economic and Social Affairs, United Nations, *The World Population Situation in 1970-1975,* (St/ESA/Series A/56) (New York: 1974), p. 25.

As one might expect, irregularities and even perfectly normal features of a nation's age profile affect nuptiality and the three main processes — mortality, fertility and migration.

A variation in a nation's age-sex structure can affect nuptiality as follows: When a sudden increase in fertility produces a bulge in the age profile, the possibilities of marriage for men and women are affected some twenty years later. Normally females select partners a few years older than themselves. In 1974, for example, the median age at marriage in Canada was 23.5 for bachelors and 21.3 for maidens. The average age at marriage was 24.7 for men and 22.4 for the females. If a baby boom such as the post-war one is preceded by a period of low fertility, the number of girls born during the early years of the baby boom will have difficulties in finding eligible mates some twenty years later because their potential mates were born in low-fertility years. The females born in 1946 faced the problem of having to find males born in the depleted cohorts of 1944. This ''marriage squeeze'', as the phenomenon is called, occurred in the 1962-1966 period in Canada when the baby boom females were trying to select appropriate grooms born during the depression and early war-years period. The sudden drop of fertility which occurred during the 1960s is bound to produce the reverse situation. The girls born during the early sixties when fertility dropped will select their partners from the larger cohorts born at the end of the baby boom. As a result the marriage prospects of those girls look relatively bright.

Other things being equal, a population with a large proportion of young adults will have a higher birth rate than a population with a smaller percentage of people of reproductive age. Since about 1962 the baby boom cohorts born after the war have entered the reproductive age. Throughout the 1970s the Canadian and American populations will still be characterized by relatively large cohorts reaching the prime childbearing years. This relative prevalence of young adults is a factor which tends to raise the birth rates even if the number of births per married woman is low.

Likewise, crude death rates are influenced by the age of the population measured either by median age or the proportion of 65 and above. Just as the C.D.R.

must be higher in a nursing home than in a prison, death rates are bound to move up when a population grows older. Growing older is the inevitable fate of populations which have moved through the demographic transition. Graying is basically a consequence of declining fertility which produces relatively small cohorts of infants thereby raising the median age. A further decline in mortality may counterbalance declining fertility because improvements in medicine and health care produce the greatest increase in survival among the young. Demographically speaking there is no difference between saving a child's life and producing another one. However, most modernized nations including Canada have by now practically reduced infant and child mortality levels which exhaust the possibility of increased survival among the very young. Aging is further enhanced by the decline in mortality of people in their fifties and sixties. All in all the proportion of high-mortality risk people (65+) rises and other things being equal the death rate is influenced upwards. In 1969, for example, the crude death rates for Taiwan and Singapore were in the 5% range. The respective figures for Sweden and Austria were 10.4% and 13.4%. Such differences in crude death rates are not to be explained by differential health care but by the dissimilar age structures of these Asian and European populations.

Its population profile must also predispose a nation to emigration or immigration. When the European nations were in the earlier phases of the demographic transition, they sent large waves of young adults to North America. The population structure of 19th century Europe was indeed marked by large percentages of young adults not always able to find suitable employment at home. Between 1872 and 1970 France allowed some five million immigrants to enter the country. The heavy casualties of World War I in particular transformed France into an area pulling in immigrants in large numbers. The two largest senders of migrants to the U.S.A. are now Mexico and the Philippines, both characterized by exploding populations and large numbers of young adults looking for work. Canada is also getting larger amounts of Asians, Africans, and Central Americans. Jamaica alone sent 8,211 people in 1975. Again, what characterized these countries of origin was a strong push factor consisting of fast growth of the proportion of youngsters and relatively few employment opportunities.

## *Economic Age Categories*

Another way of looking at the age composition of a population is in terms of producers and dependents. It is obvious that every member of a population is a consumer or at least a potential one while not every person is a producer. The relationship between the very young and very old non-producing consumers on the one hand and the adult active population on the other has important economic implications. If relatively large proportions of the population are economically active, the maintenance and improvement of a given living standard is facilitated. Large proportions of dependants constitute a heavy burden on those who are actively employed.

It is customary to divide the dependants into two categories, i.e., those who are supposedly below working age and those too old to work. The first group is the population between age 0 and 14, the second class are those aged 65 and above. The economically active population therefore is aged 15-64. It goes without saying that not all citizens between 0 and 14 and 65 and above are non-working dependents. Some do in fact support themselves. It is equally obvious that some members of the category aged 15-64 need support. In the latter case we merely estimated the *potential* workers by looking at this age group.

In order to evaluate a nation's dependency burden we compute three ratios: the old age dependency ratio (OADR), the youth dependency ratio (YDR) and the total dependency ratio (TDR). The total dependency ratio is calculated by computing the ratio of the number of persons in the age groups 0 - 14 and over 64 years of age to the number of persons in the age group 15 - 64 multiplied by 100. Thus:

$$TDR = \frac{P_{0\text{-}14} + P_{65+}}{P_{15\text{-}64}} \times k$$

For Canada in 1971 we obtain:

$$TDR = \frac{6{,}380{,}895 + 1{,}744{,}410}{13{,}443{,}005} \times 100 = \frac{8{,}125{,}305}{13{,}443{,}005} \times 100 = 60.4$$

The YDR and the OADR are calculated in the same way. The total dependency ratio then answers the question how many unproductive dependents there are for every hundred persons of working age.

TABLE 52. Trends in Dependency Ratios, Canada 1881-1976*

| Year | Total | Youth | Old-Age |
|---|---|---|---|
| 1851 | 90.8 | 85.7 | 5.1 |
| 1861 | 83.6 | 78.0 | 5.6 |
| 1871 | 82.7 | 76.0 | 6.7 |
| 1881 | 74.9 | 67.7 | 7.2 |
| 1891 | 69.2 | 61.5 | 7.7 |
| 1901 | 65.1 | 56.8 | 8.3 |
| 1911 | 60.3 | 52.9 | 7.5 |
| 1921 | 64.4 | 56.6 | 7.9 |
| 1931 | 59.2 | 50.3 | 8.8 |
| 1941 | 52.6 | 42.4 | 10.2 |
| 1951 | 61.5 | 49.0 | 12.5 |
| 1961 | 71.2 | 58.1 | 13.1 |
| 1971 | 60.4 | 47.5 | 13.0 |
| 1976 | 52.3 | 39.1 | 13.3 |

***Source:** 1971 Census of Canada, *Profile Studies . . .*, p. 22.
1976 Census of Canada, *Population: Demographic Characteristics*, pp. 1, 2.

FIGURE 22. Dependency Ratios, Canada 1851 - 1981*

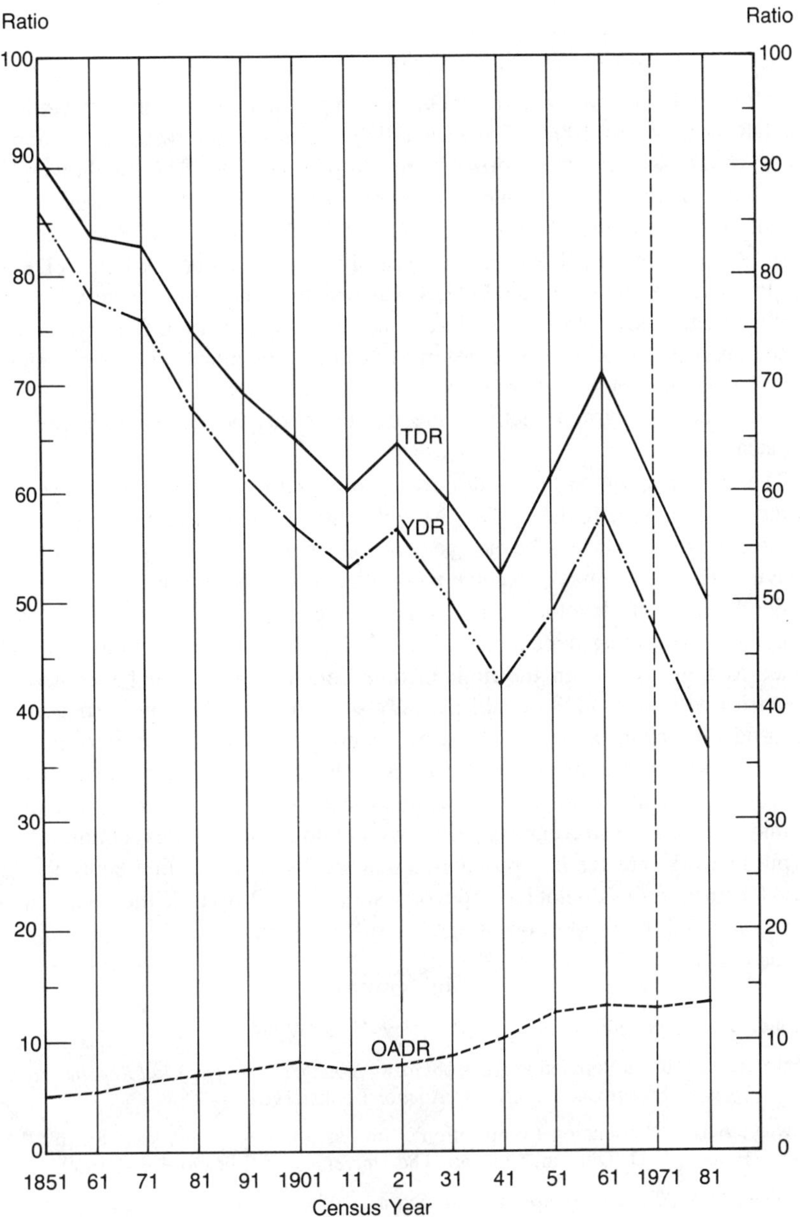


***Source:** Stone, *et al., The Population of Canada* . . ., p. 37.

A major demographic difference between the more and the less developed countries is that in the 1970s most less developed nations have substantially higher dependency ratios than the modernized industrialized countries. Table 52 and Figure 22 present the three dependency ratios for Canada between 1851 and 1976. It is shown that both the YDR and the TDR have had the tendency to decline during the period except after the two world wars which is to be explained by the post-war revivals in fertility.

Between 1851 and 1941 the YDR was approximately cut in half while the OADR increased by 100%. The TDR fell during this period because the increase in the OADR was more than offset by the drop in the YDR. The small reversal of the above mentioned trends which occurred just after World War I was due to a minor increase in fertility. Between 1941 and 1961 both the OADR and the YDR rose. As a result the TDR increased sharply as well. After 1961 the YDR fell again while the change in the OADR was insignificant. Consequently the TDR declined once more. As a general rule one can state that when fertility declines, aging takes place, while a rise in fertility causes a population to grow younger. The dependency ratios reflect these occurrences.

The preceding graph pictures the evolution of the dependency ratios in Canada.

The challenge which the more developed countries must face in the years to come is the increase in the OADR. Now that life expectancy at birth is over 70 in all modernized countries, the old age dependency burden is likely to become ever heavier. This problem will receive more attention in the following chapter. The major dilemma the developing nations are struggling with is that of a sharp rise in nonproductive young dependants. The YDR in low income nations is usually twice as high as that in the high income countries. It might be argued that countries with high YDRs could partially solve this problem by introducing or reintroducing child labor or at least by lowering the age of entry into the labor force. However, this proposition clashes with other ideals such as compulsory education, the improvement of the qualifications of the labor force and the elimination of the suffering associated with child labor. Besides, children, even if put to work, are far less productive than adults. For the time being the less developed countries do not have to worry about OADR because their populations are young and the proportion of aged is still very small.

## Bibliography

Bogue, D.J., *Principles of Demography,* New York: Wiley, 196

Coale, A.J., "How a Population Ages or Grows Younger", in: *The Vital Revolution,* Ed. by R.F. Freedman, New York: Anchor Books, 1964.

Hawley, A.H., "Population Composition", in: *The Study of Population,* Ed. by P.M. Hauser, O.D. Duncan, Chicago: The University of Chicago Press, 1959.

Momeni, D.A., *The Population of Iran,* Shiraz, 1975.

Pressat, R., *Demographic Analysis,* Chicago: Aldine-Atherton, 1972.

Sauvy, A., *La Population,* Paris: PUF, 1970.

Shryock, H.S., J.B. Siegel *et al., The Methods and Materials of Demography,* Vol. 1, Washington: U.S. Government Printing Office, 1973.

Thomlinson, R., *Population Dynamics,* New York: Random House, 1965.

Chapter 12

# *The Socioeconomic Effects of Population Change*

## A. The Economic Impact of a Rising Dependency Ratio

The previous chapter alluded to the questions associated with age structure which both more and less developed countries must face. The problem of high YDRs is at present a major obstacle to rapid economic progress in the less developed countries. The issue of ageing on the other hand is likely to become a growing topic for discussion in the more developed nations. Inevitably the process of graying will involve some drastic social, economic and political changes. The following sections will present a brief review of some of the issues at stake.

### *Youth Dependency Burden and Economic Development*

High fertility low income countries are presently burdened with a large proportion of young dependents. Sure enough, the now developed nations have faced somewhat similar problems in the earlier stages of their development. However, relatively high mortality and relatively low fertility held rates of natural increase and dependency ratios below levels now witnessed in some of the Asian, African and Latin American nations. In such countries as Canada and the United States the constant inflow of productive young workers from abroad has also helped to keep down the dependency ratio.

The following table shows the dependency ratios for selected areas.

TABLE 53. Total, Young and Old Dependency Ratios for Selected Regions, per Hundred Persons Aged 15-64, 1970*

| Area | Total | Youth | Old Age |
|---|---|---|---|
| World | 73.1 | 64.1 | 9.0 |
| MDCs | 57.4 | 42.3 | 15.1 |
| LDCs | 80.8 | 74.8 | 6.0 |
| U.S.A. | 61.3 | 45.2 | 16.1 |
| Canada ('71) | 60.4 | 47.5 | 13.0 |
| Jamaica | 108.3 | 95.8 | 12.5 |
| Iran ('72) | 95.5 | 89.4 | 6.1 |

***Sources:** World Bank, *Population Policies and Economic Development,*(Baltimore: John Hopkins University Press, 1974), p. 174.

Kayhan Research Associates, *Iran Yearbook, 1977 . . .*, pp. 38, 45.

An investigation of the relationship between C.B.R.s and T.D.R.s with the use of a scatterdiagram would show a strong positive relationship. The regression line representing the correspondence between T.D.R. and C.B.R. would be linear sloping upwards to the right as the following diagram shows.

FIGURE 23. Relation of Total Dependency Ratio and Crude Birth Rate

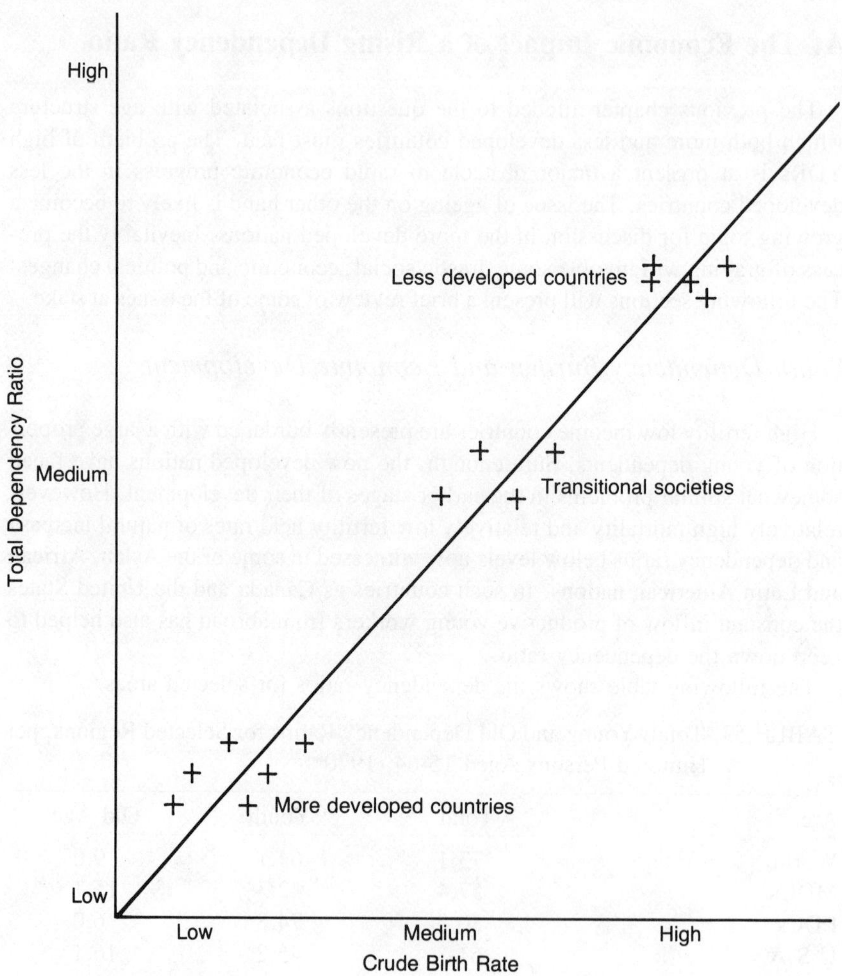

In order to understand the impact of a changing dependency ratio in developing countries fully, a distinction should be made between the transitional effect and the quasi-permanent effect of an increase in the rate of population growth. As stated earlier many developing nations introduced Western-style medicine and health technology after 1945. Mortality dropped, especially in the younger age groups and the rate of demographic increase rose resulting in a rise in the youth dependency ratio. The rather sudden increase in the proportion of unproductive dependents has two effects. During the first fifteen years after the drop in mortality and the resultant higher rate of population growth the increment in population consists almost entirely of non-productive young dependents. Although the imported health measures may save the lives of some productive workers too, no major changes can be expected to take place in the size of the labor force. Other things being equal, with a non-changing labor force total output will not grow, but that output will have to be shared among more members of the population. Forcibly, per capita output or income will be affected negatively. In other words, the per capita share of income will be smaller than before the increase of the proportion of dependents. This will tend to be true both at the micro level of the family and at the macro level of the nation as a whole. This occurrence is called the "transitional" effect.

When the transitional effect is over we find a population with a high YDR relative to a population where the proportion of young is smaller. The case of Iran is relevant here. Between the two censuses of 1956 and 1966 the population of below 15 years increased from 42.2% to 46.1%. The economically active population (population of 10 years and over) declined from 47.5% to 46.1% and this in the face of an increased female participation in the labor force.

This new situation will affect the proportion of the national income which can be saved and invested.[1] Much saving occurs in families although corporations and even government can also save. If mortality is reduced and more children survive, families will be larger than before the mortality decline. With more surviving dependant children per family the basic consumption requirements of the family increase. A larger percentage of the family income will have to be spent on food, clothing and other consumer items. This implies that a smaller proportion of the income is saved. As the economic textbooks tell us, disposable family income is either consumed or saved. Saving is a residual activity and whatever is consumed cannot be set aside for later use. Adding up all the families which are now burdened with more surviving, income-consuming dependents yields the aggregate. Other things being equal, at the macro-level of the nation, the capacity to save is reduced by the rise in the proportion of the young dependents. This is termed the "quasi-permanent" effect. Most available studies of saving patterns suggest that saving and family size at each given income level are inversely related. We must add, however, that all those studies have been carried out in developed nations. Yet, it is not unreasonable to assume that in the less

---

[1]Investment here means the building and accumulation of productive equipment which assists labor, increasing its productivity. Investment is identical to capital formation.

developed countries similar patterns prevail, although perhaps to a lesser extent because of the greater participation of children in economic activities.[2]

With regard to public saving one may add that a high dependency ratio also reduces the government's powers to tax the public or borrow from it in order to finance such infrastructural items as schools, transportation systems, power plants, irrigation projects and the like. It may actually be that the government has to subsidize basic items such as food in order to prevent extreme misery of part of the population. This is common practice in a number of low income nations.

While high dependency ratios tend to reduce per capital savings, the investment requirements are usually increased in such a situation (see next section). The relationships discussed above are summarized by the following diagram (see also subsequent section).

## B. Population Growth and Capital Investment

In developed and underdeveloped nations alike, population growth increases the capital requirements or the necessary stock of productive equipment and tools if current productivity levels are to be maintained. In order to understand the impact of population growth on capital requirements properly we must introduce here a new concept named the capital-output ratio. This notion relates the value of a nation's total capital stock in a year to the annual output which it produces jointly with labor. If for instance the constant capital-output ratio is three, that means that in a year three dollars of capital will produce one dollar of output. If the marginal or incremental c/o ratio is also three, then three dollars of extra capital will produce one dollar extra output. Numerous observers believe that in the developed nations the c/o ratio is close to four while in the developing countries it is nearer to three.

If a population grows, more houses and farm buildings have to be built. Extra schools and hospitals are needed and new infrastructure such as roads and bridges are also required. Population increments result ultimately in growth of the labor force. The additions to the labor force must also be equipped with plant, workshops, machines and tools of all kinds if current productivity levels are to be maintained.

Let us now suppose that a given population grows by one percent. If existing living standards are to be maintained the total national product should also grow by 1%. This increment in output requires an expansion of the capital stock. With

---

[2]Professor Caldwell makes the point that in a number of developing societies the net life-time flow of goods and services is from child to parent. Children perform many tasks and render many important services including the carrying of fuel and water and the transportation of goods to the market. They dust the house, look after siblings and help to process food for household consumption. In the developing world such services are the very core of real standards of living. The benefits of children outweigh their costs and high fertility is perfectly rational. See J.C. Caldwell. "Towards a Restatement of Demographic Transition Theory", *Population and Development Review,* September/December 1976, p. 321-366.

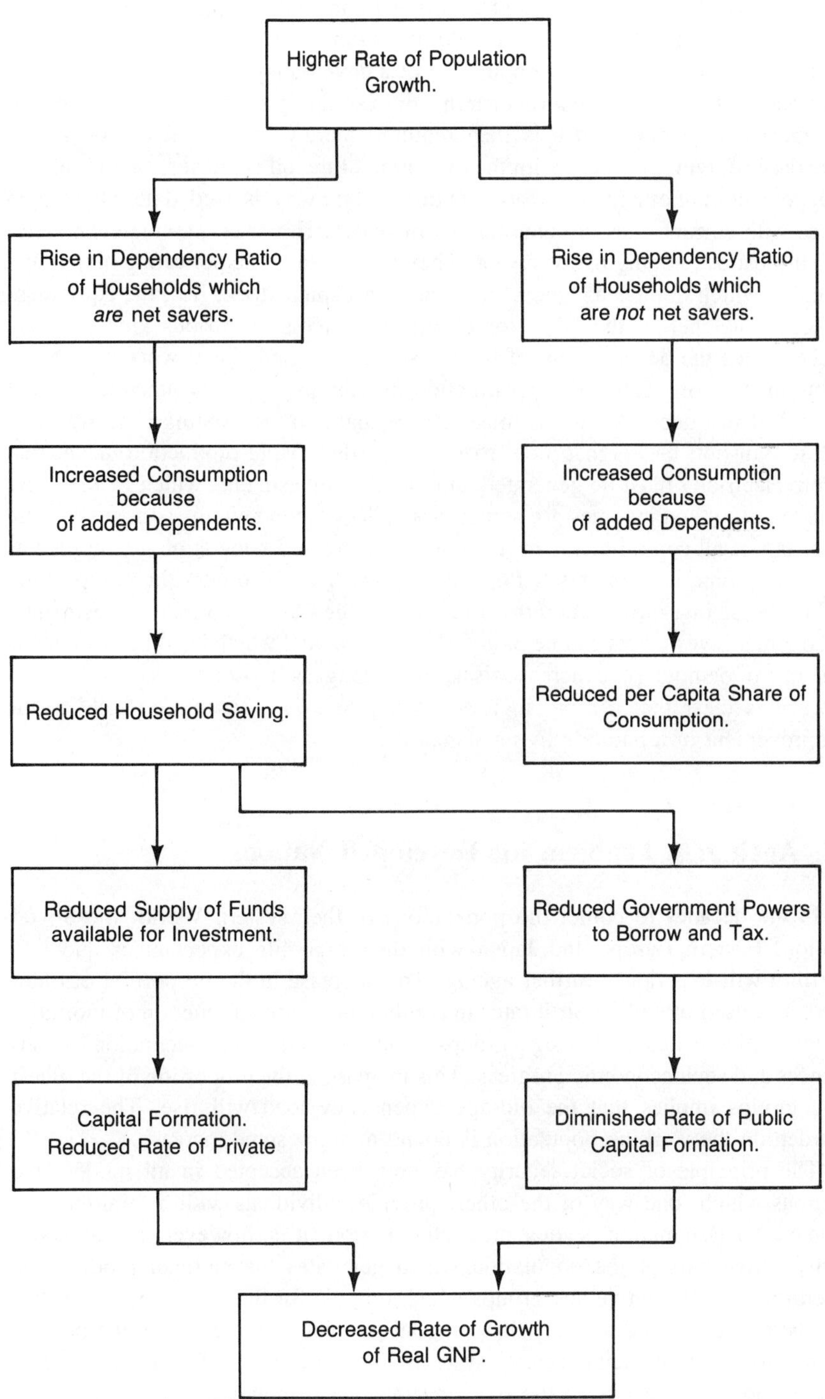
Higher Rate of Population Growth.
Rise in Dependency Ratio of Households which *are* net savers.
Rise in Dependency Ratio of Households which are *not* net savers.
Increased Consumption because of added Dependents.
Increased Consumption because of added Dependents.
Reduced Household Saving.
Reduced per Capita Share of Consumption.
Reduced Supply of Funds available for Investment.
Reduced Government Powers to Borrow and Tax.
Capital Formation. Reduced Rate of Private
Diminished Rate of Public Capital Formation.
Decreased Rate of Growth of Real GNP.

a c/o ratio of 3/1, three percent of the national income has to be saved and invested to obtain the one percent addition to the national product.

It is not uncommon that a population of a developing country grows by three percent. In 1977 the population of Iran, for example, grew by 3%. An expansion of the capital stock of 9% is then required merely to prevent a drop in the standard of living. Perhaps with the exception of the oil countries, saving nine or ten percent implies a major effort. Yet this is often what is needed merely to keep pace with current rates of demographic increases. However, staying even is not what most developing nations want. They wish to increase per capita output and income which implies a ''deepening'' of their capital stock, i.e., the equipment of each member of the labor force with more tools of various kinds. It also necessitates the development of human skills, knowledge and work capacities. This in its turn implies the construction of schools, colleges, universities and technical institutes. Additions must also be made to the existing infrastructure. More transport means that more roads are needed. More production means that more electricity must be generated and the like. Investments which increase per capita output and incomes are sometimes called ''economic investments'' while the sum of all commitments necessitated by increased population are defined as ''demographic investments''. Population growth tends to alter the composition of the total investment activity to the advantage of demographic investments. Economic investments can be thought of as a residual which becomes smaller as the rate of demographic increase rises, other things being equal of course. Therefore it is clear that a rapid increase in numbers is a serious obstacle to the improvement of a nation's living standards.

## C. Ageing: A Problem for Developed Nations

In the decades to come, the populations of the Western World, the Soviet Union, Eastern Europe and Japan with their high life expectancies and low fertility will experience further ageing. This increase in the proportion of older people caused by falling birth rates in combination with a reduction of mortality among middle and higher age groups results directly from technological advances and socioeconomic progress. This increase in the proportion of the oldest age groups implies that the old-age dependency load will rise. The relative burden on the working population is bound to show some increase.

The principle of social security has now been accepted in all modernized nations which, one way or the other, provide individuals with a minimum income after termination of their productive period. It is, however, the economically active part of the population which generates the national product and therefore it is the active age groups which provide for the old to the extent that the latter are allowed to share that national product with the rest of the population. Most current social security systems imply a transfer of real income from the economically active to the old, or from one demographic group to a very distinct alternate group. In a number of nations the pay-as-you-go system has been used to produce this transfer of income from the working population to the aged.[3] The system has worked so far because the number of contributors has been large relative to the number of old-age dependents. If because of a change in the age structure the real burden on the active population increases, the modernized nations will face a new problem requiring some fresh thinking.

## *Solutions to the Problem of Ageing*

It would seem that if the proportion of retired people increases while that of the providers does not, the existing redistribution system cannot be maintained. Either the economically active must raise their contribution or the pension benefits to the aged must be lowered. The standard of living of one of the two groups must suffer unless of course the production per worker is raised. An alternative solution lies in the expansion of the quantum of workers.

An increase in production per worker can be achieved in two ways. First, it is possible to increase the number of working hours per day. This solution is commonly employed in wartime circumstances when production must be increased at all costs. In peacetime, however, most people would agree that this solution is politically not acceptable and probably not even necessary. The public should be informed, however, that ageing of the population is hardly compatible with a regular decrease of the number of hours worked per week. Second, an increase in productivity is an ideal solution for this problem (as for many others). An increase in the amount produced per man-hour usually results from technical and organizational advances, qualitative improvements of the labor force in terms of individual health and skills and from an increase in the capital/labor ratio (the amount of productive equipment per man). As will be emphasized again in the following section, the decline in fertility does facilitate the accumulation of human and physical capital as the need for demographic investments lessens.

## *Expansion of the Labor Force*

How can an increase in the labor force be brought about? The first way to do this almost instantaneously would be by means of immigration. As most immigrants are young and active, an enlargement of the immigration flow would make the old age dependency ratio drop. A tempting solution indeed, but immigration generates other problems such as an increase in population density, a heavier burden on the existing stock of exhaustible resources and the environment in general and so on.

A higher participation rate of the women in the labor force is a second solu-

---

[3]Pay-as-you go means that the current benefits of the retired are financed by a flat rate payroll tax levied on the working population. The Canadian pension plan is financed in this manner.

tion. Although everybody between 15 and 64 is a potential worker not all members of that age group do in fact participate in career activities outside the home. The participation rate of women has in fact improved over the last decades but the available reservoir can still be tapped more intensively. Improved education and training now permit unmarried and married women to participate more fully in the economic life of the country. It increases the nation's output and helps the family to earn additional income. If young mothers devote several years to the rearing of their children as long as these are young, while rejoining the labor force when their maternal responsibilities diminish, no harm to the children's health and care occurs. The only danger is that increased participation in the labor force will reduce fertility even further in the developed countries, but it seems that we will have to live with this problem as with so many others.

A third and last means to increase the number of workers consists simply of prolonging the period of full occupational activity. If everybody continued to work until age 70, the annual output would be increased by about 16%. Although a large number of uninformed people would consider the lengthening of the active period as a regressive measure, it might equally well be asserted that the extension of the active period of life is equivalent to an improvement. For many people an abrupt break with customary activities and the sudden realization of social uselessness is disastrous.

The concept of retirement at 65 is something of more than forty years' standing. To take the example of the United States, life expectancy at birth for both sexes taken together was 59.7 years in 1930. Forty years later it had risen by at least ten years and stood at 70.9 years. In the 1930-32 period Canada's life expectancy at birth leveled at 61 years (again for both sexes taken together). Forty years later it had risen to 72.9 years (figure for 1971). Again it had advanced by more than ten years. And what had happend to the mandatory retirement age? — nothing! Life expectancy has been going up constantly and health conditions have continuously improved. A sixty-year-old man or woman today may be in as good shape as the fifty-year-old only a few decades ago. The rising length of life implies better chances of maintaining physical and mental health as well as greater fitness and vigor lasting until an advanced age. Besides, at present the physical demands on the labor force which most jobs make are rather limited. Under these circumstances there is no reason to assume that all members of the labor force should, or even would wish to retire at 65.

Another important change over the past is the prolongation of the period of instruction. With the increase of life expectancy at birth the learning period has been lengthening too. In premodern societies with most people living on household farms, economic activity starts early. Children help on the farm of their parents or work for others when they are still quite young. This changes in the transitional society which is characterized by rapid transformations in the way of life. Education becomes compulsory, child labor is abolished and the entry into the labor force occurs at a later age. This trend builds up in the modernized society. The period of instruction and training becomes ever longer and consequently the entry into a fully active life occurs consequently later. One could argue that this prolonged educational period, which after all required a considerable investment, should be compensated by a longer active period. Government officials, trade union czars and corporate bureaucrats have accumulated a tremendous body of law, policy and practice keyed to retirement at 65 without giving the employee an option. Inflexible as those functionaries often tend to be, the main obstacle to change is likely to be a man-made one.

At present the pensionable age is perhaps too rigidly defined and a mandatory retirement age of 65 will probably make even less sense in the future. The question which arises is how the situation can be improved upon.

Common sense would suggest two solutions. Now that life expectancy at birth is over seventy in all modernized nations (and will probably keep rising) the retirement age could simply be raised to 68 or 70. A second idea would consist of a phased-in retirement scheme. Instead of forcing people out of their jobs at 65, 68 or whatever age, a more gradual transition to non-activity could be planned for. The employee's workload would then be progressively lightened as his working forces decline. Many peasants, artisans and other independent workers slowly decrease their activity as their potential drops. Why could such a solution not be tried for the average employee? Allowing the worker to retire gradually with his workload and hours reduced over a period of years would probably amount to a wiser management of our human capital rather than continuing the existent system. The administration of such a plan might raise some difficulties. People who would work part-time would have to receive a partial payment of their pension to compensate for the loss in earnings resulting from their lighter workload. However, once society is won over to such a plan, its administration will probably turn out to be perfectly feasible.

## D. Some Implications of Zero Population Growth

If the present fertility decline continues in developed countries such as Canada, the rate of natural increase will keep dropping. A zero rate of population growth will become inevitable and the days of the numerophiliacs will be over. It would seem now that in Canada this will not happen until after the year 2000. The stationary population which is likely to emerge in the future will be characterized by low mortality and fertility levels, the latter being voluntarily kept low.[4] The birth rate will probably be in the neighborhood of 13% while the death

[4]From a strictly theoretical point of view we can distinguish between a stable and a stationary population. Assuming in- and out-migration to be zero, a stable population is a population which has experienced a fixed schedule of age-specific mortality and fertility rates over a long period of time. As a result the age composition has assumed a fixed distribution with all age groups maintaining the same relative size. If the stable population increases or decreases, all age groups change at the same percentage rate. The stationary or life table population is a stable population in which the deaths are exactly balanced by the number of births, hence the rate of increase is zero. The total size of the population as well as the number living in each age group never changes. In this discussion, however, we use the concept of stationary population in a rather loose sense. Here it simply means the kind of zero-growth population which is likely to emerge in such countries as Canada after the year 2000.

rate will have risen to a level just about matching it. Because of the increasing proportion of older, high-mortality risk people, mortality is bound to increase in the future even if health conditions continue to improve. In the stationary population which may emerge in Canada after the year 2000, life expectancy at birth for both sexes taken together may reach the level of some 77 years. The median age will probably be around 37 years. Some 17% of the population may be older than 65 while about 20% will be younger than 15. This leaves some 63% of the population as potential labor participants. In other words the age pyramid will have become almost rectangular with almost equal numbers in each age group until age 70. The advent of a stationary population entails advantages and disadvantages. The following sections will briefly survey some of them.

## *Advantages and Disadvantages of a Stationary Population*

A first benefit of the stationary population will be the relatively large fraction of the population which will be of working age. As fertility declines the youth dependency ratio drops too. In the stationary population to come, about 60% of the population is potentially able to work. Between the present period and the advent of the stationary population the young age dependency ratio will keep dropping. The old age dependency ratio, however, will rise but at a relatively low rate. This means amongst other things that *before* we reach the stationary state a period of exceptionally favorable circumstances will prevail. But even under stationary conditions the proportion of potential workers is satisfactory. At the same time, with low fertility prevailing, mothers are less tied to the home and will therefore enjoy greater opportunities to pursue professional interests. Educational facilities and the possibility of taking refresher courses should be at least as good as, and probably better than, at present. Hence, mothers whose skills have become a little rusty while rearing their children should still be employable again. As a result the ratio of employed labor to the population of working age has every chance to be very favorable. Therefore, the conditions for a satisfactory per capita output definitely exist from our point of view. It may of course be possible that man-made obstacles will occur. As stated before the trade unions may, for example, successfully bargain for the debarring of the older workers from the labor force, shorter work weeks and other exclusion devices. From the purely demographic viewpoint, however, there is no reason to fear that the number of potential labor force participants will be too small in a stationary state, especially if we prolong the economically active period by a few years.

A second benefit of the stationary population will be that with the low young age dependency ratio the possibilities for family saving will improve. Therefore, the capital formation potential of the low fertility, stationary population will be high.

Thirdly, the demographic investments in a stationary population are zero. All available investible funds can be used for economic investments, which increase the capital/labor ratio in the private sector and the per capital amount of public amenities. Other things being equal, the potential per capita growth of output should be higher in a stationary than in a growing population. Other things, of course, *may not* be equal. It is also possible that part of the increase in productivity will be consumed in the form of leisure.

A fourth advantage of zero population growth will be that a whole set of problems related to population expansion will cease to get worse.[5] To cite one example, the rate of increase in consumption of depletable raw materials will tend to drop. The pressure on the environment will tend not to worsen. Certain forms of political turbulence due to the existence of a large proportion of young adults in the population will cease to occur. Yet it must be admitted that a stationary population also has its problems.

A first disadvantage of the stationary population is that vertical mobility is likely to slow down. A growing population definitely induces promotion and upward mobility provided it is accompanied by a flourishing economy. Suppose, for instance, that there are 10,000 highly desirable positions in a country and that it takes about thirty years to make it to the top in an average organization or corporation. If the population grows at 2.3% per year and doubles in 30 years, some 20,000 desirable positions could exist by the time the individual and his cohort reach the top. All positions will have doubled but not the cohort which would have accumulated sufficient experience to occupy such posts. Looking at it from the point of view of one organization or corporation, the slowing down of the rate of expansion due to demographic stabilization reduces the number of new openings created at the executive level. Older people will, by right of seniority, occupy the preferred jobs. Death no longer creates many openings so the very large majority of older persons will stay in those superior positions until they retire. This relatively unchanging job structure associated with the stationary state reduces access to executive positions. This may also negatively affect work incentives. It could even sharpen intergenerational conflict. But the problem is not entirely without solution. One way to soften the whole problem would consist of weakening the relationship between age on the one hand and reward and position on the other. A large number of current income differentials are determined by convention rather than performance. It might be advisable to decrease inequality in the earnings structure up to the point that work incentives would no longer be adversely affected. It may also be necessary to reorganize public and private managerial hierarchies in such a manner that they will contain permanently a sufficient proportion of people below 40 and 50, certainly not an impossible piece of organization innovation. To some extent the problem may take care of itself. Whatever is scarce has value and if the younger, more adaptable and dynamic people are in short supply, some organizations and corporations may be eager to hire them at attractive conditions. This will make the

---

[5]For more detailed account of such problems see: J. Overbeek, *The Population Challenge*, Westport: Greenwood Press, 1976.

young more receptive to migration from firm to firm. Those companies and organizations which lose their younger administrators and employees because of their inflexibility will then be obliged to adjust.

A second problem associated with a stationary population is that of interoccupational balance. When a population grows, the labor force grows as well. The number of annual entrants exceeds the outgoers when each cohort is followed by a larger one. This tends to make the economy flexible and adaptable. It is the young entrants who tend to orient themselves towards the new industries and occupations. Thus the new trades and lines of work can always secure an adequate supply of workers. In a stationary population the quantity of annual entrants in the labor force will approximately equal the number of withdrawals. The cohorts of younger people seeking jobs will no longer be as important, relatively speaking, as in the expanding society. This reduced primary mobile labor reserve will make it more difficult for the growing trades and occupations to find an adequate supply of manpower. Nonetheless, transfers of labor remain necessary in a technologically dynamic society. The maintenance of an optimum interoccupational balance will then depend upon those who are migration prone and those who leave the declining industries. Carefully selected foreign immigration may be of some help in such circumstances. Increased participation of women in the labor force may also provide some relief. Information about expanding branches of activity should be made more readily available. More refresher and retraining courses will probably become necessary and, last but not least, the trade unions should not be allowed to interfere with inter-industry mobility.

A final problem related to a stationary population is that the demand for certain items will cease to grow while the demand for some other goods and services will actually decline. No doubt, with fertility dropping to replacement levels the demand for baby products and youth related items is bound to shrink. The demand for soft drinks, blue jeans and certain kinds of records which symbolized the youth market of the 1950s and 1960s will decline. A predominantly middle-aged society, however, will witness an expanding demand for other products entailing anything from color T.V. sets to prune juice. The fact remains that Canadian and other Western businessmen will have to adjust to the fact that markets will no longer automatically expand on account of population increase. The building industry and the educational sector are especially likely to suffer. The slump in primary education has started already. Since the nineteenth century, continued population growth has always underpinned our socioeconomic expectations. The type of society associated with a stationary population will require a different ideology, that of stability rather than growth. Since throughout most of mankind's history population grew very slowly or not at all, we really do not have to adjust to an entirely new situation. We must rather abandon recently acquired habits.

## Bibliography

Daric, J., *Vieillissement de la Population et Prolongation de la Vie Active,* Paris: PUF, 1948.

Kuznets, S., *Population, Capital and Growth,* New York: Norton, 1973.

Myrdal, G., *Population, A Problem for Democracy,* Cambridge: Harvard University Press, 1940.

Morss, E.R., R.H. Reed, eds. *Economic Aspects of Population Change,* Vol. II of U.S. Commission on Population Growth and the American Future Research Reports, Washington, D.C.: Government Printing Office, 1972.

Olson, M., H.H. Landsberg eds., *The No-Growth Society,* New York: Norton, 1973.

Spengler, J.J., *Declining Population Growth Revisited,* Chapel Hill: Carolina Population Center, 1971.

Spengler, J.J., *Zero Population Growth: Implications,* Chapel Hill: Carolina Population Center, 1975.

Steschenko, V.S., V.P. Pishunov, ''Evaluating Population Ageing'', *International Social Science Journal,* Vol. XVI, No. 2, 1974.

# Chapter 13

# *Population Policy*

## A. Definition and Problems

The whole concept of population policy specifically designed to modify demographic behavior is of fairly recent origin. It is true, however, that in the distant past some attempts have been made to increase fertility levels among specific groups of people. The oldest known endeavors in this direction were the *Lex Julia* (18 B.C.) and *Lex Poppae* (9 A.D.) enacted during the Roman Empire.

In the sixteenth and seventeenth centuries a number of European nations tried again to raise their population sizes by such measures as encouragement of immigration and fiscal privileges for large families. It was, however, in the twentieth century that some fascist countries ventured upon more comprehensive population policies purposefully directed at raising fertility levels. In the 1930s such fascist nations as Germany, Italy and Japan had already gone through the earlier stages of the demographic transition. Especially in Germany and Italy, fertility had fallen to relatively low levels which clashed with these nations' needs for large reserves of manpower required for their plans of world domination.

During the 1960s and 1970s it became increasingly clear that fertility levels in the developing countries, if allowed to prevail for a sufficiently long period, would seriously mortgage the quality of life of present and future generations. Obviously more had to be done to bring existing fertility levels in line with rapidly declining mortality. However, in the mid-1970s most population policies, in so far as they existed at all, still lacked clear goals and strong convictions.

Population policy is sometimes differentiated from population control. Population policy itself has been defined as a set of measures specifically designed to change demographic behavior or reach specific demographic goals. Professor F. Lorimer has characterized such policy as the will and commitment to deal realistically and effectively with the demographic variable in all national planning. Population control is a narrower concept and has as its sole objective restraining the population growth. It involves not only the regulation of fertility but also the control of migration.

A population policy can have a number of goals such as the reduction of mortality. But, at the moment, the most pressing problem in the developing nations is excessively high fertility. It is clear that most propositions dealing with curbing such fertility will only have a delayed impact at the macro-level. The effects of prevented births on the size of the cohorts entering primary school are only felt after 5 or 6 years. Present changes in the number of entrants in the labor force are never related to current demographic events but rather to what happened 15 or 20 years earlier. But at the micro-level of the family or household the beneficial effects of a drop in fertility will be immediate. Prevented births imply a smaller family size, improved health of the mother, a lower dependency burden and the possibility of increased savings.

## B. Population Policy in the Less Developed Countries

### *The Ethics of Population policy*

If population policy implies the modification of demographic behavior, the question may be raised whether such steps can be justified on ethical grounds. If we lived in an ideal world in which the reproductive decisions made by couples would produce an aggregate number which happily coincided with an optimum population maximizing the community's welfare broadly defined, no population policy would be needed.

Unfortunately we do not live in such a blissful universe. Usually couples do have the freedom to decide about their family size. Such decisions, however, are made without reference to the rights and interests of other people. Yet the reproductive choices of couples *do* affect the freedom and well-being of the remainder of the population. The quality of life in a society for an individual, his educational and employment opportunities, the rewards he will obtain for his work, the political stability he will enjoy, the amount of recreational space at his disposal, just to mention a few examples, are largely determined by demographic processes which in turn reflect individual reproductive decisions made at some point of time in the past.

The concept implicit in this discussion is that of "external diseconomies" or "negative externalities". They occur when an action undertaken by one individual results in uncompensated costs to others. A well-known example of such external diseconomies occurs in the case of pollution. Pollution often occurs because a producer is allowed to shift part of his costs of production to others. If, for instance, a factory releases untreated smoke into the air, surrounding houses have to be painted more often, while the inhabitants of the area may also be forced to have their clothes cleaned more frequently. In other words, the factory displaces part of its production costs onto others. From a societal point of view the social costs of production exceed the private costs. Because the individual producer can shift part of his production costs to others, he is likely to produce a greater volume of output than he would have if he had been held responsible for all the costs of his actions including those of treating the smoke.

Obviously couples can also transfer part of the costs of reproduciton to others since they are not held responsible for all the societal implications and expenses of their reproductive decisions. The concept of diseconomies is central to the justification of government intervention. Returning to the example of pollution, the environment will become clearner only if the legal authorities force the manufacturers to "internalize" the "externalities". In the same sense individual reproductive decisions must not be allowed to handicap the well-being of present and future generations. If somehow couples were forced to bear a greater share of the full costs of reproduction, they would undertake such reproductive actions less often.

## *Family Planning*

A first step towards nationwide fertility reducing consists of setting up an effective family planning program. Nothing else can be attempted unless governments provide full access to the modern means of fertility control. Family planning as an ideology does not attempt to modify the motivations of couples. It merely wants them to have the desired number of children. In other words, it aims at eliminating unwanted births. This "desired" number of children, however can be disastrously high and is often close to four and above in developing nations. In Iran the wanted number of children is about 5 (1977 figure). Yet as a first step family planning is probably still the best. By pointing to the beneficial effects it has on the health and welfare of mothers and children, its political acceptability is greatly enhanced. Supplying the full range of fertility control services implies basically three things.

(1) Providing the broadest possible selection of available contraceptive techniques including pills, I.U.D.s and condoms. Abortion and sterilization services should also be made available. Whether legal or not, abortion is one of the most ancient and widely practised means of birth limitation. The annual number of abortions in the world has been estimated at about 40 million. In such nations where it is still regarded as illegal the activity often becomes a clandestine operation performed by unqualified persons. Such a situation results in the mass maiming and killing of women. If performed under good medical conditions, preferably during the first three months of pregnancy, the operation is less dangerous to women than normal parturition. Male and female sterilizations (vasectomies and tubal ligations) are nowadays safe methods requiring only a minor surgical intervention with no known side effects.

(2) The second prerequisite of a comprehensive family planning program would consist of the establishment of an adequate delivery system by which parents and couples can obtain the services they need. Informational assistance must also be furnished. We can think here of the setting up of family planning clinics (mobile or not), sterilization centers, the provision of educational materials such as booklets, the use of paramedical workers in the villages in order to provide contraceptives as well as information, etc. Whenever possible the existing commercial distribution network (consisting of pharmacies, drug stores and even the small general store in the village) should be used to supplement what-

ever facilities the government chooses to provide. Commercial outlets can even be used if the government decides to subsidize contraception. As an example, contraceptives can be provided free to the private commercial sector which then could sell them at an agreed upon price covering the dealers' costs while including a reasonable profit. This might be a cheaper solution than selling these devices via special government operated establishments.

(3) The last need of a successful family planning program would lie in the active support for accelerated research for improved, more effective and cheaper contraceptives. If birth control technology improves, the psychic and monetary costs of contraception fall. Therefore, further advances in birth control techniques will facilitate the realization of small family size norms.

The per capita costs of providing the full range of family planning services in a developing country have been estimated at about one dollar per year per head of the population. Costs per user are higher but only a fraction of the population is at risk — hence it evens out at a dollar per capita in an average developing nation (United Nations Fund for Population Activities estimate). Excluding mainland China, the costs of universal provision of family planning services would be around two billion dollars per annum. If half of this sum could be provided by the developing countries themselves and the remaining fifty per cent by the international community, only one billion dollars would be needed in the form of international aid. This is a relatively modest sum compared to the annual $200 billion armaments bill which the world now offers itself each year. At the moment only about $250 million is annually devoted to family planning.

## *The Need For An Antinatalist Institutional Framework*

Once the family planning benefits are provided we must create an environment conducive to the use of the available services. This implies a number of institutional reforms designed to alter people's demographic behavior.

## *Understanding Our Pronatalist Past*

A first step towards the creation of a new low-fertility environment consists in the recognition of the pronatalist constraints in which we have lived until recently. In the past death rates were high sometimes leveling temporarily above the birth rates. Life expectancy at birth was short. Each society had to mobilize the reproductive potentialities of its members to the full to match the prevailing high mortality. Those societies which have not been able to ensure high levels of reproduction have disappeared and cannot even be studied. Practically all communities which have survived so far have done so because over the last thousands of years they have evolved a complex system of values, customs and policies pressuring people into marriage, child-bearing, caring for and raising of children. The custom of early marriage, for example, lengthens the period of exposure to pregnancy of the females. The habit of arranged marriages, still so customary in the third world, ensured that everybody did in fact get married quickly. The extended family relieved parents of some of the cost of raising the children. The linking of sexual roles and parental functions again coaxed almost everybody into marriage because parenthood has been, and still is, in many countries implicit in the very definition of feminity and masculinity. The fact that no career alternatives to those of marriage, homemaking and childrearing were open to women again encouraged universal and early marriage. Such values, customs and social pressures do not fail to be internalized by young individuals who are practically brainwashed into their acceptance from birth onwards. Although it is the individuals themselves who make choices with regard to mating and reproduction, such choices are free and voluntary in a limited sense only. Now that mortality is low and declining, the whole pronatalist framework which has allowed us to survive so far has suddenly become useless, nay burdensome and offensive, to the attainment of the good society. A lifting or deassembling of the existing reproductive coercions and inventives must rank high in any antinatalist population policy if it is to be successful.

## *Manipulation of Taste*

A large part of the present world population still lives with pronatalist values and norms which are premodern in the sense that they reflect the high death rates of the past. If modifications in demographic behavior are to be brought about, substantial changes in attitudes toward marriage and childbearing are essential. The media will have to pay an essential role in the process. Countries such as Hongkong, Taiwan and Singapore have already successfully experimented with the media. Films, the transistor radio, T.V. posters, leaflets, exhibits, newspapers and the like can all be used to dramatize the realities and implications of exponential population growth, to provide information with regard to contraceptive practices, and to disseminate the small-family norm. Population related information should also be incorporated in the school curricula and textbooks. If political and religious leaders, national celebrities and prominent persons in general were to endorse the new population ethic in their public addresses the effect on public thinking and attitudes could be considerable. A prime minister announcing his vasectomy in public could work wonders. If the preferences of couples can be changed successfully, parents would produce *and* prefer smaller families. Conformity between fertility performance and fertility preference would be maintained and the diseconomies which provoked the manipulation of taste in the first place would disappear.

## *Raising the Minimum Age of Marriage*

Early marriage is a typical arrangement biased toward encouraging fertility. As in many Asian and African countries marriages are still often contracted when the marriage partners are young. Raising the age of marriage for girls to at least 18 years and that of males to 20 would help significantly to dampen fertility. Such measures shorten the period during which females are exposed to pregnancy and give them more time for training and education which in themselves are known to be inversely associated with fertility. In countries such as Iran, Pakistan and India it is often the parents who decide upon the marriage partner for the girl and not the young lady herself. A simple but effective legislative change in this context would consist of conferring the legal right to all females of all ages to refuse to marry a partner chosen for her by her parents or other family members.

## *Prohibition of Child Labor and Compulsory Education*

Assuming that the costs and benefits of the additional child have some effect on fertility decisions, the number of desired children would obviously drop with any increase in the costs of the added child and/or a decline in their benefits. When the children have to be sent to school and cannot be hired out for gainful employment until say their early adolescence, their importance as income earners declines. They contribute less to the family income either in real terms or with money earned elsewhere, yet they have to be provided with food, clothes, shelter and education equipment. Such a shift in costs and benefits may induce parents to want fewer children.

## *The Role of Women*

The classical role assigned to girls and women has been that of marriage and parenthood. With no genuine alternatives existing, females had every inducement to get married and do so early. If the existing pronatalist machinery is to be dismantled all the laws, customs and regulations involving sex discrimination must be stricken from the books. The legal status of women has to be improved. Appropriate property laws, inheritance and divorce laws, regulations giving women the right to vote and to share in the decision-making process are essential elements here. Schools and institutes of vocational training should be opened to girls whose chances of admission should be made equal to those of men. There are still too many nations where the women's chances for education and training do not match the opportunities for the men. Schools and public information programs should explain to girls that being the mother of a large and poor family is neither beneficial to her nor to the nation and that alternatives exist. All available data indicate an inverse relationship between education and fertility and there is no doubt about the fact that participation in the labor force also diminishes the woman's desire for children. One obvious reason is the prevalence of indirect or opportunity costs (foregone social activities, relinquished salary, etc.) associated with the additional child. Child rearing is time and money consuming. The extra child may tie a women to the home for at least four more years during which period she must abandon her gainful employment and chances for promotion. The higher the level of education the larger the salary the woman is likely to earn, hence the more substantial the opportunity cost of the added child.

As soon as we have set up an antinatalist institutional framework we are ready for the next step: the adoption of a scheme of financial incentives and disincentives designed to encourage parents to have small families while dissuading them from being prolific.

## *Incentives and Disincentives*

We may define incentives and disincentives as conditions or arrangements which induce certain types of behavior at the expense of others. Suppose we want families not to exceed a target number of say two children. We can then reward those parents who comply with the norm and penalize those who do not conform. The incentives may consist of monetary objects such as cash, tax rebates, bonds and bonuses or goods and services, of which food, housing priorities and medical services are prime examples. Incentives and disincentives, promising as their application may be, do have their problems too. Some are politically sensitive, others are difficult to implement and all of them require the allocation of scarce administrative talents and financial resources. Surely, government should measure the sacrifice of implementing them against the much greater costs of not doing so. In spite of their disadvantages the benefit-cost ratio of incentive programs is likely to be high. A common argument against the use of disincentives is that they may punish the children as well as the parents. Yet the fact is that the absence of disincentives may result in a larger number of higher order births per family which often penalizes the lower order children and may even increase their mortality chances.

## *Positive Incentives*

At the moment a large number of propositions are in existence of which we will discuss here only a few. A first proposal consists of an annual bonus to be given to the man or women who postpones marriage by another year. If, for instance, the legal minimum age of marriage for women has been fixed at 18, she would be entitled to a first disbursement on her 19th birthday if at that moment she were still a maiden. The main idea, of course, is to reduce the reproductive period of the woman. The extra years of celibacy can be used for additional training or education while the bonus will help to defray its costs. A problem with this proposition is that rewards will be given to females whose behavior will not be different in the absence of such a bonus plan. This actually is a main problem with all bonus schemes.

A second suggestion consists of awarding an allowance to married couples for each year of non-pregnancy. The premium could be granted at the end of each year or after a two or five-year period. It is also possible to deposit the payments in a blocked savings account to be released at the end of the reproductive period of the woman. It is likely, however, that the majority of people to be reached would prefer immediate or annual disbursements. A major difficulty inherent in this type of plan lies in its administration. Administrative know-how is a scarce commodity in all developing nations.

A third idea consists of rewards being given to individuals who agree to be sterilized, with vasectomy being the obvious target. The compensation can be given in cash or kind. An example of the latter would be a transistor radio or a bag of rice. Such schemes can also be tried at the level of the community. A village can be offered a water pump, a well, or a cash award if a given percentage of the qualified men accepts a vasectomy. This proposition would result in group pressure but since not every eligible man in the village would have to accept sterilization, the resulting allocation could perhaps minimize the amount of individual sacrifice to be made.

If the plan is tried on an individual basis it is possible to pay a flat rate or a graduated one for every sterilization. In a vasectomy project one could, for example, deny sterilization to men not having at least two children. Fathers of two descendants would then get the highest compensation were they to accept the operation. Fathers of three would get a somewhat smaller reward and so on. Such a plan would encourage those most likely to have many more children to accept permanent sterility.

Existing surveys show that parents often want numerous children — especially sons — because they are a guaranteed source of material assistance and help in old age. Parents of larger families are thus often better off in old age than heads of smaller households. A plan which would neutralize this particular advantage of having many descendants would consist of making a special pension payment to those couples willing to limit their offspring. If support were given to those couples who restrict their families to say two or three children and not to the others, all parents would be placed on equal footing. The parents of the larger families could rely on their sons; parents of smaller families would qualify for (social security) support. In a variant of this plan all people having reached a certain age would be eligible for support. However, the parents of small families would qualify for higher benefits than the more prolific couples.

There have also been many suggestions to reward parents at the time of retirement or at the end of the childbearing period if they have not exceeded a target (n) number of children. Economist Ronald Ridker has proposed giving a bond to all couples who agree to limit the number of children to two or three. The bond would mature at the end of the woman's reproductive period. If the couple has more than *n* children the bond becomes void automatically. The administration of the scheme would not tie up too many resources. Only two contacts with the executive authorities are needed. First when the married couple accepts the bond which can be fingerprinted on that occasion. The second contact would occur at the end of the childbearing period. A specific advantage of such deferred payment schemes is that they reach the parents and avoid harm to children. Such plans also leave the parents free to decide upon their own contraceptive method. However, there is some evidence that recipients prefer immediate disbursements to future compensation even if the bonds are more valuable.

## *Disincentives*

Disincentives penalize parents of large families. Let us suppose that a nation officially proclaims that it considers a family consisting of more than *n* children socially undersirable. It may then set up a number of social and financial arrangements aiming at dissuading couples to exceed the *n*th child. An advantage of negative incentives is that they cost little to the taxpayer. Some may actually add to tax revenues. But, they will obviously be a great deal less popular than the positive ones.

It has been argued that disincentives might penalize the poor rather than the more prosperous sections of society because low-income groups are usually the least quick to restrict their progeny. There is also the danger of punishing innocent children rather than the parents. Such dilemmas are real but governments must weigh such disadvantages against the immeasurably greater burdens in store for societies which fail to arrest population growth in time. A first disincentive would be a tax on higher order children. We could imagine a policy of not taxing the first two or three children. However, for each additional descendant parents would be obliged to pay a given percentage tax on their combined adjusted gross income. The tax would be effective until the age of retirement. The tax, justified as it might be, does run the risk of meeting to much political opposition to be acceptable. In the developing countries, moreover, the low-income groups subject to paying such charges are likely to be too poor anyway to bear the expense. Besides, the costs of collecting such dues may simply be too high.

Housing opportunities and school admission priorities can be redesigned to favor small families. In Singapore families with only two children enjoy priority over larger families when it comes to qualifying for public housing. If educational facilities are limited, the children of small families could be given priority, or the first two children of any family, large or small. The latter proposal seems fairer and could still generate some effect.

Income tax laws can be reframed as to limit the number of personal exemptions allowable for children to only the first two descendants. Maternity leaves and benefits could be allotted only for the lower order children. In Singapore, where 80% of all births take place in government-run hospitals, delivery fees rise steeply after the second child. However, such fees are waived if one of the two parents accepts sterilization after the birth of the last child. If we set our minds to it we could certainly design many more disincentives, but such measures will have to be adapted to different environments. What may succeed in one country may fail in another.

### *Coercion*

If governments fail to act in time (as they do), coercive methods will ultimately become unavoidable. Not many examples exist as yet, but the future is likely to see direct limitations on family size as well as sanctions to enforce them. One proposition likely to be adopted in the future is obligatory sterilization after the *n*th child. It goes without saying that incentive systems are preferable and much easier to live with than coercive methods. However, many governments have already waited too long to be able to solve their population problems by relying only on the milder propositions outlined in earlier sections. Presently most existing population control programs show little commitment and conviction and even less imagination.

## C. Population Policy and the Developed Countries

In the more developed nations fertility seems to move ever closer to replacement levels. As a result much of the need to manipulate aggregate birth rates has evaporated. At present it may be enough to agree that there is no solid case for encouraging further population growth or fertility above replacement levels. Such a consent would merely call for "neutral" social policies, that is to say, policies without a specific pronatalist bias.

Many nations in the West including such densely population countries as Belgium, the Netherlands and England have set up social policies characterized by tacit pronatalist leanings. On top of such procedures the same nations have permitted the entry of larger numbers of foreign workers in order to "cure" alleged labor shortages. The latter question will be discussed in greater detail in a subsequent section.

Often enough such social arrangements as the collective financing of education were not intended to encourage natality *per se*.

Yet, *de facto*, they did put a premium on having children as existing restraints on childbearing were further removed. What should perhaps receive consideration is the rescinding of the pronatalist machinery incorporated in existing social legislations.

A first idea consists of the elimination of the requirement for wives and husbands to file tax returns jointly. This obligation does in certain countries result in a situation whereby the wife's contribution to the family income is assumed to begin where that of the husband ends. Under the graduated income tax applying to the joint return, the wife's earnings are then subject to a higher marginal tax rate than the husband's. In Canada the incomes of wives and husbands in a two-earner family are now taxed separately. The ideal situation consists of taxing wives, husbands and single persons at identical rates, thus putting an end to the discrimination against wives' earnings.

Another idea would consist in holding the parents financially responsible for the education of their children. If parents were obliged to account for the costs of schooling and education, they would become better off by having smaller rather than larger families. To the extent that the state meets the costs of education parents cannot gain by reducing their fertility in this respect. If under the current system parents choose to increase the quality of their children's educations by sending them to private schools, they are actually financially penalized. First, they must settle the private school fees; second, they are forced to pay taxes in order to finance the state school system they have opted not to use. Such harsh treatment not only discourages the smaller family size, it also dissuades parents to substitute quantity for quality in matters of progeny.

Many developed countries actually go so far as to give family allowances, which usually imply a direct money transfer from the low fertility to the high-fertility families. Again low fertility is punished, high fertility is rewarded. Those who argue in favor of free schooling, subsidized medical services, family allowances and the like usually state their case by arguing that such social arrangements "improve" the existing income distribution by effectuating a greater equalization of revenues. The obvious answer here is that if society opts to redistribute or equalize incomes to a greater extent, it could do so by methods other than those consisting of honoring the most fertile sections of the population.

A remaining question is: "what should be done if fertility in a developed country such as Canada drops well below replacement levels and stays there?" Although at the moment this question is still somewhat theoretical it may well become an issue in the future. Since working women tend to be less fertile than non-working women some of the following measures might be contemplated.

(1) Public creches and nurseries could be provided at low or zero cost in order to reconcile employment with a moderate-sized family. If children are well taken care of, working women might find it easier to accept an additional birth.

(2) Employers may be given tax concessions if they agree to employ females on more flexible conditions (especially with regard to working hours) than is common for male employees.

(3) Maternity grants and related provisions might be improved. A working woman can be given her full wage for a period before and/or after the birth of her child, perhaps up to a stretch of time of three months.

(4) It could be made illegal in the public sector as well as the private to dismiss a single girl for getting married or a married woman for getting pregnant.

## D. The Policy Debate on Immigration: Crisis and Long-term Perspective

If an attempt is made to assess the advantages and disadvantages of immigration in a country like Canada, we must do so in terms of the welfare of those already living within its borders. Foreign applicants for entry presumably want to establish themselves in the country of destination because they anticipate improving their position by doing so.

As stated earlier immigration has demographic, social and economic effects. Canadian immigration policies in the past and present have often responded to supposed economic needs amongst which the requirements of Canada's labor market always loomed high. It is thus legitimate to devote primary attention to economic criteria in the discussion which follows.

## *Benefits of Post-War Immigration*

The overall effect of post-war immigration in Canada has probably been beneficial. The reasons are as follows:

(1) One of the weak points of the Canadian economy in the post-war period was the existence of a high dependency ratio. The proportion of population under 15 years of age increased from a low of 28% in 1941 to a high of 34% in 1961. The Y.D.R. rose from 42.4 in 1941 to 58.1 in 1961. The minimal fertility of the 1930s (Depression Years) produced deficient cohorts. Immigration during that period had also been kept at low levels. The revival of fertility which occurred after 1944 produced the well-known "baby boom" and the youth dependency burden was increased. Most post-war immigrants, however, were young adults (refugees excepted), eager and able to join the labor force immediately after entry. The effect of their admission was to increase the proportion of workers in the population and thus to raise the productive potential of the nation.

(2) A second positive factor of immigration was the fact that many immigrants moved to the basic sectors such as agriculture, forestry, mining, metallurgy, building and the like, where skilled and unskilled labor were in short supply. Although the majority of foreign immigrants settled in densely populated areas (usually the bigger cities), substantial numbers did move to the relatively new and untouched regions, assisting the development of the natural resource industries. This also benefited Canada's export position as many raw materials were sold abroad (iron, oil, lumber, etc.).

(3) The post-war arrival of immigrants provided the country with some badly needed skills, thus adding to the quantity and variety of skills and aptitudes. Many bottlenecks were prevented from occurring. Bottlenecks come about when some vital skills are lacking in a firm or organization thus preventing the remaining employees from performing their jobs properly. The result is loss in output and incomes. Skilled immigrants often filled key positions when no local residents were available or willing to be trained. Immigrants also helped to fill job vacancies which occurred because Canadians moved up to better paid jobs or left for the United States.

(4) Finally, immigrants made an indirect contribution to economic growth by increasing the size of the domestic markets for goods and services. This market grew steadily through the arrival of immigrants animating the entire economic system while making a larger number of activities economically rewarding and viable. Many economic ventures which otherwise might have failed now could grow and prosper because of the ongoing expansion in potential clients. One only

has to compare the rather sleepy Toronto of 1945 with the thriving metropolis of the 1970s.

## *Problems with Immigration*

Immigration also had its drawbacks. Immigration tends to make labor cheaper than it otherwise would have been. This enables a number of marginal, inefficient, high-cost firms to survive. With a smaller supply of labor and the consequent higher wages, employers would have been under stronger pressure to resort to labor-saving devices. Their quest for labor-saving equipment would have provided an incentive for research and production. In that sense immigration slowed down the rate of technical progress. One could argue that immigration contributed to the maintenance of regional inequalities in Canada. Without the inflow of foreign workers, wages in the metropolitan centers would probably have risen faster. This might have induced some corporations and business firms to leave such centers in search for cheaper labor (and land). Low-income regions such as the Maritimes might have benefited from such developments. Since the early 1970s this type of adjustment seems to have been occurring in the U.S.A. American firms have left the northern and eastern regions heading towards the South. This move can be partly explained by lower wages, less aggressive trade unions and inexpensive land in the southern states. One might also raise the question of how real the much decried labor shortage of the 1960s really was. During that period the level of business activity in nearly all Western countries was high. Producers often sold off their shelves and were therefore tempted to increase output while hiring more production factors such as laborers. Such endeavors put the labor market under pressure and if full employment prevailed employers would exercise pressure on the government to liberalize immigration in order to "combat" the alleged "labor shortage". A closer look at the Western World of the 1960s reveals a substantial rate of inflation with little enthusiasm on the part of the governments to take corrective action. If the total annual demand in a nation, consisting of consumer demand by citizens, private investment demand for equipment by firms, foreign demand and the purchase of goods and services by government (mirrored by its level of expenditure), exceeds the output capacity of the nation, producers discover that they can raise their prices and still sell all their goods and services. Demand-pull inflation thus occurs. One way to combat it is to reduce the level of government expenditure in order to bring aggregate demand and supply back into balance. During the 1960s no Western nation had the courage and discipline to cut back its own level of spending significantly. In most cases governments actually spent much more than they received from taxes and other sources. The deficits which thus occurred in their budgets had to be financed with money borrowed from Central Banks and other sources. More money was introduced into the economy and the rate of inflation rose again. The correct solution would have consisted in disciplined and orderly fiscal and monetary policies, but governments found it easier to encourage immigration in order to ''solve'' the alleged labor shortages. The pursuance of vigorous anti-inflationary policies was postponed partly because governments did not wish to antagonize powerful vested interests.

From the macro point of view, it was sometimes argued that if there existed a problem of excess demand, immigration could provide a partial solution because it helped to expand production and aggregate supply, thus closing the gap between spending and production. There can of course be no doubt that immigration often helps to increase production but workers do not only produce, they also consume. They will spend most of their income on goods and services, which increases consumer demand. Their entry into the labor force may encourage firms to spend more on capital-widening types of investment needed to equip labor force entrants. Immigration also involves other types of capital demand because newcomers require homes and other facilities. Their successful absorption into the country of destination calls for infrastructural support; means of transport, hospitals and the like must be provided. Their children will increase the demand for nurseries, schools, vocational training institutes, libraries and so on. All this tends to increase government outlays again. Demand may once more outrace supply, labor shortages may occur anew and additional foreigners will have to be admitted. A self-perpetuating inflationary situation can and did in fact develop this way until the rate of inflation reached double-digit figures in the early 1970s, which finally alarmed public opinion. Reluctantly governments began to dampen their own level of spending and corrective monetary policies were adopted. This had the effect of reducing the so-called labor shortages and even of creating some unemployment. This latter phenomenon was reinforced by the entry into the labor force of the middle cohorts of the baby boom. In many industrial nations the return flow (outflow or migrants towards the area of origin) increased but numerous were those immigrants who stayed. To the extent that they lost their jobs and had to be supported they became an additional burden on the taxpayer.

## *Present versus Future Immigration*

Now that we are approaching the end of the 1970s much of the earlier enthusiasm for immigration has evaporated. The Green Paper talks in somber tones about the negative implications of migration and tells us that many of the former arguments in favor of immigration have now lost much of their validity. Yet there are still certain public figures, such as the Canadian internationalist Maurice Strong, who hold the ''heroic'' view that Canada possesses a disproportionate portion of the world's territory and natural resources which imposes upon her the moral obligation to increase her population, in particular through the absorption of more immigrants from the high-fertility developing countries. Against this view, it may be argued that although Canada looks big on the map, the amount of usable territory is relatively small. Besides, why should Canada be obliged to absorb immigrants from countries which most of the time are unwilling to put their own house in order? The number of developing countries which have a meaningful population policy is less than 15 at the moment.

Another author by the name of Warren E. Kalbach, who has produced several excellent demographic studies of the Canadian population, has suggested that a "logical" immigration policy for Canada would consist of admitting enough immigrants to raise the Canadian rate of population increase to world levels. Hence if the population of Canada grew by 0.5% and that of the world by 2%, this country would have to admit enough immigrants to produce the remaining 1.5% increase. And the author calls this a "realistic" policy. Whatever one may think of such propositions it should be remembered that with an unparalleled population explosion going on in Asia, Africa and Latin America it must be frankly recognized that migration can no longer ease the population problems of those regions. The world net rate of increase is about 73 millions per year, most of it occurring in the developing countries. Where could they go? Who would want such quantities?

When it comes to Canada proper, and the same could apply to the United States, there is a purely demographic argument which would militate for restricting the immigration movement now while being perhaps a bit more expansionist in the somewhat distant future. During the 1944-1964 period large cohorts of babies were born. Many of them have already entered the labor market while others are still being trained and educated. Fertility in Canada dropped after 1964-65 and the cohorts born in subsequent years became smaller. In the near future, the young-age dependency ratio and the total dependency ratio will be relatively low. As a result the investments needed to parry the increase in population will be small, thus creating the proper demographic and economic conditions for a spurt in economic growth. However, around the year 2010 the first cohorts of the baby boom will begin to retire. By 2030 the Canadian age pyramid will almost have taken on the shape of a light bulb, unless of course present fertility conditions change again. With relatively small economically active groups and a relatively large burden of oldsters, the existing welfare arrangements will experience enormous pressure and could actually collapse. As we noted earlier the choice is then to reduce the support to the aged or increase the tax burden on the economically active. Continued immigration *now* of people born during the baby boom period will worsen the situation after the year 2010.[1] From the point of view adopted here it would make more sense to reduce immigration now to a relatively small flow. Just before or at the very moment the baby boom begins to retire (around 2010), the influx of productive young workers could be made a little easier. The tax base would be broadened, the dependency ratio would drop and more favorable conditions to support ageing Canadians would be created. This proposition, however, relies on the long-term view. Canada's immigration policies however, have usually been dictated by short-term considerations.

---

[1]We remind the reader that most immigrants are young adults.

## Bibliography

Bickel, W., "Foreign Workers and Economic Growth in Switzerland", in: United Nations, Department of Economic and Social Affairs, *Proceedings of the World Population Conference* (E/Conf. 41/5), Vol. IV, New York: 1967.

Blake, J., "Coercive Pronatalism and American Population Policy", in *Aspects of Population Growth Policy,* Edited by R. Parke and C.W. Westoff, Washington D.C. Government Printing Office, 1972.

Brown, L.R., In *The Human Interest,* New York: Pergamon Press, 1974.

David, K., "Population Policy: Will Current Programs Succeed?", *Science* Vol. CLVIII, November, 1967.

Demeny, P., "Welfare Considerations in U.S. Population Policy", in *Aspects of Population Growth Policy,* Edited by R. Parke and C.W. Westoff, Washington D.C. Government Printing Office, 1972.

Lorimer, F., "Issues of Population Policy', in *The Population Dilemma,* 2nd ed, Edited by P.H. Hauser, New Jersey: Prentice Hall, 1969.

Mishan, E.J., *21 Popular Economic Fallacies,* New York: Praeger Publishers, 1973.

National Academy of Sciences, *Rapid Population Growth,* Vol. I, Baltimore: The John Hopkins Press, 1971.

Passaris, C., "The Cost-Benefit Impact of Immigrants on Economy", *International Perspectives,* September-October, 1975.

Spengler, J.J., "Population Problem, In Search of a Solution", *Science,* Vol. CLXVI, Dec. 1969.

World Bank Staff, *Population Policies and Economic Development,* Baltimore: The John Hopkins Press, 1974.

# Index